Seven Myths of the Civil War

MYTHS OF HISTORY: A HACKETT SERIES

Seven Myths of the Civil War

Edited, with an Introduction, by Wesley Moody

Series Editors
Alfred J. Andrea and Andrew Holt

Hackett Publishing Company, Inc.
Indianapolis/Cambridge

20 19 18 17   1 2 3 4 5 6 7

For further information, please address
    Hackett Publishing Company, Inc.
    P.O. Box 44937
    Indianapolis, Indiana 46244-0937

www.hackettpublishing.com

Cover design by Rick Todhunter and Brian Rak
Interior design by Elizabeth L. Wilson
Composition by Aptara, Inc.

Library of Congress Cataloging-in-Publication Data

Names: Moody, Wesley, editor.
Title: Seven myths of the Civil War / edited, with an introduction, by Wesley Moody.
Description: Indianapolis : Hackett Publishing Company, Inc., 2017. | Series: Myths of
history: a Hackett series | Includes bibliographical references and index.
Identifiers: LCCN 2017009569| ISBN 9781624666360 (pbk.) | ISBN 9781624666377
    (cloth)
Subjects: LCSH: United States—History—Civil War, 1861–1865—Historiography. |
    Confederate States of America—Historiography.
Classification: LCC E468.5 .S48 2017 | DDC 973.7—dc23
LC record available at https://lccn.loc.gov/2017009569

CONTENTS

SERIES EDITORS' FOREWORD

Publication of *Seven Myths of the Crusades* in 2015 inaugurated Hackett Publishing Company's Myths of History series, which is dedicated to exposing and correcting some of the misconceptions, misjudgments, distortions, exaggerations, outdated interpretations, fallacies, seductive canards, and blatant lies that stick like superglued Post-it notes to so many of history's most significant events and actors.[1] The editors and authors involved in this work do not believe that they are presenting pure *truth* or claim they are rendering the final word on the issues under examination. The craft of history does not allow its practitioners to speak with the voice of unquestionable authority. Rather, each historian involved in this series offers a counter-narrative that reflects the best, most up-to-date scholarship on one or more so-called myths.

The reason for engaging such "myths" is simple. The past is neither dead nor forgotten. An understanding of our shared past informs our understanding of who we are and our place in the here and now. This never-ending dialogue between the present and the past—a process we term "history"—is vital to our lives, our societies, our cultures, and our world, and it is incumbent upon us to understand that past on its own terms and as clearly and correctly as the evidence and our fallible intellects allow.

Although the initial book in this series focused on seven myths, in large part as an homage to Matthew Restall's ground-breaking *Seven Myths of the Spanish Conquest*, there is nothing sacred about the number seven—at least as far as this series is concerned.[2] To be sure, Wesley Moody, the editor of the book under present consideration, chose to involve six colleagues in investigating seven of the more popular myths of the American Civil War. Forthcoming books in the series, however, might center on more or fewer myths. The range and complexity of human history and its variations are sufficiently vast to allow great latitude to our editors and authors.

Despite such latitude, *Seven Myths of the Civil War* must necessarily confront head-on the core myth of so much of the Southern memory of the War Between the States (or War of Northern Aggression)—the Lost Cause. It is to Moody's credit that he—a Southerner by birth, education, and residence—has not only taken on the Lost Cause in this little book, but he has actively furthered our collective understanding of the Civil War through his scholarly publications, which are reflected in his introduction and the chapter on Sherman's March to the Sea. Similar praise is due the six other author-contributors—Michael T. Bernath, Edward Bonekemper, Benjamin Cloyd, Ian Hunt, Barton A. Myers, and Brooks D. Simpson. Each is a published specialist in

---

1. Alfred J. Andrea and Andrew Holt, eds., *Seven Myths of the Crusades* (Indianapolis: Hackett, 2015).
2. Matthew Restall, *Seven Myths of the Spanish Conquest* (Oxford: Oxford University Press, 2003).

The Robert Gould Shaw and 54th Massachusetts Volunteer Infantry Regiment Memorial, Beacon Street entrance to the Boston Common. Unveiled in 1897, this sculpture by Augustus Saint-Gaudens depicts Colonel Shaw and his African American regiment marching up Beacon Street on May 28, 1863, on their way to embark at Battery Wharf for combat operations in the South. Above Shaw and the soldiers is an allegorical female figure bearing the laurel branch of victory and poppies that symbolize death. As depicted in the movie *Glory* (1989), Shaw and a significant number of his troops were killed in the assault on Fort Wagner, South Carolina, on July 18, 1863. A Latin inscription on the memorial reads, "Omnia Relinquit Servare Rempublicam" (He gives up everything to serve the Republic). Photo courtesy of A. J. Andrea © 2017.

the area on which he has written and is acknowledged by his peers as a skilled practitioner of our art. Thanks to their individual and collective efforts, a bit of the fog of mythic history has been lifted.

The Lost Cause and its consequent mythic spin-offs is not the only Original Myth writ large. One of the two editors of this series is a New England Yankee who knows all too well the countervailing myth—the Noble Cause—which is embedded in the rocky soils of his native and adopted states, Massachusetts and Vermont. By being blind to the ambiguities, contradictions, and inherent horrors of the Civil War, many Northerners continue to this day to look upon that conflict as a Manichean struggle between Absolute Good and Incarnate Evil. The tone of self-evident righteousness that pervades the stirring lyrics of "The Battle Hymn of the Republic" reveals that sentiment, as do the almost innumerable memorials to the Grand Army of the Republic that dot the Northern landscape. Benjamin Cloyd has it right in Chapter 5 where he cites Robert Penn Warren's insightful comment that the North accepted with certainty the notion that its victory was an inevitable consequence of its "Treasury of Virtue."

The Vermont State House, for example, is a virtual Civil War museum. Contained within its walls are war-scarred battle flags carried into combat by Vermont units in the years 1861–1865 and several large, nineteenth-century paintings that memorialize the martial deeds of Vermont troops. One of them, *The Battle of Cedar Creek* by Vermonter Julian Scott, the first Union soldier awarded the Medal of Honor for valor on the battle-field, dominates the south wall of the State House's reception hall. Titled the Cedar Creek Room, the hall commemorates not only the battle of October 19, 1864, in which the First Vermont Brigade led a crucial counterattack, but all the actions of Vermonters in that bloody war. A plaque at another location in the State House reads:

> At Gettysburg, the Wilderness, Cedar Creek and other battlefields of the Civil War, Vermont soldiers fought magnificently. The first state to out-law slavery, Vermont played an outsized role in the great war that defeated slavery and preserved the Union. When it ended in victory, the state motto of "Freedom and Unity" seemed fulfilled.

The sentiment is understandable, but the historian asks, "Is it the full story? Where is the ambiguity and nuance?"[3]

In no way do we intend to demean the dedication and sacrifices of the more than two million blue-clad individuals who marched to war, including almost 200,000 African American soldiers and sailors for whom the war was an intensely personal struggle for freedom and recognition of their full humanity. And this certainly includes the roughly 34,000 Vermont volunteers, who constituted a bit more than 10 percent of the state's official 1860 population. More than 5,000 of them died in service to their cause. In like manner, we do not deny the equal dedication and sacri-fices of the men-at-arms who wore gray and a variety of home-spun uniforms. Likewise, the devoted support of so many on both home fronts was real enough. Yet to wrap either side in this fratricidal bloodletting in the false colors of unalloyed nobility, chivalry, and self-sacrifice is to blind ourselves to the brutal realities and complexities of this war. To reduce it to "this" or "that," "yes" and "no" choices is to distort the multi-hued history of the war and to rob all of us of a more complete understanding of this defining moment in U.S. history.

The seven authors of this little book have not failed in their mission to shed the light of sober scholarship on key aspects of the Civil War, thereby enlightening us further regarding a heritage that belongs to all citizens of this nation, no matter their region or circumstances.

Alfred J. Andrea
Andrew Holt

---

3. Howard Coffin, *Something Abides: Discovering the Civil War in Today's Vermont* (Woodstock, VT: Countryman Press, 2013), is also emblematic of the continuing fascination in Vermont with the Noble Cause.

EDITOR'S PREFACE

Seven Myths of the Civil War was a great idea, but it was not mine. I am fortunate to have an office down the hall from Andrew Holt, the coeditor of the Myths of History series, who recruited me to create this book. I was a witness as he created the first book of the series, *Seven Myths of the Crusades*.

The crusades fall well outside my specialty area, and I hate to admit that I believed many of the myths the authors dispelled. I was very disappointed to find one of

The Civil War was sometimes a "children's crusade." John Lincoln Clem joined the 22nd Michigan Volunteer Infantry at the age of ten. He was decorated for bravery at the battles of Perryville and Chickamauga. He remained in the army until 1915, when he retired as a major general. Image courtesy of the Library of Congress.

my favorite stories of European history in his book, the Children's Crusade. We can become attached to our myths. As the evidence against a thirteenth-century invasion of the Middle East made up of and led by children mounted, I was as heartbroken as those fictional parents whose mythical children marched off to war. Having suffered this pain, I am more sympathetic toward those who hold dear the myths of the Civil War than when I wrote my first book dispelling many of the myths that surround General William T. Sherman.

The loss of the Children's Crusade left a hole that was quickly filled with an even more interesting story, the tale of how the many fictional elements that surround this crusade were invented and came to be widely believed. This is what we have tried to do in *Seven Myths of the Civil War*: not only show that a cherished belief is not true but also tell the story of how it emerged. The process is known as "historiography" (the study of how history is written), and it is as important as the original event in helping us understand our past, our present, and ourselves.

I would like to thank the authors of this book, whose knowledge, patience, and hard work made this possible. I also need to thank series coeditor Alfred J. Andrea, whose experience and eye for detail made this a much better book. Rick Todhunter and the staff at Hackett Publishing Company have made this a wonderful experience. I am extremely proud to have my name attached to their first Civil War title. Of course, I need to thank my colleague and friend Andrew Holt, who had the idea for this project and refused to take no for an answer.

Wesley Moody

INTRODUCTION

The Continuing Battles of the Civil War

One common and reasonable criticism of modern historians is that we overspecialize. In the case of the Civil War, we often over-sub-specialize, and this can lead to problems in our scholarship. For example, some of the great historians who have written about Lee's campaigns in the East have a poor grasp of the war west of the Appalachian Mountains, and vice versa. And when one of those historians writes about the conflict more broadly, she or he risks lending well-earned prestige and support to a myth, misunderstanding, or outdated notion that he or she would have otherwise dismissed had it been within that historian's specialty area. In turn, future historians, writing outside their area of expertise, cite that earlier scholar's work as evidence that they have done their due diligence on the subject; in this way the original error is recycled and perpetuated. Additionally, there are a large number of amateur historians and popular writers working in the field of Civil War history—perhaps more than in any other field of history—and although some of them have produced outstanding work, they are perhaps more susceptible to some of these myths than trained academics would be. But, as already suggested, even the professionals are mere mortals, and no historian, no matter his or her expertise, is immune to error. We have all been guilty, to greater or lesser extents, of creating or disseminating myths. The object of this volume of essays is, in a humble way, to confront and perhaps correct some of the myths, misconceptions, exaggerations, errors, fabrications, and deliberate lies that have taken hold over the 150 years following the end of the American Civil War.

The second goal of this work is to encourage the reader to view all historical work, from any source, with a more critical eye. Regardless of their prior experience or understanding of a given topic, many students enter introductory-level history courses embracing the single greatest myth in the field of history: that history is a stagnant, never-changing, and exact record of past events. And from that follows the mistaken notion that there is no difference between the history class their parents took twenty to thirty years ago and the one they themselves are about to start. Nothing could be further from the truth. Our understanding of history changes as the world, and our knowledge of it, changes. It is true that some of these changes to our understanding of the historical record are driven by the latest archaeological or archival discoveries. But at a more fundamental level, these changes are related to the mind-set and experiences of the historian, the lens through which the past is perceived and interpreted. Any interpretation of the past tells us as much about the historian writing it as it does about the historical events under scrutiny. For example, an American writing during the Second World War, when the United States and Great Britain were close allies, would most likely have had a different view of the American Revolution than one writing during a period when relations between the two countries were not as positive.

In his 1954 book *Americans Interpret Their Civil War*, Thomas J. Pressly compares our understanding of history to our appreciation of art. He points out that in the sixteenth century, the *Mona Lisa* was praised for its stunning realism. In the nineteenth century, the painting was admired for its mystery and symbolism. In the twentieth century, Sigmund Freud found a way to psychoanalyze Leonardo da Vinci through the painting. The oil and the canvas did not change, only the observer.[1]

As a Civil War historian, it is tempting for me to assert that no other series of events better demonstrates changing views of historical events over time than does the American Civil War. However, all fields of history are subject to constant re-evaluation, and the deeper one digs into any aspect of our past, the more that person will see that the writing of that history is a story unto itself. Americans, both Northern and Southern, still hold deeply personal beliefs about the Civil War, and these beliefs often color their thinking on the subject. I have often been asked, "Was the war about slavery or states' rights?" That seems straightforward enough. Yet this question is always asked with a specific, predetermined answer in mind. My response (when flight is not acceptable) is that few historical realities can be so tidily summed up.

Why the Civil War?

More than 2.1 million men fought for the Union, and more than a million fought for the Confederacy. Eleven states tried to leave the United States of America. This was not a decision made by a handful of politicians alone. In an attempt to avoid being seen as revolutionaries—and to give the proceedings a sheen of legality—pro-secession forces, liberally interpreting their states' constitutions, left it to the voters to decide whether or not to leave the Union. The combined free populations of those eleven states numbered more than 5.5 million. Of course, women and children were not allowed to vote, but more than a million white men cast their votes on the issue, and the majority chose secession. Unfortunately, there was no television news network performing exit polling, so we do not know which issue the voters would have said was most influential in guiding their decision. But if we had this information, it seems highly unlikely that many people would have given just one or two answers as their reason for supporting such a monumental change as breaking up the United States of America.

---

1. Thomas J. Pressly, *Americans Interpret Their Civil War* (Princeton, NJ: Princeton University Press, 1954), vii.

The war was an equally complicated issue for the millions in the North who supported it with blood, sweat, money, and votes, and many Americans on both sides embraced shifting opinions of the war as the years dragged on. It is possible that a historian willing to be selective in his or her use of the sources could make a convincing argument for almost any cause. But to do so would not only be disingenuous; it would constitute invalid historical research, and it would certainly result in a flawed view of the past.

The Southern Perspective

To anyone who might demand that we stuff into a neat little package the entire messy political, social, economic, and military situation that was the Civil War, we could say that the war was fought to avoid change. This argument is most easily made about the Southern states' reasons for going to war.

Generally speaking, Southerners believed their unique social, economic, and political system was under assault. Based on the production of cotton, this entire system rested on the need for slave labor. The system was an aristocratic one: Southerners at the very top of the system benefited greatly from it, and those at the lower levels benefited less but held hopes of upward mobility, and they could at least gain some comfort in knowing they were not at the very bottom—the spot reserved for African slaves.

Just as the Southern system was beginning to solidify, there was increased resistance to a perceived assault on the South. Many Southerners viewed a challenge to any part of the system as an attack on their entire way of life. Thus any challenge to the Southern system—a tariff levied against imported manufactured goods or abolitionists' calls for a ban on slavery—was considered an assault on the whole Southern world, and it had to be resisted. To debate slavery versus states' rights as the origin of the Civil War, as it is so popular to do, misses the point. The two issues cannot be considered separately—to do so would be equivalent to arguing over whether it is the eggs or the flour that makes a cake.

The question for Southerners was how best to resist. The famous, oft-quoted statement of the military theorist Carl von Clausewitz (1780–1831) that "war is a mere continuation of policy by other means"[2] is a truism that aptly describes the American Civil War. Defense of the Southern way of life began in the halls of Congress long before the first shots were fired and continued long after the last volley. The wealthiest Southerners, those with the most to lose, were the most loath to resort to armed conflict. White Southerners toward the bottom of the socioeconomic scale were also reluctant to fight for a system that they were beginning to realize did not benefit them.

---

2. Carl von Clausewitz, *On War*, trans. J. J. Graham (London: Kegan Paul, Trench, Trubner, 1908), 1:23.

Photographed in 1937, these six men were born into slavery but because of the American Civil War spent the majority of life as free men. Regardless of the cause, the war meant only one thing to them. Image courtesy of the Library of Congress.

It was in the poorest areas of the South, the mountain country of north Georgia, West Virginia, east Tennessee, and the pine country of southern Mississippi, where resistance to the Confederate government grew as the war dragged on and partisan warfare broke out. In Chapter 4, "The Myth of the 'Great' Conventional Battlefield War," Barton A. Myers addresses the issue of partisan warfare and other forms of irregular military conflict in the Civil War.

Of course, the Southerners at the very bottom of the socioeconomic ladder were the 3.5 to 4 million African slaves. Since the Civil Rights movement of the late 1950s and 1960s, an increasing amount of literature has been produced about the role of slaves in the war, and most of these histories are well researched and well written. But the disheartening paucity of sources written by former slaves presents a challenge to any historian researching African Americans in the Civil War.

Ironically, many Southerners who supported secession and the forming of a Southern nation believed secession would be the only way to avoid armed conflict. Many more Southerners came to hold this belief following the radical abolitionist John Brown's failed attempt to start a slave revolt in Harpers Ferry, Virginia, on October 16–18, 1859. Only by being independent, so the theory went, and therefore free to defend their borders, could they prevent further incursions by militant abolitionists. To most Southerners the word "abolition" meant slave revolt and the type of slaughter that occurred in Haiti at the end of the eighteenth century. Prior to the Civil War, the Haitian Revolution was foremost in every slave owner's mind and the cause of innumerable fears and numerous restrictive laws.

Beyond the fear of slave revolt, there were those who favored a Southern nation for the same reasons that so many other peoples have sought, and continue to seek, self-determination. They saw themselves as radically different from their Northern counterparts, whom only the accident of history placed under the same flag. If fear of being murdered in their sleep by a revolting slave drove some Southerners into the camp of the Southern nationalists, the same nationalists were not above playing on those fears. These Southern nationalists, or Fire Eaters as they are more commonly called, were willing to mislead the public to reach their goal. As Michael T. Bernath illustrates in Chapter 1, "Confederate States' Rights: A Contradiction in Terms," the very Southern leaders who openly championed the preservation of states' rights against an overreaching central government in Washington, D.C., showed no hesitation in creating a strong Confederate central government.

The Northern Perspective

Considering the earth-shattering effects of the Union victory, it might be hard for us to accept the idea that Northerners were also fighting to prevent change. Northerners shared their Southern counterparts' desire to maintain the old order, and that went beyond fighting to preserve the Union. It is true that Northern abolitionists were pushing for a major change—the end of slavery—but they were a minority. The majority of Northerners felt that, while they might not approve of slavery, what happened in the South was not their concern, as long as it stayed in the South. The fear that drove Northern men first to vote for an abolitionist candidate (see Chapter 2, "Was Abraham Lincoln a Racist?") and then to take up arms was the fear that slavery would not stay in the South.

Northerners feared that slavery would expand and that, with its expansion, the Southern aristocracy that slavery supported would take over the U.S. government.

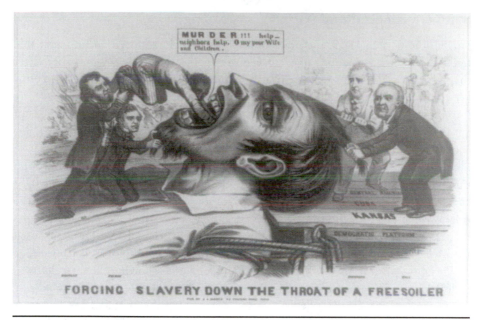

An 1856 political cartoon showing the fear many Midwesterners had about the expansion of slavery. Image courtesy of the Library of Congress.

After all, the Southern aristocracy already maintained a level of representation in Congress that was disproportionate to the size of the free Southern population. The phrase used (just prior to the war and in the literature of the period just following the war) to describe this perceived threat was "the great slave power conspiracy." The major political—and sometimes physical—fight in the halls of Congress at the time was over the expansion of slavery into the new territories. With a bang of the gavel in 1857, the Southern-dominated Supreme Court issued the infamous *Dred Scott* decision, which allowed for the expansion of slavery into the free territories and states. This included the states that had been part of the old Northwest Territory, where slavery had been banned during the Washington administration.

Southern defenders of slavery often argued that slaves were far better off than the "wage slave" laboring classes of the North, and this argument had to make commoners in the North nervous. If slavery was such a superior institution for maintaining a well-organized and cost-effective laboring class, why not enslave white factory workers? Moreover, while Southerners felt safer by separating from the North, Northerners felt threatened by a South unmoored from the federal government. To Northerners, a slave-owning aristocratic nation on their southern border, free to make alliances with like-minded nations, would represent a constant threat of invasion and conquest, and the destruction of their social and economic system. Thus fear of change, on both sides, led to four years of brutal warfare.

Southern Expectations

For Southerners in 1865, the previous four years had produced an unimaginable result. Southern predictions of victory made in the prewar years, and soon after the fighting began, had been disastrously wrong. Many Southerners perceived Yankees to be either soft, money-grubbing businessmen or slum-dwelling trash recently immigrated from the pest-ridden streets and famine-plagued corners of Europe. In any case, they did not believe that Northerners of this type would ever actually fight. Many Southern politicians uttered some variation of "I will drink every drop of blood spilled in this war," suggesting a quick, easy, and fairly bloodless confrontation. (Asking who first uttered this phrase, and in what form, can easily start a fight at a roundtable of Civil War enthusiasts.) No Southerner could have predicted the tidal wave of blood to come.

Many Southerners further believed that even if these unmanly Northerners roused themselves to battle, they would be unable to stomach a full-blown war once they had been bloodied in their first real fight. Consequently, following the First Battle of Bull Run, many Southerners thought the war was all but done. As the Union quickly began to rebuild its army in the East, this was clearly not the case, and developments in the West would eventually lead to a Union victory. Further, when the Lincoln government announced its plan for a naval blockade—the goal of which was to cut the South off from outside resources, including food—the announcement was greeted by laughter and derision from Southerners. How, they asked, could an agricultural nation be starved by a blockade? Yet by the end of the war, there were food riots in most Southern cities.

The "Lost Cause"

Looking back, after four years of war and eventual defeat, Southerners had to ask themselves why their predictions had been so wrong. Southern culture prided itself on its martial qualities. To quote the opening lines of the movie *Gone with the Wind*, "There was a land of Cavaliers and cotton fields." It was unthinkable to Southerners that Northern factory workers had defeated their knights, so Southerners developed a series of myths to explain their defeat. These myths came to be called collectively the "Myth of the Lost Cause." According to this all-embracing myth, the South lost not because its armies were beaten on the battlefield or because a democratic people overpowered a slaveholding aristocracy; instead, the South's loss was attributed to a combination of pre-existing factors, inherent Yankee characteristics, and Northern ways of waging war, all conceived of as reflecting the inferiority of Northern culture.

Adherents to this myth have posited the notion that the South's war efforts were doomed from the start, crippled by deficiencies in manufacturing and population; the fact that the South even came close to victory showed the superiority of the Southern fighting man. Moreover, "Lost Cause" believers held (and continue to hold) the idea that Northerners did not fight by the rules of civilized nations—that they fought "dirty"—and this is an argument that I dissect in Chapter 7, "Marching through Georgia: The Myth of Sherman's Total War." There was (and is) even a belief that Northern forces simply threw wave after wave of poor immigrants into the fray to be slaughtered on the battlefield until their numbers simply overwhelmed the gallant but outmanned and outgunned armies of General Lee and other Confederate leaders. In Chapter 6, "The Lost Causers' Favorite Target: Grant the Butcher," Edward Bonekemper subjects this view to close scrutiny as he examines the strategy and tactics of Ulysses S. Grant. In brief, the "Myth of the Lost Cause" asserts that Union armies never actually outfought or outthought their Confederate opponents. In putting forth this narrative, its advocates have worked hard to disprove the old cliché that the victors write history.

Why This Little Book?

Many contemporary Southerners must feel as though they are unjustly picked on or singled out for unfair treatment by Civil War academics. I know many Southerners who groan every time they hear the term "Lost Cause" because they view it as the signal that their ideas are about to be attacked. If Southerners feel as though they are being singled out, such treatment has been earned. Southern historians dominated the writing of Civil War history for more than a century following the war. As a result, parts of the Lost Cause mythology have become deeply entrenched in our popular culture to the point that even historians who would never identify themselves as Lost Causers have inadvertently embraced and perpetuated many elements of the myth. Any historian attempting to set the record straight must engage the Lost Cause.

In choosing myths for this book, I have made a number of hard choices. I have tried not to favor one region over the other. (Benjamin Cloyd's chapter on the myth of Civil War prisons might well anger both Northerners and Southerners.) There are also a number of myths that are simply too complicated and even problematic for a work of this nature and size. I have tried to at least touch on some of these—including the overall cause of the war and the inevitability of Union victory—in this Introduction. Other myths have been left out because they have been covered so well, and in depth, in other works. For example, though some myths about Robert E. Lee are still religiously accepted, Lee's reputation as a brilliant field commander is treated here only as a secondary-level myth in the chapter on Ulysses S. Grant. Any chapter on Lee could not help but rehash Thomas Connelly's excellent study of the legend of Robert E. Lee.[3] Pickett's Charge and Gettysburg have been covered as thoroughly in scholarly literature as perhaps any event in American history. The former's place in myth and

---

3. Thomas L. Connelly, *The Marble Man: Robert E. Lee and His Image in American Society* (Baton Rouge: Louisiana State University Press, 1977).

memory is discussed extremely well in Carol Reardon's aptly titled *Pickett's Charge in Myth and Memory*, and so there is no reason to summarize her work here.[4]

Although several of the essays in this volume incorporate and discuss elements of the Lost Cause myth, that myth does not dominate the chapter selection as it would have had this book been published a decade or two ago. With that noted, the myths about Generals Sherman and Grant are mainstays of the Lost Cause narrative that seem to have staying power, and each was justifiably selected for inclusion among the sacred seven myths.

Old Wine in New Bottles: Some "New" Myths

Unfortunately, some of the perhaps lesser-known myths addressed here appear to be gaining traction in public consciousness. When examined closely, these "new" myths are revealed to be new twists on older myths. Two of these have to do with race, as great an issue in the twenty-first century as it was in the nineteenth.

Many Southerners who, naturally, do not want to be on the wrong side of history insist that the war was about something other than a defense of slavery. In Chapter 3, "African Americans in Confederate Military Service: Myth and Reality," Brooks D. Simpson considers the claim that significant numbers of African American soldiers served in the Confederate army and the corresponding conclusion that if black men wore gray, the war could not have been fought over issues of race and slavery. According to a second, closely related myth, the war could not have been about race or slavery because Lincoln himself did not care about the issue: at best, he was indifferent to the plight of the slaves; at worst, he was racist. Two different groups champion this myth, and I have had it repeated to me by a member of the Sons of Confederate Veterans with a Robert E. Lee tattoo as well as a young African American college student wearing a Malcolm X t-shirt. It is not hard to imagine why both would want to accept this myth. For too long African Americans were portrayed in the historical literature as the passive recipients of freedom. Historians arguing against this view should be applauded; however, it has led to the belief that if more credit is to be given to African Americans, credit must be taken from others. Lincoln is becoming the major victim of this redistribution of credit. And for Southerners who look upon the Confederacy as a proud part of their heritage, a certain pride in identity is likely validated by a belief that Lincoln was nothing more than a wily politician who acted out of a sense of expediency rather than moral fervor. If they were not defeated by the moral "right," then how can they be considered "wrong"? In Chapter 2, Ian Hunt, historian of the Lincoln Presidential Library, addresses Lincoln's abolitionist credentials and puts into its proper context his famous statement about saving the Union without freeing a single slave.

---

4. Carol Reardon, *Pickett's Charge in Myth and Memory* (Chapel Hill: University of North Carolina Press, 1997).

The Enduring Civil War

The American Civil War remains at the forefront of American consciousness for a number of reasons, and it seems highly unlikely that this will change anytime in the near future. It was, after all, a war fought between Americans on American soil. Moreover, regional rivalries continue to sustain the unpleasant memories of old grievances. One does not have to travel very far in the South to see a historical marker of the Civil War. The scars of defeat take a long time to heal, and each new generation of Southerners has seemed to hunt for salt to rub into its wounds. Victory can also be bitter. Memorials to fallen Union soldiers and sailors can be found throughout towns and cities in the North.

Race and Slavery

Race and slavery, of course, were the central issues of the Civil War. Three and a half to four million African American men, women, and children who were held in bondage in 1861 became free people when the war concluded in 1865. That statistic alone shows that one cannot ignore race and slavery when studying the Civil War. Even now, race remains an extremely divisive social and political issue avoided by scholars much braver than I. Yet we must address it head on. For though it might be tempting to oversimplify the political situation in 1860 and claim that the main political battle between North and South was centered on the question of strong central government versus individual (or states') rights, the fact is that slavery was the main political issue, the one on which the American people voted. Southerners took up arms because the central government was in the hands of those who disagreed with them on the slavery issue, as Bernath demonstrates in Chapter 1. But to many Americans even today, Southerners' taking up arms against a government they considered oppressive was no worse or different than angry colonialists arming themselves against the British Crown or the current Tea Party movement challenging a federal bureaucracy its supporters consider to be overbearing. Yet when we understand the values and system that many Southerners were determined to protect from federal regulation, to claim that the Confederates were simply carrying on an American tradition of "fighting the good fight" against an unchecked and oppressive power appears fallacious.

After 150 Years

Several years ago I was involved in a discussion with a group of senior Civil War historians. It was the sesquicentennial anniversary of the war, and these scholars were lamenting the fact that this 150th anniversary had not been recognized in the same way as the Centennial had been recognized in 1961–65, a time when these men were at the beginning of their careers as historians. In the 1960s, their mentors were (or soon thereafter became) celebrities with best-selling books. Now, fifty years later, a now-senior generation of historians felt it was its turn for a celebration. It did not turn out that way. The Centennial had come at just the right time to capture the public's attention. The Second World War was a recent memory in the early 1960s, and large numbers of now-middle-aged veterans were fascinated by the common experience of war that they shared with their ancestors. For many Southerners, there was also something eerily familiar about the decade leading up to the Centennial. The Republican then in the White House—Dwight Eisenhower—had used the power of the central government in 1957 to interfere with race relations by federalizing the Arkansas National Guard and deploying paratroopers from the U.S. Army to enforce the desegregation of public schools in Little Rock. It was not exactly Lincoln and the Emancipation Proclamation, but many Southerners perceived this forced desegregation of public schools—many of which were named after prominent Confederate leaders—as an attack on their society and culture. Current events then and now have power to awaken the passions and grievances of a bygone era that is not so bygone.

Yes, even now, the memory of the Civil War and the myths that emerged in its wake stir up old controversies, antagonisms, and passions over issues of race and politics. Why is this, and what does it say about us as a society?

Once, long ago, it was an unwritten rule that professional historians would allow seventy-five years to pass between an event and their study of it, in order to let passions cool before a supposedly unbiased history could be written. In the case of the Civil War, this seventy-five-year rule has been problematic on several counts. First, gun barrels had scarcely cooled when partisans on both sides began writing memoirs and histories that set in popular memory the myths and misconceptions that became standard wisdom in the North and South. And is this not often the reality concerning any controversial current event? The myths that skew our understanding of an event and that feed our ever-growing misperceptions become entrenched while the historian waits to take up the pen. As noted above, the passions of the Civil War show no signs of cooling after more than a hundred and fifty years; seventy-five years was clearly not enough time.

Is it not possible that it is precisely an event that does stir the passions of people—historians or not—that should be examined and reexamined, both early on and well into the future? Indeed, the study of such events over time has more to tell us about those events and about ourselves as keepers of a collective memory than any supposedly unbiased, apparently definitive account could ever convey.

Wesley Moody

1. Confederate States' Rights: A Contradiction in Terms

Michael T. Bernath

> The Southern people desire to retain from the wreck in which their constitutional views, their domestic institutions, the mass of their property, and the lives of their best and bravest were lost the knowledge that their conduct was honorable throughout and that their submission at last to overwhelming numbers and resources in no way blackened their motives or established the wrong of the cause for which they fought.[1]
>
> —The Confederate Veteran, *1897*

> If a monument is ever erected as a symbolical gravestone over the 'lost cause' it should have engraved upon it these words: "Died of State Rights."[2]
>
> —*Frank Owsley, historian, 1925*

The origin of the myth of Confederate states' rights—that is, that Confederates fought to defend the constitutional principle of states' rights during the Civil War and that the Confederacy itself both upheld and epitomized states' rights ideology—is no great mystery. Indeed, it is the seemingly logical, if mistaken, extension of the belief that the Civil War arose from a dispute over states' rights. If Southern states seceded in order to protect states' rights, then, presumably, the Confederacy fought for states' rights during the war itself, or so the assumption goes. But this myth also serves a larger purpose central to the Lost Cause, the term popularized by Southern newspaperman Edward Pollard in an 1866 book of the same title, which came to represent the interpretation and memory of the Civil War and the Confederacy promoted by white Southerners during the late nineteenth century and beyond.[3]

---

1. "Patriotic School Histories," *Confederate Veteran* 5 (September 1897): 450.

2. Frank Lawrence Owsley, *State Rights in the Confederacy* (Chicago: University of Chicago Press, 1925), 1.

3. Edward Pollard, *The Lost Cause: A New Southern History of the War of the Confederates* (New York: E. B. Treat, 1866). On the Lost Cause, see Rollin G. Osterweis, *The Myth of the Lost Cause, 1865–1900* (Hamden, CT: Archon Books, 1973); Charles Reagan Wilson, *Baptized in Blood: The Religion of the Lost Cause* (Athens: University of Georgia Press, 1980); Thomas L. Connelly, *The Marble Man: Robert E. Lee and His Image in American Society* (Baton Rouge: Louisiana State University Press, 1977); Thomas L. Connelly and Barbara L. Bellows, *God and General Longstreet: The Lost Cause*

One of the key tenets of the Lost Cause holds that Confederates, honorable and brave as they were, had been overwhelmed by the superior numbers and resources of a centralized, industrialized North. Those doomed Confederates had remained united around a noble cause, and that cause was not the institution of slavery but rather the constitutional principle of states' rights. This myth has survived, in the popular imagination at least, because of mistaken notions about the causes of the war; an inaccurate, whitewashed understanding of the Confederate war effort, including failure to recognize the internal Southern resistance to that effort; and fundamental confusion over what "states' rights" actually means. There remains a striking disconnection between historians and the public, or at least a particular segment of the public that continues to posit certain values and virtues of the Confederacy that are largely creations of the postwar period or even the modern day. Many confidently maintain that white Southerners fought against a centralized federal power that threatened their state, local, and personal liberties, without recognizing that the central government threatening those liberties during the war was located in Richmond, not Washington. They assert a false dichotomy wherein the Confederacy was the bastion of traditional states' rights and the federal government of the United States represented central and

---

and the Southern Mind (Baton Rouge: Louisiana State University Press, 1982); Alan T. Nolan, *Lee Considered: General Robert E. Lee and Civil War History* (Chapel Hill: University of North Carolina Press, 1991); Gaines M. Foster, *Ghosts of the Confederacy: Defeat, the Lost Cause, and the Emergence of the New South, 1865 to 1913* (New York: Oxford University Press, 1987); Gary W. Gallagher, *Jubal A. Early, the Lost Cause, and Civil War History: A Persistent Legacy* (Milwaukee: Marquette University Press, 1995); Gary W. Gallagher and Alan T. Nolan, eds., *The Myth of the Lost Cause and Civil War History* (Bloomington: Indiana University Press, 2000); W. Fitzhugh Brundage, *The Southern Past: A Clash of Race and Memory* (Cambridge, MA: Harvard University Press, 2005); Karen L. Cox, *Dixie's Daughters: The United Daughters of the Confederacy and the Preservation of Confederate Culture* (Gainesville: University Press of Florida, 2003); Caroline E. Janney, *Burying the Dead but Not the Past: Ladies' Memorial Associations and the Lost Cause* (Chapel Hill: University of North Carolina Press, 2008); Caroline E. Janney, *Remembering the Civil War: Reunion and the Limits of Reconciliation* (Chapel Hill: University of North Carolina Press, 2013); David W. Blight, *Race and Reunion: The Civil War in American Memory* (Cambridge, MA: Belknap Press of Harvard University Press, 2001); John M. Coski, *The Confederate Battle Flag: America's Most Embattled Emblem* (Cambridge, MA: Harvard University Press, 2005); W. Scott Poole, *Never Surrender: Confederate Memory and Conservatism in the South Carolina Upcountry* (Athens: University of Georgia Press, 2004); William A. Blair, *Cities of the Dead: Contesting the Memory of the Civil War in the South, 1865–1914* (Chapel Hill: University of North Carolina Press, 2004); Sarah E. Gardner, *Blood and Irony: Southern White Women's Narratives of the Civil War, 1861–1937* (Chapel Hill: University of North Carolina Press, 2004); Anne E. Marshall, *Creating a Confederate Kentucky: The Lost Cause and Civil War Memory in a Border State* (Chapel Hill: University of North Carolina Press, 2010); Terry A. Barnhart, *Albert Taylor Bledsoe: Defender of the Old South and Architect of the Lost Cause* (Baton Rouge: Louisiana State University Press, 2011); William C. Davis, *The Cause Lost: Myths and Realities of the Confederacy* (Lawrence: University Press of Kansas, 1996). On late twentieth-century manifestations of the Lost Cause, see Tony Horwitz, *Confederates in the Attic: Dispatches from the Unfinished Civil War* (New York: Vintage, 1998).

centralizing power. The reality was that both nations experienced similar wartime transformations, both moved toward becoming modern centralized states, and, in some ways, the Confederacy was the more centralized of the two.

The idea that Confederates fought for states' rights following their secession from the Union immediately raises some perplexing questions. One might ask, Fighting against whom? States' rights as opposed to what? If, as they claimed, the Confederate States were no longer part of the Union and thus no longer beholden to Washington, then what were these states' rights, and who threatened them? This is not to say that states' rights rhetoric or ideas were absent from the Confederacy, as will be shown, but states' rights were not the cause for which Confederate armies fought. There were Southerners who stood up and even fought for states' rights during the war, but those who did are not the figures often celebrated in Confederate lore. The champions of states' rights in the Confederacy were the obstructionist governors who hoarded supplies, issued exemptions to keep the men of their states out of the Confederate ranks, and undermined the Confederate war effort at nearly every turn. They were the legislators and judges who opposed Jefferson Davis, as often for personal as for political reasons, and who beat the states' rights drum to thwart his policies and to bolster their own political fortunes. They were the draft dodgers, the planters who refused to grow food instead of cotton, those who traded with the Yankees, those who resisted impressment or refused to pay their taxes. They were the disgruntled, the disaffected, and, quite often, the disloyal.

And so, the myth of Confederate states' rights is not so much a myth, really, as a misdirected, misappropriated, and mis-credited concept. Historians see states' rights as an obstacle to Confederate independence—a force of resistance and division within the Confederacy itself. While they might disagree about the extent to which states' rights ideas and obstruction actually hindered the Confederate war effort, they all agree that, from the perspective of Confederate leaders, it was a problem to be overcome and not the unifying cause that would come to be held in reverence by latter-day Confederate supporters. At least in terms of the internal dynamics of the Confederate South, the Confederate war effort was in many ways a fight against states' rights. Even if secession and the coming of the Civil War had been a struggle over states' rights (and it wasn't, at least not primarily), the conduct of the war, the experience of the war, and the struggle for Confederate independence itself mandated that Confederates repudiate their states' rights ideology by their actions, if not their words.

States' Rights in the Antebellum South

Still, it is easy to see how the myth arose and survived. Strict constructionism and the belief that the national government possessed only those powers specifically granted to it in the Constitution, with the rest reserved to the states, had a long history—though hardly an exclusively Southern one. By the time of the Civil War,

John C. Calhoun (1782–1850), former vice president and senator. Calhoun was a strong supporter of states' rights and a defender of slavery. Image courtesy of the Library of Congress.

states' rights had long been in the Southern air, and antebellum Southerners had breathed it in deeply. Jefferson and Madison had championed such ideas in the Kentucky and Virginia Resolutions in 1798. Since the 1830s, Southern advocates, particularly Southern radicals, and especially those in South Carolina, had talked incessantly about states' rights. John C. Calhoun, the antebellum South's foremost political thinker, had devoted the latter decades of his career to an impassioned defense of Southern interests through the vehicle of states' rights. His theory of nullification, his advocacy of the concept of concurrent majority, and, later, his insistence that Northerners capitulate to Southern demands were all rooted in his desire to protect the rights of a Southern minority within an American democracy premised upon majority rule.

Still, Southerners had always had a funny relationship with states' rights. Certainly, they invoked the rhetoric with increasing frequency and vehemence during the 1840s and 1850s as the growing power and population of the North threatened to block the expansion of and perhaps, it was feared, even the existence of slavery. But when judged solely from a strict constructionist states' rights position, Southerners proved to be remarkably inconsistent thinkers. Certainly, they raised few objections when federal power was used to advance Southern interests, when activist federal judges and justices issued expansive pro-Southern rulings, or when the states' rights of Northern states were infringed upon (as with the Fugitive Slave Act, for instance). After all, the "Slave Power Conspiracy" that Northerners so decried was the alleged Southern dominance of the national government and national political parties employed to suppress Northern states' rights. The truth was that states' rights had never been the South's true guiding star. Such rhetoric had always been a means to an end. For there was one state right that mattered above all else, and that was the right to hold slaves.

4

When it came to slavery and its protection, Southern leaders demonstrated great consistency. When states' rights rhetoric served the interests of slavery, as it usually did, they were adamant states' rights men. When it did not, they were content to raise no doctrinal objections.

States' Rights, Secession, and the Birth of the Confederacy

Likewise, when it came time to justify their secession from the United States, those individual states that issued declarations certainly drew on states' rights principles, but in every case, threats to slavery and the white racial order were what drove them to action. In its lengthy declaration of the "immediate causes" of its secession, South Carolina, the first to secede, invoked the Declaration of Independence, the Articles of Confederation, the United States Constitution, and all the states' rights rhetoric that it could muster before focusing on its true grievances: Northern threats to slavery and the election of Abraham Lincoln. Unlike South Carolina, Mississippi, the second to secede, saw little reason to dance around the issue: "Our position is thoroughly identified with the institution of slavery—the greatest material interest of the world. . . . There was no choice left us but submission to the mandates of abolition, or a dissolution of the Union, whose principles had been subverted to work out our ruin."[4] And this was the public face that white Southerners put on their decision to secede. As historian Charles Dew has so well documented, when speaking to each other, as in the case of the secession commissioners who were dispatched to persuade other, more reluctant, states to act, Southerners were far less veiled in identifying what they saw as the true stakes of the secession crisis: the preservation of slavery and, even more vitally, the maintenance of white supremacy. Lincoln's election was "an open declaration of war" against the South, Alabama secession commissioner Stephen F. Hale told Kentucky's governor, Beriah Magoffin, one that threatened to unleash "all the horrors of a San Domingo servile insurrection, consigning her citizens to assassinations and her wives and daughters to pollution and violation to gratify the lust of half-civilized Africans." Make no mistake, Hale warned,

> the slave-holder and non-slaveholder must ultimately share the same fate;
> all be degraded to a position of equality with free negroes, stand side by
> side with them at the polls, and fraternize in all the social relations of life,
> or else there will be an eternal war of races, desolating the land with blood,
> and utterly wasting and destroying all the resources of the country.[5]

---

4. J. L. Power, *Proceedings of the Mississippi State Convention* (Jackson, MS: Power and Cadwallader, 1861), 47.

5. Charles B. Dew, *Apostles of Disunion: Southern Secession Commissioners and the Causes of the Civil War* (Charlottesville: University Press of Virginia, 2001), 98.

Since this chapter is concerned with the myth of Confederate states' rights rather than the even more prevalent and pernicious myth of states' rights as the cause of the Civil War, we will focus specifically on the war years, on the Southern nation's short four-year life, and on how states' rights ideology actually affected the course and conduct of the war, the actions of the Confederate government, the nature of internal resistance to that government, and life within the Confederate States of America generally. At the outset, it seemed that Confederate states' rights stood on a firm foundation. After all, white Southerners had consciously decided to call their new nation a "Confederacy"—though, to be fair, that name had long been in circulation among Southern sectionalists and there was little question at the time over what the name would be. When representatives of the seven states of the Deep South, those that had seceded in response to Lincoln's election in November 1860, met in Montgomery, Alabama, in February 1861, to form their new nation and draft their constitution, states' rights, it would seem, were front and center. The legal and constitutional, as opposed to the revolutionary, justification for secession was grounded upon the original sovereignty of the individual states, the nature of the compact between them, and the rights and powers they had retained within the old Union. States' rights were enshrined in the new Confederate Constitution's preamble ("We, the people of the Confederate States, each State acting in its sovereign and independent character . . .") and reinforced, albeit with some ambiguity, throughout that document through key revisions to the language of the original U.S. Constitution.

But whatever their rhetoric about states' rights in the old Union, whatever they said in their constitution, and despite President Jefferson Davis' solemn oath to "preserve, protect, and defend" that constitution, the newly formed Confederate government almost immediately proceeded to amass power at the expense of the states and to assume ever greater control over the economy, the loyalty, and the lives of its citizens, quickly growing to become a far bigger, more powerful, and more intrusive central government than the one Southern states had seceded to get away from. Indeed, the story most historians tell of the Confederate government is not that of a loosely connected confederation of independent sovereign states but rather that of a rising, modern centralized nation-state with all the trappings, bureaucracy, and powers therein.

This transformation was not the result of duplicity or conspiracy, and the speed with which change occurred and the muted public response to, and even enthusiastic support for, the Confederate government's appropriation of sweeping new powers suggest that Confederate leaders, and Confederates generally, had other things on their minds than the protection of states' rights during the war. Davis himself had been a strong states' rights man as a Mississippi senator, but now he, as president of the Confederacy, with little sense of contradiction, proceeded to amass great power in his hands and within the Confederate government, all at the expense of the states and all, seemingly, at odds with the doctrine of states' rights.

There were immediate pressing needs facing Confederate leaders, and whatever their original intentions, those needs simply could not be met within a states' rights framework. Whether white Southerners could have maintained (or even would have wanted to maintain) a nation predicated upon states' rights in tranquil times without outside threat or interference is a matter of conjecture, but the truth is that the all-encompassing war for survival, which defined their nation's short life, simply would not permit it. Had the Confederacy truly fought for states' rights and had Confederate political and military leaders restricted their activities and limited their powers accordingly, the war would have been over very soon, and the Confederacy would have died an even quicker death.

The "Revolution" of 1860

The experience of fighting the Civil War produced a series of profound internal changes, revolutions even, within the Confederate States, even before defeat overtook them and with it the most revolutionary change of all: the final destruction of slavery. Many of these changes came at the expense of states' rights and individual rights as traditionally understood and passionately defended by antebellum Southerners. This was not the plan at the outset. Following Lincoln's election in November 1860, the radical *Charleston Mercury*, the South's foremost fire-eating paper, proudly proclaimed that "the revolution of 1860 has been initiated."[6] But if this was a "revolution," it was intended to be a very specific type of revolution. For in seceding and then forming their own nation, Southern leaders were not seeking rapid, fundamental change (a conventional definition of revolution). Indeed, they seceded to protect the South from change, to protect the "Southern way of life" and, above all, to protect the institution of slavery, upon which that way of life depended. It was the Northern states that had changed, Southern spokesmen argued, and white Southerners simply sought to uphold the original vision of the Founders, to restore and safeguard the proper balance of government, and to protect their own cherished individual and states' rights. The numerically superior North had become fanatical and dangerous, as clearly evidenced by the recent election of Abraham Lincoln, and the seceding Southern states simply desired to remove themselves from this diseased body before the infection could spread further. Thus, Southern secessionists sought to destroy the United States government in order to preserve it, or at least the Southern part of it.

This was intended, therefore, to be a conservative revolution, even a counter-revolution, and Confederate leaders were divided over whether they should even use the word "revolution" when describing Southern independence. Social revolution and threats to the white racial order were what they most feared, and some political elites worried about the impact that revolutionary rhetoric might have on groups for which they did not intend it to apply, such as slaves, free blacks, or even non-slaveholding whites. History taught them that revolutions, once begun, had a tendency to spin out of control.

---

6. "The News of Lincoln's Election," *Charleston Mercury*, November 8, 1860.

Alexander H. Stephens (1812–83), the only vice president of the Confederate States of America. He was a strong supporter of slavery and a vocal critic of President Jefferson Davis and the government in Richmond. Image courtesy of the Library of Congress.

As such, many Confederate leaders in the wake of secession sought to downplay or deny any revolutionary implications, and they used the language of constitutionalism, traditionalism, and states' rights to do it. Confederates were defending existing institutions, not seeking to create new ones, they staunchly maintained. Secession was a legal, constitutional right, not a revolutionary one, that was firmly and conservatively grounded upon the original nature of the compact between sovereign states. President Jefferson Davis said so explicitly. As he later explained in an 1864 speech, "Ours is not a revolution. . . . We are not engaged in a Quixotic fight for the rights of man; our struggle is for inherited rights."[7] The South's most eminent theologian, Reverend James Henley Thornwell of South Carolina, writing in 1861, agreed: "We are not revolutionists; we are resisting revolution. We are upholding the true doctrines of the Federal Constitution. We are conservative."[8] For proof of this conservatism, Southerners could point to the Confederate Constitution itself, which retained almost the exact structure and even much of the same language as the United States Constitution.

Others, like the new vice president of the Confederacy, Alexander Stephens of Georgia, were not afraid to use the word "revolution," but they made it very clear that their revolution was a creature very different from the liberty, equality, and fraternity model of the French Revolution or the liberal democratic European revolutions of 1848. As Stephens

---

7. "Speech in Augusta, Georgia," October 3, 1864, in William J. Cooper, Jr., ed., *Jefferson Davis: The Essential Writings* (New York: Modern Library, 2003), 346.

8. J. H. Thornwell, *Our Danger and Our Duty* (Columbia, SC: Southern Guardian Steam-power Press, 1862), 5.

declared in his most often quoted and infamous speech, the "present revolution" was to preserve "the proper *status* of the negro in our form of civilization." The American Declaration of Independence's assertion of manhood equality was wrong, dead wrong. "Our new government," Stephens explained, "is founded upon exactly the opposite idea; its foundations are laid, its corner-stone rests upon the great truth, that the negro is not equal to the white man; that slavery—subordination to the superior race—is his natural and normal condition. This, our new government, is the first, in the history of the world, based upon this great physical, philosophical, and moral truth."[9] Thus, in Stephens' view, the Confederacy's revolution was a counter-revolution, not just against the North but against the entire tendency of the age; one dedicated to protecting, preserving, and conserving those rights and ideas that had come under threat by an increasingly liberalized and, in his judgment, irreligious world.

But whether they used the word "revolution" or not, Confederate leaders agreed that secession and the formation of the Confederacy were intended to protect Southern society from change, to preserve its character, its institutions, and its rights. Despite these avowedly conservative intentions, however, revolution is what they got. Confederates quickly found that the necessities and exigencies of war would force radical change upon them and that the steps that the Confederate government had to take in order to fight that war would destroy the status quo that Southerners had set out to preserve. One of the consequences, indeed one of the goals, of the myth of Confederate states' rights is to conceal the degree to which Southern society, its economy, and its government changed during the war and to obscure what historian Emory Thomas memorably called "the Confederacy as a Revolutionary Experience."[10]

Confederate Revolutions

Politically, over the course of its short life, the Confederacy experienced an irresistible movement toward centralized national power at the expense of the states. The theory of states' rights, as championed by antebellum Southern leaders, maintained that the individual states always had remained sovereign within the old Union and that the central national government, while necessary, had to be tightly restrained, performing only its specifically enumerated functions with the balance of power reserved to the states. It was on this basis that secession was legally and constitutionally justified, and the framers of the Confederate Constitution in Montgomery adopted some key revisions to the language of the United States Constitution designed to bolster states' rights and to safeguard them from encroachment (as well as to offer explicit

---

9. Henry Cleveland, *Alexander H. Stephens in Public and Private with Letters and Speeches, before, during, and since the War* (Philadelphia: National Publishing, 1866), 721.

10. Emory Thomas, *The Confederacy as a Revolutionary Experience* (Englewood Cliffs, NJ: Prentice-Hall, 1971). The next several paragraphs are indebted to Thomas' formulation.

federal protections to the institution of slavery). Nevertheless, the Confederate government, once constituted, quickly came to exercise powers that far exceeded those of the United States government prior to 1861.

This political revolution was driven by the necessities of war and national defense. The Civil War presented a new military reality to both sides. The armies that fought the war were exponentially larger than any that had ever been marshaled on American soil before. The military theater was enormous, and the logistical and strategic difficulties of moving and coordinating armies over such vast distances and keeping them fed, supplied, and reinforced confronted political and military leaders with challenges the scale of which no American government had ever faced. In order to meet those challenges, the Confederate government required the power to enlist long-term volunteers who could be moved from place to place independent of state control or oversight. It required the power to compel those soldiers to remain in the ranks and, as soon became obvious once initial war enthusiasm began to wane, even the power to compel them to enter the ranks. The Confederacy would resort to a draft before the United States, with the Confederate Congress passing the first national conscription act in American history in April 1862. Under its terms, all white males between the ages of eighteen and thirty-five were placed in national service unless occupationally exempted or they provided a substitute. Later, the ages would be extended to all males between seventeen and fifty, substitutions would be prohibited, and the number of exemption categories reduced. Through a combination of volunteers, who now would be compelled to serve for the duration of the conflict, and conscripts, the Confederacy raised a national army composed of the overwhelming majority of its white male population of military age. The creation of that army, its organization and deployment, its ability to compel men to stay at their posts and to punish or force the return of those who left, and especially the draft, all represented significant increases in the power of the central Confederate government as well as dramatic erosions of states' rights as traditionally understood.

It was not just the military. Similar centralizing tendencies were evident in the dealings between the Confederate government and its civilian population. The Confederate government assumed control over suppressing dissent and disloyalty on the home front, and Southern civilians soon found that their freedoms of movement, speech, and assembly were subject to the oversight and restriction of Confederate officials. As Mark Neely has shown, the constitutional rights of Confederate citizens were severely curtailed as the war progressed, and, for the most part, Southerners readily accepted such restrictions in the name of wartime necessity and internal security.[11] Unlike his rival in Washington who seized the power and sought congressional approval only after the fact, in 1862 Jefferson Davis received authorization from the Confederate Congress to suspend the writ of habeas corpus, which protected citizens from arbitrary arrest. And although this authorization was subject to renewal, Davis

---

11. Mark E. Neely, Jr., *Southern Rights: Political Prisoners and the Myth of Confederate Constitutionalism* (Charlottesville: University Press of Virginia, 1999).

was given great latitude. For instance, he immediately placed the capital city of Richmond under martial law and used his sweeping powers to curtail internal dissent and arrest disloyal elements. Indeed, though Lincoln has received far greater scrutiny in this regard, Davis' record on domestic civil liberties was quite similar, though given long-standing Southern suspicions of centralized power, perhaps even more shocking. Still, no matter which president wielded his powers more widely or wisely, the Confederate government's assumption of control over Southern disloyalty represented a further erosion of states' rights and Southern civil liberties.

The Confederate government also took increasing control over the Southern economy and transportation infrastructure. Through a combination of prodding and coercion, the central government helped to usher in the rapid industrialization of the Confederate South as well as the dramatic transformation of its agricultural economy. The War Department stimulated, subsidized, and directly managed large segments of the Southern war industry. It opened factories, operated mines, and constructed laboratories, munitions works, powder mills, and foundries, and it encouraged various new domestic manufacturers. Once the draft went into effect in 1862, all private manufacturing and industry effectively came under national control. Through the granting of exemptions, the detailing of men, and the awarding of contracts, the Confederate government decided which businesses remained in operation and what their products would be. And, even though the Confederate Constitution specifically forbade financial aid from the central government for internal improvements (a long-standing states' rights issue in the old Union), the Confederate government oversaw and paid for the construction of new railroad lines and the completion of old ones.

But the nationalization of the Confederate economy did not stop there. Individual citizens too felt the direct power of the Confederate government. The practice of impressment—that is, the taking of food, crops, animals, implements, and even slaves from Confederate citizens for military purposes—while necessary for the war effort, was widespread and much decried. "The sorest test of [the people's] patriotism and self-sacrificing spirit," impressment was a "harsh, unequal, and odious mode of supply," Confederate Secretary of War James Seddon admitted.[12] For those unfortunate citizens who received a visit, or multiple visits, from the impressment officer, these requisitions often had devastating consequences on their personal finances and household production.

The deeply unpopular draft exemption of one white man on every plantation with twenty or more slaves (also known as the Twenty Negro Law), later reduced to fifteen slaves, in addition to exciting class tensions between slaveholders and non-slaveholders and leading to the cry that this was a "rich man's war but a poor man's fight," had the less publicized effect of placing planters under government oversight and later forcing them to sell food to the government at government-set prices. While introduced too

---

12. James A. Seddon to Jefferson Davis, November 26, 1863, in *The War of the Rebellion: A Compilation of the Official Records of the Union and Confederate Armies*, comp. United States War Department (Washington, D.C.: Government Printing Office, 1880–1901), ser. 4, 2:1009.

late (in 1863) and never adequately enforced, to arrest the crippling financial woes facing the Southern nation, the Confederacy's comprehensive tax system included a graduated income tax, a tax on all agricultural products, license taxes of all kinds, and a very unpopular tax in kind, and represented, by virtue of its very existence, yet another sweeping new federal power at the expense of the states.

In sum, just like Lincoln's government in Washington, Jefferson Davis' government in Richmond became a modern centralized state as a result of the course and conduct of the Civil War, and the Confederate government had the bureaucracy—the hallmark of all centralized states—to prove it. By 1863, the Confederate government employed some seventy thousand civil servants, which was more than even Washington had.[13] Whether they liked it or not, Jefferson Davis and Confederate leaders overrode many of the states' rights principles that the Confederacy was supposedly called into existence to protect, and they did so in response to the demands of a full-scale and all-out war for national survival.

By the war's end, Confederate leaders were even willing to interfere with the most precious states' right of all: the institution of slavery. What had begun with Alexander Stephens declaring slavery to be the cornerstone of Southern civilization ended with Jefferson Davis and the Confederate Congress endorsing the recruitment and arming of slaves as Confederate soldiers. In March 1865, with the Confederacy teetering on the edge of oblivion, the Confederate Congress authorized the enlistment of 300,000 slaves with the promise of freedom in return for their service. It never happened—only a handful of would-be African American soldiers came forward, and Richmond soon fell to Ulysses S. Grant's forces—but the fact that limited emancipation was even contemplated, let alone approved, at the highest levels of the Confederate government represented a repudiation of the core principle of antebellum Southern society and a violation of the ultimate states' right.[14]

The Confederacy versus States' Rights

These sweeping changes to the relationship between Southern citizens and the Confederate state did not happen painlessly or without resistance. Indeed, resistance to the Confederate government's policies seemed to come from every direction at once, and much of it took the form, or at least the guise, of protection for states' rights. Much of the historical scholarship of the Confederacy has focused on the nature, the sources, and the effectiveness of this resistance, and historians have

---

13. Thomas, *The Confederacy as a Revolutionary Experience*, 70; Richard F. Bensel, *Yankee Leviathan: The Origins of Central State Authority in America, 1859–1877* (Cambridge: Cambridge University Press, 1990), 103.

14. See Bruce Levine, *Confederate Emancipation: Southern Plans to Free and Arm Slaves during the Civil War* (New York: Oxford University Press, 2006).

vigorously debated the extent to which internal divisions, obstruction, and outright disloyalty hampered the Confederate war effort and perhaps even bore responsibility for Confederate defeat.[15] Almost a century ago, Frank Owsley, who is quoted at the head of this chapter, concluded that the obstructionism of Confederate governors and other political leaders was so damaging to the South's war effort that the Confederacy had, in fact, "died of state rights."[16] David Donald revised Owsley's thesis, arguing instead that the Confederacy had "died of democracy," meaning Southern individualism and localism.[17] Other historians subsequently have offered their own "died

15. The literature is vast. Some key books include Stephanie McCurry, *Confederate Reckoning: Power and Politics in the Civil War South* (Cambridge, MA: Harvard University Press, 2010); William W. Freehling, *The South vs. the South: How Anti-Confederate Southerners Shaped the Course of the Civil War* (Oxford: Oxford University Press, 2001); Carl N. Degler, *The Other South: Southern Dissenters in the Nineteenth Century* (New York: Harper and Row, 1974); Richard E. Beringer, Herman Hattaway, Archer Jones, and William N. Still, Jr., *Why the South Lost the Civil War* (Athens: University of Georgia Press, 1991); Wayne K. Durrill, *War of Another Kind: A Southern Community in the Great Rebellion* (New York: Oxford University Press, 1990); Paul D. Escott, *After Secession: Jefferson Davis and the Failure of Confederate Nationalism* (Baton Rouge: Louisiana State University Press, 1992); Richard Nelson Current, *Lincoln's Loyalists: Union Soldiers from the Confederacy* (Boston: Northeastern University Press, 1992); Drew Gilpin Faust, *Mothers of Invention: Women of the Slaveholding South in the American Civil War* (Chapel Hill: University of North Carolina Press, 1997); Armstead L. Robinson, *Bitter Fruits of Bondage: The Demise of Slavery and the Collapse of the Confederacy, 1861–1865* (Charlottesville: University of Virginia Press, 2005); Albert Burton Moore, *Conscription and Conflict in the Confederacy* (New York: Macmillan, 1924); Mark A. Weitz, *More Damning than Slaughter: Desertion in the Confederate Army* (Lincoln: University of Nebraska Press, 2005); David Williams, *Bitterly Divided: The South's Inner Civil War* (New York: New Press, 2008); David Williams, *Rich Man's War: Class, Caste, and Confederate Defeat in the Lower Chattahoochee Valley* (Athens: University of Georgia Press, 1999); James Alan Marten, *Texas Divided: Loyalty and Dissent in the Lone Star State, 1856–1874* (Lexington: University Press of Kentucky, 1990); Thomas G. Dyer, *Secret Yankees: The Union Circle in Confederate Atlanta* (Baltimore: Johns Hopkins University Press, 1999); Margaret M. Storey, *Loyalty and Loss: Alabama's Unionists in the Civil War and Reconstruction* (Baton Rouge: Louisiana State University Press, 2004); John C. Inscoe and Robert C. Kenzer, eds., *Enemies of the Country: New Perspectives on Unionists in the Civil War South* (Athens: University of Georgia Press, 2001); John C. Inscoe and Gordon B. McKinney, eds., *The Heart of Confederate Appalachia: Western North Carolina in the Civil War* (Athens: University of Georgia Press, 2000); Phillip S. Paludan, *Victims: A True Story of the Civil War* (Knoxville: University of Tennessee Press, 2004); Victoria E. Bynum, *The Free State of Jones: Mississippi's Longest Civil War* (Chapel Hill: University of North Carolina Press, 2001); Judkin Browning, *Shifting Loyalties: The Union Occupation of Eastern North Carolina* (Chapel Hill: University of North Carolina Press, 2011); Martin Crawford, *Ashe County's Civil War: Community and Society in the Appalachian South* (Charlottesville: University Press of Virginia, 2001); Kenneth W. Noe and Shannon H. Wilson, eds., *The Civil War in Appalachia: Collected Essays* (Knoxville: University of Tennessee Press, 1997); Jonathan Dean Sarris, *A Separate Civil War: Communities in Conflict in the Mountain South* (Charlottesville: University of Virginia Press, 2006); and Barton A. Myers, *Rebels against the Confederacy: North Carolina's Unionists* (New York: Cambridge University Press, 2014).

16. Owsley, *State Rights in the Confederacy*, 1.

17. David Herbert Donald, "Died of Democracy," in *Why the North Won the Civil War*, ed. David Herbert Donald (Baton Rouge: Louisiana State University Press, 1960).

of" pronouncements with many laying responsibility at President Jefferson Davis' feet.[18] In more recent years, the role that states' rights played in the destruction of the Confederacy has been absorbed into contentious debates surrounding the strength or weakness of Confederate nationalism, which in turn has fed the even more expansive debate over whether the Confederacy was crushed from without (by the North) or crumbled from within.[19] Counter to Owsley and Donald, historians have argued that, in fact, the forces of centralization and nationalism prevailed, that obstruction by the individual states and governors was both less effective and less widespread

---

18. For instance, see Escott, *After Secession.*

19. The foundational studies of Confederate nationalism remain David M. Potter, "The Historian's Use of Nationalism and Vice Versa," in *The South and the Sectional Conflict* (Baton Rouge: Louisiana State University Press, 1968); and Drew Gilpin Faust, *The Creation of Confederate Nationalism: Ideology and Identity in the Civil War South* (Baton Rouge: Louisiana State University Press, 1988). Important recent books exploring different aspects of Confederate nationalism include Robert E. Bonner, *Mastering America: Southern Slaveholders and the Crisis of American Nationhood* (Cambridge: Cambridge University Press, 2009); Robert E. Bonner, *Colors and Blood: Flag Passions of the Confederate South* (Princeton: Princeton University Press, 2002); Anne Sarah Rubin, *A Shattered Nation: The Rise and Fall of the Confederacy, 1861–1868* (Chapel Hill: University of North Carolina Press, 2005); Paul Quigley, *Shifting Grounds: Nationalism and the American South, 1848–1865* (Oxford: Oxford University Press, 2011); Michael T. Bernath, *Confederate Minds: The Struggle for Intellectual Independence in the Civil War South* (Chapel Hill: University of North Carolina Press, 2010); John D. Majewski, *Modernizing a Slave Economy: The Economic Vision of the Confederate Nation* (Chapel Hill: University of North Carolina Press, 2009); Peter S. Carmichael, *The Last Generation: Young Virginians in Peace, War, and Reunion* (Chapel Hill: University of North Carolina Press, 2005); Victoria E. Ott, *Confederate Daughters: Coming of Age during the Civil War* (Carbondale: Southern Illinois University Press, 2008); Jason Phillips, *Diehard Rebels: The Confederate Culture of Invincibility* (Athens: University of Georgia Press, 2007); Aaron Sheehan-Dean, *Why Confederates Fought: Family and Nation in Civil War Virginia* (Chapel Hill: University of North Carolina Press, 2007); Coleman Hutchison, *Apples and Ashes: Literature, Nationalism, and the Confederate States of America* (Athens: University of Georgia Press, 2012); and Ian Binnington, *Confederate Visions: Nationalism, Symbolism, and the Imagined South in the Civil War* (Charlottesville: University of Virginia Press, 2013). Major works in the strong vs. weak Confederate nationalism debate include Escott, *After Secession*; Beringer et al., *Why the South Lost the Civil War*; Durrill, *War of Another Kind*; Freehling, *The South vs. the South*; Robinson, *Bitter Fruits of Bondage*; Gary W. Gallagher, *The Confederate War: How Popular Will, Nationalism, and Military Strategy Could Not Stave Off Defeat* (Cambridge, MA: Harvard University Press, 1997); William Alan Blair, *Virginia's Private War: Feeding Body and Soul in the Confederacy, 1861–1865* (New York: Oxford University Press, 1998); Faust, *Mothers of Invention*; Emory Thomas, *The Confederate Nation, 1861–1865* (New York: Harper and Row, 1979); George C. Rable, *Civil Wars: Women and the Crisis of Southern Nationalism* (Urbana: University of Illinois Press, 1989); George C. Rable, *The Confederate Republic: A Revolution against Politics* (Chapel Hill: University of North Carolina Press, 1994); Williams, *Rich Man's War*; David Williams, Teresa Crisp Williams, and David Carlson, *Plain Folk in a Rich Man's War: Class and Dissent in Confederate Georgia* (Gainesville: University Press of Florida, 2002); Brian Steel Wills, *The War Hits Home: The Civil War in Southeastern Virginia* (Charlottesville: University Press of Virginia, 2001); Jacqueline Glass Campbell, *When Sherman Marched North from the Sea: Resistance on the Confederate Home Front* (Chapel Hill: University of North Carolina Press, 2003).

than Owsley had argued, and that the Southern populace largely acquiesced in, and even vigorously demanded, the Confederate government's ever-greater involvement in their daily lives. But regardless of where scholars fit in this debate, essentially everyone agrees that the issue of states' rights was a problem from the Confederate point of view, an obstacle to victory, a force of division, not a unifying cause. Where they disagree is over just how big an obstacle it was. While few today would follow Owsley in granting such a central role to states' rights ideology in explaining Confederate defeat, many maintain that internal divisions within Southern society and outright opposition to the Confederate government and the war effort—be it by non-slaveholders, women, slaves, Southern Unionists, and so on—weakened and ultimately disintegrated the Confederacy from within. But no matter their particular arguments and no matter the relative importance they assign to various modes or groups of internal opposition, all of this scholarship runs counter to the myth of Confederate states' rights, and it has highlighted the degree to which the Confederacy battled against, not for, states' rights.

The rhetoric of states' rights did serve as a blanket cry of opposition against Jefferson Davis and the Confederate government. Those who voiced it ranged from the strictly doctrinaire to the cravenly opportunistic to the generally disgruntled. Certainly there was a strong states' rights tradition within Southern politics, and Southern leaders were deeply steeped in it. Set in their ways and in their thinking, some Southerners, it was true, had a knee-jerk reaction against encroaching centralized power, and they found it difficult to adjust to the new wartime and political realities presented by Confederate independence. As South Carolinian Laurence Keitt complained in January 1864, "[I] fear that our people have not risen to the height of this present crisis. . . . They have cherished state pride and exclusiveness for eighty years, and no changes however great, no ruin however appalling, could make them forget it for a moment. Our people will not move out of the old forms and routine."[20]

But some Southern politicians also consciously and strategically deployed states' rights rhetoric in order to weaken Jefferson Davis or advance their own political agendas and personal careers. They accused Davis of seeking to be a dictator and plotting to destroy the rights of the states. They rejected his claims that the war required unusual, extreme measures. Or as his own vice president, soon turned vociferous critic, Alexander Stephens, warned a Crawfordville, Georgia, audience in November 1862, "Away with the idea of getting independence first, and looking for liberty afterward. Our liberties, once lost, may be lost forever."[21]

Confederate governors posed the biggest internal political obstacle to Jefferson Davis' policies and conduct of the war. Not only did the governors retain a great deal of power, but also they were the Confederate politicians who had the most to lose from

---

20. As quoted in Bell Irvin Wiley, *The Road to Appomattox* (1956; repr., Baton Rouge: Louisiana State University Press, 1994), 117.

21. Cleveland, *Alexander H. Stephens*, 760.

the expansion of Confederate authority and the most to gain by agitating states' rights issues. Unlike Davis, their focus was the well-being and defense of their individual states, not the nation, and it was politically expedient, if not far-sighted, to build up their own popularity by appealing to the narrower, state-focused concerns of their constituents. Many governors, troubled by, even jealous of, the growing prerogatives and prestige of the national government, did obstruct or at least raise objections to Davis' actions at various times throughout the war. Historians have drawn pointed contrasts between the provincialism of Confederate governors and the national vision and sacrificing spirit of some of Lincoln's great wartime Northern governors: men like John Andrew of Massachusetts, Oliver Morton of Indiana, and Andrew Curtin of Pennsylvania. To be fair, however, these Northern governors never faced the same challenges as did their Southern counterparts. They were never confronted with the same degree of suffering, the dire shortages, or the existential threat of invading and occupying armies (except for Curtin's Pennsylvania, briefly). Two Confederate governors in particular, Joseph Brown of Georgia and Zebulon Vance of North Carolina, proved especially difficult for Davis, and they have subsequently attracted much historical attention.

A die-hard defender of state sovereignty, meaning his own personal sovereignty, Joseph Brown had been a thorn in Davis' side from the very beginning. Following Georgia's secession, Brown had even dispatched his own diplomatic officer abroad to represent and negotiate for Georgia as an independent republic. Throughout the war, Brown did everything he could to thwart Davis' policies, to keep as many Georgia men as possible out of the Confederate army and under his own jurisdiction, and to deny the Confederate military badly needed supplies and assistance in the name of state sovereignty and local defense. As Georgian editor and harsh Brown critic Joseph A. Turner wrote in disgust in July 1863, "We, for one, are tired of being the subject, or the citizen of two governments. We do not wish to have two sovereigns—Gov. Brown and President Davis, for instance—claiming our allegiance."[22] Even Edward Pollard of the *Richmond Examiner*, who, during the war, loathed Jefferson Davis with a passion not to be matched, later condemned Brown as the "coarse, obese prince of Southern demagogues."[23]

Zebulon Vance's record as a states' rights obstructionist was far more mixed. Certainly, he represented growing war frustration in North Carolina beginning in 1862. He complained that Davis favored Democrats and secessionists over ex-Whigs and former Unionists like himself. Vance often has been tarred with the same die-hard states' rights obstructionist brush as Brown, and certainly some of his actions, such as exempting as many state officers and local defense forces as he could and hoarding military supplies within his state, hurt the Confederate war effort. At the same time, although often at odds with Davis, Vance did support the Confederate cause, especially toward the end.

---

22. Joseph A. Turner "Gen. Toombs in Hancock. No. 1," *Countryman*, July 7, 1863.

23. Edward Pollard, *Life of Jefferson Davis* (Philadelphia: National Publishing, 1869), 212.

When confronted with a true anti-Confederate opponent in the person of William Woods Holden, who ran against Vance for governor in 1864 as a "peace candidate," Vance railed against antiwar sentiment in his state and overwhelmingly won reelection. Even Davis threw his support behind Vance as the lesser of two evils.

But the governors were not the only Southern voices crying foul in the name of states' rights. There were doctrinaire states' rights diehards, the former Fire Eaters, who opposed the growing power of the Confederate government on principle: men like William Yancey of Alabama and Robert Rhett, owner of the radical *Charleston Mercury*. For example, in May 1864 the *Mercury*, in characteristic fashion, thundered

Zebulon Vance (1830–94), governor of North Carolina and critic of Jefferson Davis and the government in Richmond, yet still a loyal supporter of the Confederacy. Image courtesy of the Library of Congress.

that "from the commencement of the war, the Confederate Government, in every sort of way, has endeavored to establish a despotic authority over the people of the Confederate States."[24]

Then there were those who came to embrace states' rights ever more strongly as the war progressed, not out of principle but out of frustrated political ambition and outright personal animosity toward Jefferson Davis (though, it should be said, Davis was an easy man to dislike). Robert Toombs of Georgia, who had been in the running for Davis' office and continued to believe that he could do a far better job than the current president, was one of these. So was Confederate vice president Alexander Stephens, also of Georgia, who initially supported Davis but soon became his bitter enemy. After 1862, Stephens spent less and less time in Richmond, but from Georgia he kept up a constant rhetorical barrage against the man whom he came to regard

---

24. "Usurpation Again," *Charleston Mercury*, May 14, 1864.

as "weak and vacillating, timid, petulant, peevish, obstinate."[25] Both former Whigs, Toombs and Stephens never forgot their old political battles against Davis and the other Southern Democrats. Known more for their pragmatism than their doctrinaire states' rights stances before the war, they now seized on states' rights as their most effective weapon against the man whom they both reviled—a convenient cloak for their own animus and political disappointment.

States' rights opposition also arose as a result of the Confederacy's unique party system, or rather the lack thereof. At the birth of the Southern nation, politicians consciously decided not to revive their former political parties in the name of national unity and nonpartisan cooperation. But what was intended to be a source of strength and cohesion proved to be a force of division. Historians continue to debate just how crippling the Confederacy's no-party politics were to the Confederate government and the conduct of the war, but there can be little doubt that the absence of formal national parties encouraged a state-focused perspective among Confederate elected officials at the expense of national interests.[26] In the absence of a party structure and the ties of loyalty, patronage, and self-interest that went with it, Jefferson Davis had little institutional means of rallying support for his policies. With little reason to look up the ladder, Confederate politicians naturally looked down to their individual state interests as the best way to promote their own political success. As a consequence, opposition to Jefferson Davis quickly became petty, factional, parochial, and extremely personal. There is no space here to examine the intricacies of Confederate politics, but suffice it to say that the lack of national political parties helped to foster states' rights–based opposition within the Confederate and state legislatures to a significant degree.

Recruitment, Conscription, and Habeas Corpus

While opponents of Davis' administration deployed the weapon of states' rights in many different contexts, there were three particular issues that attracted the most fire: the recruitment, deployment, and arming of troops; conscription; and the suspension

---

25. Alexander Stephens to H. V. Johnson, April 8, 1864, in *The War of the Rebellion*, ser. 4, 3:279.

26. See Rable, *The Confederate Republic*; David M. Potter, "Jefferson Davis and the Political Factors in Confederate Defeat," in Donald, *Why the North Won the Civil War*; Eric McKitrick, "Politics and the Union and Confederate War Effort," in *The American Party Systems: Stages of Political Development*, ed. William N. Chambers and Walter D. Burnham (New York: Oxford University Press, 1967); Bensel, *Yankee Leviathan*; Alexander B. Thomas and Richard E. Beringer, *The Anatomy of the Confederate Congress: A Study of the Influences of Member Characteristics on Legislative Voting Behavior, 1861–1865* (Nashville: Vanderbilt University Press, 1972); Kenneth C. Martis, *The Historical Atlas of the Congresses of the Confederate States of America: 1861–1865* (New York: Simon and Schuster, 1994); Daniel W. Crofts, *Reluctant Confederates: Upper South Unionists in the Secession Crisis* (Chapel Hill: University of North Carolina Press, 1989); and Wilfred Buck Yearns, *The Confederate Congress* (Athens: University of Georgia Press, 1960).

of habeas corpus. From the beginning, Jefferson Davis had stressed the need for a national army, one firmly and solely under central control, or as he himself explained in 1863, "Our safety—our very existence—depends on the complete blending of the military strength of all the States into one united body, to be used anywhere and everywhere as the exigencies of the contest may require for the good of the *whole*."[27] The war required that the recruitment, control, discipline, and disposition of soldiers be placed under central Confederate authority, he argued, thus justifying his attempts to bypass state governors or limit their power. For their part, the governors rightly saw Davis' actions as infringements on their traditional authority, and they attempted to maintain control over the recruitment of troops in their own states or, failing that, to ensure that they could either recall troops as needed or maintain a reserve military force (essentially state armies) to defend their states from external invasion or internal (slave) insurrection. Governors also stood on states' rights ground when it came to the arming and provisioning of troops, insisting that supplies held in their states be used by their own men and refusing to turn over their stockpiles of weapons and equipment to Confederate authorities. While understandable, such actions and obstructions impeded the total mobilization of Confederate forces and kept badly needed soldiers and materials from where they were needed most. As the frustrated acting secretary of war, Judah P. Benjamin, complained to General Braxton Bragg in November 1861, "The difficulty lies with the governors of the States, who are unwilling to trust the common defense to one common head. . . . Each Governor wants to satisfy his own people, and there are not wanting politicians in each State to encourage the people to raise the cry that they will not consent to be left defenseless at home. The voice of reason, which would teach them that their home defenses would be best secured by a vigorous attack on the enemy on his own frontier is unheeded."[28]

But it was conscription, the draft, that produced the greatest outcry as the most flagrant and dangerous violation of states' rights. First enacted in April 1862, the Confederate draft was far more sweeping than subsequent conscription in the North. Unless exempted, every Southern man of military age was placed in the national army. Unlike in the North, no lottery names were drawn, few bounties or other incentives were offered, commutations were not permitted, and substitutions were later prohibited. Instead, the Confederacy relied upon compulsion. Conscription officers roamed the countryside, rounding up men and delivering them to the army. Through compulsory reenlistment, volunteers found their terms of service extended indefinitely, and every Confederate soldier would be made to serve for the duration of the conflict until he was killed, wounded to the point of incapacitation, captured, or discharged or

---

27. Jefferson Davis to senators and representatives from Arkansas, March 30, 1862, in *Jefferson Davis, Constitutionalist: His Letters, Papers, and Speeches*, ed. Dunbar Rowland (Jackson: Mississippi Department of Archives and History, 1923), 5:462.

28. Judah P. Benjamin to Braxton Bragg, November 4, 1861, in *The War of the Rebellion*, ser. 1, 6:763.

he deserted. While necessary to carry on the war, conscription, both the thing in itself and the way it was enforced, was denounced as subversive of states' rights and indicative of tyranny. States' rights advocates charged that it was unconstitutional to destroy or appropriate the state militias. They warned that it was dangerous to concentrate so much power in the hands of the president. While all the governors were decidedly lukewarm toward the draft, its leading critics, not surprisingly, were Zebulon Vance and especially Joseph Brown. "No act of the Government of the United States prior to the secession of Georgia struck a blow at constitutional liberty so fell as has been stricken by the conscription acts," Brown bitterly complained to the president in October 1862.[29] One strategy to block the draft, adopted by Brown and Vance and, to a lesser extent, the other Confederate governors, was to exempt as many state officials and to promote as many militiamen to an officer's rank as possible. As a result, one Confederate general quipped, the typical Georgia or North Carolina militia regiment consisted of "3 field officers, 4 staff officers, 10 captains, 30 lieutenants, and 1 private with a misery in his bowels."[30]

Civil liberties violations also attracted the ire of Davis' states' rights opponents. Jefferson Davis relied on his suspension of the writ of habeas corpus to enforce conscription and control dissent, and to prevent local and state courts from interfering. Recognizing the dangers of appearing tyrannical, Davis had trodden somewhat carefully. As already noted, unlike Lincoln, Davis first sought permission from Congress before suspending the writ, and he had that authorization for only eighteen months during the war. Even when he had the power, he was circumspect in using it, suspending habeas corpus in limited areas, usually those threatened by invasion. Even still, opponents howled at this violation of Southern civil liberties as a betrayal of states' rights and a clear sign of Davis' dictatorial designs. Georgia, not surprisingly, took the lead, with Joseph Brown, Robert Toombs, and Alexander Stephens urging their fellow citizens to resist Davis' tyranny. As one Georgia newspaper warned, "Georgians, behold your chains!—Freeman of a once and happy country, contemplate the last act which rivets your bonds and binds you hand and foot at the mercy of an unlimited military authority."[31] Confederate Vice President Alexander Stephens tore into his chief executive in a three-hour speech before the Georgia legislature in March 1864. "Could the whole country be more completely under the power and control of one man . . . ?" he asked rhetorically. "Could dictatorial powers be more complete?"[32]

Other cases of individual or local resistance to Confederate policies often were couched in the language of states' rights, even though their opposition was really

---

29. Joseph Brown to Jefferson Davis, October 18, 1862, in *The War of the Rebellion*, ser. 4, 2:131.

30. As quoted in Moore, *Conscription and Conflict in the Confederacy*, 71n.

31. As quoted in George C. Rable, "Rebels and Patriots in the Confederate 'Revolution,'" in *In the Cause of Liberty: How the Civil War Redefined American Ideals*, ed. William J. Cooper and John M. McCardell (Baton Rouge: Louisiana State University Press, 2009), 82.

32. Cleveland, *Alexander H. Stephens*, 782.

grounded in a refusal to permit government officials (of any government) to █ with their personal business, property, or behavior rather than in a desire to u█ the traditional sovereignty of the states. Still, those seeking to thwart Confederate o█ cials were not inclined to split ideological hairs, and resistance to tyranny and states' rights were seen as two sides of the same coin. Planters who continued to grow cotton instead of food in defiance of government mandates, those who secretly (and some not so secretly) sold cotton to the Yankees, those who hid their crops, animals, and especially their slaves from impressment officers, and those who refused to pay the new Confederate taxes all drew on a tradition of Southern state, local, and individual rights to justify their noncompliance. But in all cases, states' rights, contrary to the myth, were not a cause that bound Southerners to the Confederate nation. Rather, states' rights set them at odds with it.

States' Rights in the Confederacy

The point here is not to overemphasize the role that states' rights played in Confederate defeat. It is well worth noting that in the end, Jefferson Davis and the Confederate government got their way in almost every case. Nor should the individual Southern states be seen solely, or even primarily, as impediments to Confederate victory. While they might have grumbled, and in a few cases outright resisted, Southern governors did make vital contributions to the Confederate war effort. State governments not only supplied the men for the Confederate armies and the materials to support them, but they also provided essential services at home to alleviate suffering and bolster home front morale, without which the Confederacy would have collapsed much sooner. However, if the theory of states' rights did not kill the Confederacy, there can be little doubt that it did wound it.

The myth of Confederate states' rights need not be a myth at all. The ideology of states' rights was certainly alive, and it played a significant role in the Confederate story. What it was not was the unifying, noble cause for which Southerners fought and died. For the myth to become the reality, we merely need a change of cast and an alteration of trajectory. The defenders of states' rights in the Confederacy were not Jefferson Davis, Robert E. Lee, Stonewall Jackson, or any of the other venerated heroes of the Lost Cause. They were, instead, obstructionist governors, anti-Davis legislators, defiant planters, recalcitrant slave owners, and disgruntled, disaffected, and, in some cases, outright disloyal Confederates. And what an examination of states' rights in the Confederacy truly reveals is not wartime Southern unity, but a significant force of division within the Confederate South.

2. Was Abraham Lincoln a Racist?

Ian Patrick Hunt

> By omissions and evasions, by half-truths and quarter-truths and lies, by selective quotations, and suppressed quotations, by begging the question and forgetting the question and ignoring the question, by committing all the logical fallacies in the book, and by inventing new ones, by all these methods, and others, and by the biggest attempt in recorded history to hide a man, Lincoln defenders have managed to turn a separatist into an integrationist and to fool all the Black people and all the White people, save one or two, all the time.[1]
>
> —*Lerone Bennett, Jr.*

Was Abraham Lincoln a racist? For most people this question seems absurd. Lincoln throughout his life proclaimed that the institution of slavery was evil. During his extensive career as a politician on both the state and federal levels, he consistently argued that slavery could not be allowed to expand beyond where it already existed. As president he authored the Emancipation Proclamation, advocated both publicly and privately for African American voting rights, and actively employed patronage and political arm-twisting to ensure the passage of the Thirteenth Amendment abolishing slavery. Yet a small but highly vocal minority has long claimed that Mr. Lincoln was no friend of the black man; that rather than standing up for African American rights, he continually pumped the brakes on abolition until finally being forced into supporting it through pressure by both radical Republicans and abolitionists and the changing dynamics of the Civil War; that until his death he continually encouraged a policy of ethnic cleansing through deportation of both slaves and free blacks to Africa, the Caribbean, or to Central and South America; and finally, that the president's murder created an opportunity to whitewash his record while simultaneously punishing the South for the sins of slavery and the tragic costs of the Civil War. They contend that the legacy of Abraham Lincoln we have today is not one of equality and reconciliation but rather of division and abhorrence. The evidence used to support these arguments comes from a variety of sources, including various events in his life, excerpts from speeches, recollections of those who came in contact with the president, and finally these dissenters' interpretations of the period. It is worth

---

1. Lerone Bennett, Jr., *Forced into Glory: Lincoln's White Dream* (Chicago: Johnson Publishing, 2007).

Abraham Lincoln (1809–65) two months before his assassination. President Lincoln's reputation has experienced many ups and downs over the last 150 plus years. Image courtesy of the Library of Congress.

noting that more than a century and a half after the abolition of slavery, issues of race continue to haunt this country.

The Origins of the Myth

To begin, it is noteworthy that claims of Abraham Lincoln being a racist are not a modern invention. In the period leading up to and during his presidency, while many of his critics ridiculed him for his support of African American equality, a small but vocal minority of radical abolitionists frequently argued that he was a friend rather than an enemy of slavery. Angry over what some considered an overly conciliatory approach to the South and its "peculiar institution," African American abolitionist H. Ford Douglas remarked, "I do not believe in the anti-slavery of Abraham Lincoln, because he is on the side of this slave power."[2] Even as late as 1864, Wendell Phillips proclaimed that "we have the misfortune, in this great struggle of ideas, to have our standard-bearer emphatically a Southern man . . . trying to be an abolitionist."[3] Nearly all of these types of condemnation dissolved with the passage of the Thirteenth Amendment, which permanently abolished slavery, in January 1865.

In the late nineteenth and early twentieth centuries, as Jim Crow laws codified segregation in the South and violence against blacks increased, two similar schools of thought, though of vastly different origins, began to emerge, each accusing Lincoln of racism.

In the earlier of the two, neo-Confederate adherents to the Lost Cause myth began to claim, in a rather circular argument, that because Lincoln was racist, the Civil War had nothing to do with slavery. In the 1901 book entitled *The Real Lincoln*, Charles Minor contended that Lincoln expressed "no sympathy for the slave" and that he "laughed at the abolitionists as a disturbing element easily controlled, without showing any dislike to the slave-holders."[4] These types of accusations have been carried through into the modern era in books such as *The South Was Right!* and *Slavery Was Not the Cause of the War Between the States.*[5] In a comparable argument, some adherents of libertarianism claim that Lincoln simply used the issue of slavery as a vehicle to consolidate the power of the federal government at the expense of state sovereignty. In a 1966 article, Frank Meyer suggested that "Lincoln himself and most of his defenders . . . deny that the abolition of slavery was ever Lincoln's intent."[6] Such positions are a focal point for modern libertarian writers such as Charles Adams and Thomas DiLorenzo, who in 2012 wrote that Lincoln's opposition to slavery and its expansion rested solely upon a "plan of politically and economically dominating the South."[7] In the last few decades, the arguments offered by both neo-Confederates and libertarians have so overlapped that it is difficult to separate them.

The second school of thought accusing Lincoln of racism grew out of late nineteenth- and early twentieth-century African American intellectuals who had witnessed firsthand how promises of equality at the end of the Civil War failed to materialize. This led some to reevaluate Lincoln's war-time goals and motivations as they pertained

---

2. "Speech of H. Ford Douglass [sic]," *Liberator* (Boston), July 13, 1860.

3. "Speech of Wendell Phillips, ESQ," *Liberator* (Boston), February 5, 1864.

4. Charles Minor, *The Real Lincoln*, ed. Kate Mason Rowland (Richmond, VA: Everett Waddey, 1901), 50.

5. James Ronald Kennedy and Walter Donald Kennedy, *The South Was Right!* (Gretna, LA: Pelican, 1994); Gene Kizer, *Slavery Was Not the Cause of the War Between the States: The Irrefutable Argument* (Charleston, SC: Charleston Athenaeum Press, 2014).

6. Frank Meyer, "Again on Lincoln," *National Review*, January 25, 1966, 71–72.

7. Thomas DiLorenzo, *Lincoln Unmasked: What You're Not Supposed to Know about Dishonest Abe* (New York: Random House, 2006), 176. See also Charles Adams, *When in the Course of Human Events: Arguing the Case for Southern Secession* (Lanham, MD: Rowan and Littlefield, 2000).

to the issue of slavery versus the Union. In an address given in 1917, W. E. B. Du Bois claimed that had Lincoln been able to "keep the Union from being disrupted, he would not only allow slavery to exist but would loyally protect it."[8] The rise of the Civil Rights movement in the 1960s further crystallized this attitude, which was punctuated in 1968 when Lerone Bennett, Jr., an editor of *Ebony* magazine, published an essay entitled "Was Abe Lincoln a White Supremacist?" In it Bennett, condemned both the man and his policies, arguing that the Emancipation Proclamation had "all the moral grandeur of a real estate deed" and believing that had Lincoln survived his second term, Reconstruction would have been "of the white people, by the white people, and for the white people."[9] These types of charges were repeated by other African American authors, including Julius Lester, Vincent Harding, and Henry Louis Gates, Jr.[10] In 1999 Bennett greatly expanded his original essay in a book-length study of Lincoln and his relationships with African Americans entitled *Forced into Glory: Abraham Lincoln's White Dream*; a quotation from that book opens this chapter.

Some of Lincoln's detractors concede that his views on race evolved during his lifetime, especially during his presidency, while others charge that he never wavered from his hatred of African Americans. In one of the great demonstrations of how historical perspectives can shift, Lincoln's enemies throughout his life referred to him as an abolitionist (similar to being called a social anarchist today), whereas in the modern era there are those who now call him a racist.

Lincoln's Early Ideology regarding Slavery

For many today it is difficult to comprehend that while all abolitionists were antislavery, not all anti-slavery supporters were necessarily abolitionists. Abolitionism had its roots in the late eighteenth century, but it only began to gain a serious but still small foothold in the first half of the 1830s as the issues surrounding slavery began to creep into the national conscience. Most abolitionists, though they varied in their zeal, would have argued for the twin goals of the immediate abolition of slavery and social equality regardless of race. This view differed significantly from many anti-slavery advocates who were concerned that the expansion of slavery into the West would encumber free labor in that region or who feared the seemingly limitless power in the nation's capital that slavery granted to the planter aristocracy. In his youth, Lincoln

---

8. W. E. B. Du Bois, "The Problem of Problems," in *W. E. B. Du Bois Speaks: Speeches and Addresses, 1890–1919*, ed. Philip S. Foner (New York: Pathfinder Press, 1970), 261.

9. Lerone Bennett, Jr., "Was Abe Lincoln a White Supremacist?" in *The Lincoln Anthology*, ed. Harold Holzer (New York: Library of America, 2009), 752.

10. Julius Lester, *Look Out, Whitey! Black Power's Gon' Get Your Mama!* (New York: Grove Press, 1968); Vincent Harding, *There Is a River: The Black Struggle for Freedom in America* (New York: Harcourt Brace, 1981); Henry Louis Gates, Jr., *Lincoln on Race and Slavery* (Princeton, NJ: Princeton University Press, 2009).

fell somewhere within the middle ground of these arguments but gradually grew more liberal during the course of his life.

Historians have long acknowledged that Lincoln's desire to see slavery abolished was as motivated by politics as it was by his abhorrence of the South's "peculiar institution." As a young man studying the writings and speeches of Henry Clay, he fully bought into Clay's "American System," which encouraged industry and promoted internal improvements. His vision for the future of America was one in which individuals could, through hard work and self-sacrifice, evolve from employee to employer. African slavery, Lincoln would later attest, was "a war upon the rights of all working people."[11] He further believed that no one should enrich himself at the expense of another's toil.

These beliefs, however, occasionally clashed with his devotion to and reverence for the Declaration of Independence and the Constitution. Prior to 1865 the latter document guaranteed the right to own slaves. For Lincoln, the rights and privileges promised in the Declaration were the moral foundation upon which the nation had been constructed; the Constitution was the physical framework upon which those rights would be guaranteed. In his mind, the Declaration was the "apple of gold" while the Constitution was the "picture of silver" that framed it.[12] As early as 1838, Lincoln was imploring his constituents that, in "support of the Constitution and Laws, let every American pledge his life, his property, and his sacred honor."[13] Unlike some abolitionists, such as William Lloyd Garrison (who, on July 4, 1854, publicly burned a copy of the Constitution because of its protections of slavery), Lincoln believed that one simply could not discard the one while embracing the other.

Yet Lincoln also understood that while slavery was guaranteed in the Constitution in the states where it existed, its expansion was not. When, in 1854, Senator Stephen Douglas' Kansas-Nebraska Act allowed for the expansion of slavery into territories where it had previously been prohibited, Lincoln lashed out, announcing that "the theory of our government is Universal Freedom . . . the clause that covers the institution [slavery] is one that sends it *back* where it exists, not *abroad* where it does not."[14] Six-years later during his Cooper Union Address, Lincoln was even more passionate declaring that, just as the Founding Fathers had "marked it, so let it be again marked, as an evil not to be extended, but to be tolerated and protected only because of and so far as its actual presence among us makes that toleration and protection a necessity."[15]

---

11. Abraham Lincoln, "Reply to New York Workingmen's Democratic Republican Association, March 21, 1864," in *Collected Works of Abraham Lincoln*, ed. Roy P. Basler et al., 8 vols. (New Brunswick, NJ: Rutgers University Press, 1953–55), 7:259.

12. Ibid., "Fragment on the Constitution and the Union" [c. January 1861], 4:168–69.

13. Ibid., "Address before the Young Men's Lyceum of Springfield, Illinois, January 27, 1838," 1:108–15.

14. Ibid., "Speech at Springfield, Illinois, October 4, 1854," 2:240–47.

15. Ibid., "Address at Cooper Institute, New York City, February 27, 1860," 3:522–50.

For Lincoln, the ideals embodied within the Declaration of Independence could be achieved by working within the boundaries of the Constitution.

An early example of these beliefs occurred in January 1837, when Lincoln, then a twenty-seven-year-old Illinois legislator, attempted to amend a pro-Southern resolution making its way through the Illinois General Assembly. To the resolution, which cautioned Congress against abolishing slavery in the nation's capital, Lincoln attempted to add the wording "unless the people of the said District petition for the same."[16] Though the amendment to the resolution was rejected, Lincoln affirmed that the power to abolish slavery, even on a limited scale, rested with the voters.

Lincoln's hatred of slavery, however, ran deeper than simply a difference in political ideology. From the moment of his birth in 1809, negrophobia and slavery had loomed large over nearly all aspects of society and culture during his lifetime. By the time of his twenty-first birthday in 1830, he could count only four years of his life when the president of the United States was not a slave owner. In Congress, during this same period, four of the six men elected to serve as Speaker of the House were slave owners, while nine of the eleven men elected as president of the Senate owned slaves or hailed from slave states. In major Southern cities, such as Charleston, Savannah, and New Orleans, the immense wealth created by slavery drove the construction of opulent mansions and townhomes. These residences rivaled anything that could be found in larger Northern cities such as New York or Philadelphia. Slavery created "a quality of residential life that, in terms of comfort and ostentation, has seldom been surpassed by other Americans of any time or place."[17]

While little is known about his early experiences with African Americans, Lincoln mentioned in 1860 that his father's decision to move the family from Kentucky to Indiana "was partly on account of slavery."[18] While the moves to Indiana and later to Illinois might have removed him from an environment that unequivocally sanctioned slavery, large segments of the population of both of those states harbored deep resentment against African Americans. This hostility led to the passage of some of the strictest "black codes," meant to prohibit blacks from settling within their borders, in the nation.

Despite this harsh environment, Lincoln repeatedly spoke out both publicly and privately against slavery. When, in the spring of 1837, the Illinois General Assembly overwhelmingly passed several anti-abolitionist resolutions at the behest of Southern state legislators, Lincoln publicly spoke out, filing an official protest that declared "that the institution of slavery is founded on both injustice and bad policy."[19] It is worth noting that Lincoln's personal views on slavery did not remain static throughout his

---

16. Illinois General Assembly, *Journal of the House of Representatives of the Tenth General Assembly of the State of Illinois*, December 1836, 309.

17. William Kauffman Scarborough, *Master of the Big House: Elite Slaveholders of the Mid-Nineteenth-Century South* (Baton Rouge: Louisiana State University Press, 2003), 152.

18. Lincoln, "Autobiography Written for John L. Scripps" [c. June 1860], in *Collected Works*, 4:60–68.

19. Ibid., "Protest in Illinois Legislature on Slavery, March 3, 1837," 1:74–75.

life but rather grew harsher with age. One of the clearest examples of this involved a journey to Kentucky to visit the family estate of his best friend, Joshua Speed. On his return to Illinois in 1841, Lincoln wrote to his friend's sister Mary Speed to relate an encounter that had occurred during his journey. He described seeing "twelve negroes" who were "strung together like . . . so many fish upon a trot-line." He explained in detail the grim future that awaited them but that despite their "distressing circumstances . . . they were the most cheerful and happy aboard," concluding that God "renders the worst of human conditions tolerable."[20] While it is possible that Lincoln chose to end his tale on a positive note in hopes of not offending a young woman whose family embraced slavery, his description is vivid but emotionally detached. He is clearly weighing his own anxieties about his own unknown future as an unmarried, struggling thirty-two-year-old attorney against the set fate that he knows awaits the slaves.

Fourteen years later in 1855, having a deeper understanding of the divisiveness that slavery created within the nation, Lincoln wrote to Joshua Speed:

> You may remember . . . ten or a dozen slaves, shackled together with irons. That sight was a continual torment to me; and I see something like it every time I touch the Ohio, or any other slave-border. It is hardly fair for you to assume, that I have no interest in a thing which has, and continually exercises, the power of making me miserable. You ought rather to appreciate how much the great body of the Northern people do crucify their feelings, in order to maintain their loyalty to the constitution and the Union.[21]

Here the future president clearly articulates the anger growing in the North over slavery, despite claims made by some Southerners that it was a regional issue that Northerners should not concern themselves with. Fidelity to the Constitution and the nation were being taxed by continual agitation over slavery. This chapter, which is not meant to be a biography of Lincoln, will, instead, now consider the validity of the events and issues typically raised by those who argue that Lincoln harbored racist sentiments.

The Matson Slave Case

*If Lincoln was a champion for abolishing slavery,
then why did he defend a slave owner?*

Today, what is typically cited as the earliest example of Lincoln's presumed racism centers upon his work in the legal case of *Matson v. Ashmore et al. for the Use of Bryant* but more frequently called simply the Matson slave case. The particulars of the case are as follows. In August 1842, Robert Matson, a slave owner from Bourbon County, Kentucky, purchased a tract of land for farming in Coles County, Illinois. The property,

---

20. Ibid., Lincoln to Mary Speed, September 27, 1841, 1:259–61.
21. Ibid., Lincoln to Joshua Speed, August 24, 1855, 2:320–23.

which he would later dub Black Grove because of the clusters of black walnut trees on the property, sat just north of the present-day community of Oakland, Illinois. Matson immediately began housing slaves in Illinois during the growing season before moving them back to Kentucky during the winter months. In this way, Matson believed that he was circumventing the laws against slavery in Illinois by claiming that they were simply in transit through the state, which was legal. Matson repeated this process for several years, though eventually he did appoint one of his slaves, Anthony Bryant, as a permanent overseer of his Illinois holdings. In 1845 Bryant's wife, Jane, and their five children, who were all the property of Matson, were sent to Illinois for the season. However, when fall harvesting was complete, Matson failed to return the slaves to Kentucky, and they remained continuously in Illinois through the summer of 1847.

In mid-August of that year, a vicious fight erupted between Jane Bryant and a white woman, Mary Corbin, who was Matson's housekeeper and rumored mistress. Corbin reportedly threatened to have Jane and her children sold "way down South in the cotton fields" for her alleged transgression.[22] At that time, Matson had already returned one of the Bryant children to Kentucky, and Anthony Bryant, likely fearful of losing his entire family, began planning their escape. He first sought out the assistance of two local abolitionists, Gideon Ashmore, a tavern keeper, and Dr. Hiram Rutherford, who took up the family's cause and helped shelter them after they fled the Matson property. Shortly thereafter, Mrs. Bryant and her children were arrested as fugitive slaves and brought before the local justice of the peace by the county sheriff. Much to the chagrin of Matson, the family was not handed over to him but rather held in custody until the next session of the Coles County Circuit Court.

On October 16, 1847, the Bryant family had its day in court. Representing the family were two local attorneys, while Robert Matson was represented by Usher Linder and Mr. Lincoln. The case would be heard by no less than the chief justice of the Illinois Supreme Court, William Wilson, who invited Associate Justice Samuel H. Treat to assist. As was the custom of the day, both justices, when not in session in the Illinois Supreme Court, presided over state circuit courts. Ironically, of the four attorneys and two judges who would preside over the case, all with the exception of Samuel H. Treat were born in slave states.

The entire case hinged on a simple but crucial question. Had Mrs. Bryant and her children been permanently relocated to Illinois? If so, they were free. If not, they were simply in transit and therefore still enslaved. In the verdict rendered by Judge Wilson, it was decided that "by bringing Jane and her children into the State of Illinois, and domiciling them here, [Matson] has forfeited all claim to their services, and entitled them to be discharged therefrom."[23] The court's decision not only freed Mrs. Bryant

---

22. Charles R. McKirdy, *Lincoln Apostate: The Matson Slave Case* (Jackson: University Press of Mississippi, 2011), 24.

23. Daniel W. Stowell et al., eds., *The Papers of Abraham Lincoln: Legal Documents and Cases*, 4 vols. (Charlottesville: University of Virginia Press, 2008), 2:1–43.

and her family from Matson but ensured that they could not be re-enslaved by his creditors or others in the South. In the end, Matson quickly chose to sell his property in Illinois and permanently relocate back to Kentucky. The Bryants, after receiving assistance from local members of the American Colonization Society, chose to emigrate to the colony of Liberia, along the west coast of Africa.

Obviously the Bryant case raises a number of questions. Why would a man who, five years earlier in 1842, had compared the evils of alcoholism with that of slavery, announcing that "victory shall be complete—when there shall be neither a slave nor a drunkard on the earth,"[24] accept this case? Different theories have been offered over the years, ranging from a personal connection to Matson to a desire to demonstrate politically to Illinois voters that he was a moderate on this issue. Because no diaries or journals exist and Lincoln presented no explanation in any personal correspondence, all of this is a matter of conjecture. How Lincoln even ended up in Coles County that October is a matter of historical debate. One claim, later made by Matson himself, was that before the case began he had ridden the one hundred miles to Springfield because he intended to secure the services of the "greatest attorney in the country."[25] This statement, made after Lincoln's assassination, seems rather dubious. Though he was then the senior partner in the firm of Lincoln & Herndon, his most celebrated cases were still years away. A more plausible explanation would be that Lincoln was traveling with Justice Treat on the eighth circuit and that Linder, who had known Lincoln for more than a decade in the Illinois legislature, asked him to participate.

Soon after Lincoln's arrival in Coles County, the Bryants' abolitionist advocate, Dr. Rutherford, also attempted to retain his services but was refused. Rutherford later recalled that Lincoln had reluctantly informed him that he had already been retained as counsel for Matson and was ethically required to represent him unless released. In recounting the story, Rutherford stated that Lincoln went so far as to consult with co-counsel Usher F. Linder to obtain a release from representing the slave owner so that he might instead represent the Bryant family. Rutherford, however, angered over Lincoln's initial refusal, rejected his offer, and Lincoln continued in his work for Matson.

Like most things with a connection to Abraham Lincoln, the various aspects of this event in his life have been mythologized over the last century and a half. One example of this comes from some of his early twentieth-century biographers who claimed that Lincoln so sympathized with the Bryants that he failed to mount a vigorous defense and may have purposely lost the case, to ensure their freedom.[26] Yet if that had been his primary motivation, it would have been far simpler to either defend the Bryants

---

24. Lincoln, "Temperance Address, February 22, 1842," in *Collected Works*, 1:271–79.

25. Duncan T. McIntyre, "Lincoln and the Matson Slave Case," *Illinois Law Review* 1 (1906–7): 387.

26. Albert J. Beveridge, *Abraham Lincoln, 1809–1858* (New York: Houghton Mifflin, 1928), 1:396; Albert A. Woldman, *Lawyer Lincoln* (New York: Little Brown, 1937), 67–68.

or completely recuse himself from the case. The argument is further refuted when we consider that several eyewitnesses, including Lincoln's opposing counsel, Orlando Ficklin, complimented him on his strategy and eloquence while defending Matson.[27]

In a similarly lofty tone, some have claimed that this early case in Lincoln's career had much larger ramifications for the nation in the near future. In his 2010 book *The Fiery Trial*, Eric Foner wrote, "Ironically, Lincoln's position—that residence in a free state did not automatically make a slave free—was adopted, to widespread dismay in the North, by Chief Justice Roger B. Taney in the *Dred Scott* decision ten years later."[28] That statement is misleading. In the opinion written by Justice Taney in the *Dred Scott* case, Taney cites at least a half-dozen cases in making his argument but does not refer to Matson.[29] We have no evidence that Taney even knew about the Matson case. It is also critical to understand that the crux of Lincoln's argument was that the Bryants had never attained residency in Illinois and were therefore simply in transit and still subject to the slavery laws of Kentucky. Justice Taney went significantly further stating that "neither Dred Scott himself nor any of his family were made free by being carried into this territory, even if they had been carried there by the owner with the intention of becoming a permanent resident."[30] In Taney's mind it was a historical fact that African Americans were "an inferior order, and altogether unfit to associate with the white race . . . and so far inferior that they had no rights which the white man was bound to respect."[31]

Attempting to use this case or any of Lincoln's other legal cases as proof that his legal career was a reflection of his personal philosophies is unwise. On two separate prior cases, *Baily v. Cromwell* in 1841 and *Ex parte Warman* in 1845, Lincoln helped secure the release of African Americans being held as slaves. So why would Lincoln reverse course on this occasion? In his 2008 two-volume biography of Lincoln, Michael Burlingame offered the explanation that Lincoln

> would represent doctors and patients alike; he represented railroads being sued by boat owners whose vessels crashed into their bridges and also boat owners suing railroads for obstructing navigation with their bridges; he represented stock subscribers reneging on their pledges and corporations suing such stock subscribers. At least three times he was defeated because of a precedent that he had earlier helped to establish.[32]

---

27. "Reminiscence of Orlando B. Ficklin" [c. January 1885], *Papers of Abraham Lincoln*, 2:28–38.

28. Eric Foner, *The Fiery Trial: Abraham Lincoln and American Slavery* (New York: W. W. Norton, 2010), 49.

29. *Dred Scott v. Sandford*, 60 U.S. 393, 399–454 (1857).

30. Ibid., 452.

31. Ibid., 407.

32. Michael Burlingame, *Abraham Lincoln: A Life*, 2 vols. (Baltimore: Johns Hopkins University Press, 2008), 1:253.

There were several reasons for this. As an attorney and adherent of the philosophy of the Whig Party, Lincoln accepted the principle that an attorney's obligation to uphold the legal system includes a responsibility to assist individuals regardless of the morality of their cases. In short, lawyers are to trust that the legal system will separate the innocent from the guilty. One of the fundamental tenets of our judicial system is that all individuals are equal before the law and therefore deserve equal protection, including legal counsel and advocacy.

Others, however, are not so quick to dismiss Lincoln's defense as simply a professional obligation. In his essay "Emancipation and the Proclamation: Of Contrabands, Congress, and Lincoln," Robert Fabrikant offered the opinion that "it is inexplicable that a lawyer who ethically objects to a client's conduct would seek to vindicate the client's right to engage in that conduct."[33] Yet another theory offered by Charles McKirdy in his book *Lincoln Apostate: The Matson Slave Case* attempts to infuse a psychological argument into the issue. McKirdy claims that Lincoln's close friendship with Usher Linder, his co-counsel on the case, "often required Lincoln to suspend his critical judgment and to put aside his personal values and standards. That is what he did with regard to the Matson Case."[34]

A more straightforward answer as to why Lincoln might have accepted this case revolved around simple economics. Prior to the presidency, there was no point in Lincoln's life in which he could be considered wealthy. When he departed for Washington in 1861, his financial portfolio consisted of his home, a dozen or so small loans owed to him, six shares of railroad stock, and a handful of other securities. After the president's death, the administrator of his estate reported that his affairs in Springfield were resolved to the amount of $9,044.41, or less than half of one year's presidential salary. When he accepted this case in 1847, Lincoln was averaging around $10 per case (roughly the purchasing power of $286 today), and with a wife, two children, and political ambitions, he would have likely not turned down any client seeking his services.[35]

The Lincoln-Douglas Debates

If Lincoln was not a racist, why did he make those statements at the Charleston debate in 1858?

On September 18, 1858, Lincoln chose to open his remarks for the fourth debate with Stephen A. Douglas at Charleston, Illinois, with the following statement:

---

33. Robert Fabrikant, "Emancipation and the Proclamation: Of Contrabands, Congress, and Lincoln," *Howard Law Journal* 57 (2013): 50–51.

34. McKirdy, *Lincoln Apostate*, 102.

35. Harry E. Pratt, *The Personal Finances of Abraham Lincoln* (Chicago: Lakeside Press, R. R. Donnelley, 1943), 33–35.

> I will say then that I am not, nor ever have been, in favor of bringing about in any way the social and political equality of the white and black races—that I am not, nor ever have been, in favor of making voters or jurors of negroes, nor of qualifying them to hold office, nor to intermarry with white people; and I will say in addition to this that there is a physical difference between the white and black races which I believe will forever forbid the two races living together on terms of social and political equality. And inasmuch as they cannot so live, while they do remain together there must be the position of superior and inferior, and I as much as any other man am in favor of having the superior position assigned to the white race.[36]

By itself, this appears incredibly damning. He is clearly rejecting any notions of equality while advocating white supremacy. Yet when we look closer at his words, there is a certain level of ambiguity in his statement. It is assumed that his reference to "physical difference" must relate to both physical and mental capacities but in reality all he is touching upon is skin color. Contrast Lincoln's remarks at Charleston with his statement six weeks earlier in Chicago when he stated,

> Let us discard all this quibbling about this man and the other man— this race and that race and the other race being inferior, and therefore they must be placed in an inferior position—discarding our standard that we have left us. Let us discard all these things, and unite as one people throughout this land, until we shall once more stand up declaring that all men are created equal.[37]

Here Lincoln is clearly rejecting the tired arguments that blacks are either mentally or physically inferior and must be forced into a second-class status. It is important to remember that Lincoln and Douglas were engaging in an intellectual boxing match. During the course of this contest, arguments brought forward in one debate were revisited again and again with both men looking to exploit weaknesses in the other's position. They also both understood that the vast geography separating the debate sites would result in very different audiences (Freeport and Jonesboro are separated by 335 miles, farther apart than New York City and Richmond, Virginia) who would have different perspectives on the topics. In Illinois, which was divided geographically, with the southern part of the state more sympathetic to slavery while the northern half tended toward anti-slavery, the key to victory would be in the central portion of the state. Douglas knew that by portraying Lincoln as a radical abolitionist seeking full equality of the races he would be victorious. Only five years earlier, the Illinois legislature had passed a law banning the immigration of African Americans, whether

---

36. Lincoln, "Fourth Debate with Stephen A. Douglas at Charleston, Illinois, September 18, 1858," in *Collected Works*, 3:145.

37. Ibid., "Speech at Chicago, Illinois, July 10, 1858," 2:484–502.

free or enslaved, into the state. For many in Illinois, keeping slavery out of the West meant a better opportunity for the future, but that certainly did not translate into a desire to embrace equality of the races.

In the opening debate at Ottawa, Douglas spoke first and immediately attacked Lincoln on everything from the dissolution of the Whig Party and formation of the Republicans to his views on the *Dred Scott* decision. Douglas ominously painted a vision for the crowds of what would befall the state if Lincoln and his party were to be elected:

> I ask you, are you in favor of conferring upon the negro the rights and privileges of citizenship . . . allow the free negroes to flow in, and cover your prairies with black settlements . . . to turn this beautiful State into a free negro colony, in order that when Missouri abolishes slavery she can send one hundred thousand emancipated slaves into Illinois, to become citizens and voters, on an equality with yourselves?[38]

To ensure that no one would have any doubts about where Douglas stood on the topic, the senator declared that

> I am opposed to negro citizenship in any and every form. I believe this government was made on the white basis. I believe it was made by white men, for the benefit of white men and their posterity for ever, and I am in favour of confining citizenship to white men, men of European birth and descent, instead of conferring it upon negroes, Indians and other inferior races.[39]

From these statements, it is clear that Douglas' position was unequivocal: African Americans had no rights of any kind, and Senator Douglas would ensure the purity and superiority of white America.

Descriptions in some newspapers after the debate and a handful of eyewitnesses years later claimed that Douglas had won this debate. Over the course of the next two meetings in Freeport and Jonesboro, Douglas did his best to keep Lincoln bogged down by forcing him to answer questions that would either paint the Republican as a radical or require him to agree with Douglas' Democratic philosophy. He also continually hammered home the claims that Lincoln would waffle on the issues depending upon the audience, while Douglas would stay true to his racist ideals.

It was at the fourth debate at Charleston that Lincoln decided to flip the race card on Douglas and place himself on the offensive. Lincoln had now picked up the gauntlet that Douglas had thrown at his feet since the first debate at Ottawa and declared a difference between the races and a desire to see the white race in a position of superiority. It is worth noting that the *Chicago Press and Tribune* mentioned both "great

38. Ibid., "First Debate with Stephen A. Douglas at Ottawa, Illinois, August 21, 1858," 3:1–37.
39. Ibid.

laughter" and "applause" from the audience as Lincoln was making this statement.[40] What Lincoln said next, however, shifted his argument to an attack on the "slavery or total equality" dichotomy that Douglas had been pushing since the beginning. He did so by stating,

> I do not understand that because I do not want a negro woman for a slave I must necessarily want her for a wife. My understanding is that I can just let her alone. I am now in my fiftieth year, and I certainly never have had a black woman for either a slave or a wife. So it seems to me quite possible for us to get along without making either slaves or wives of negroes.[41]

Lincoln then concluded this portion of his argument by demonstrating the ridiculousness of Douglas' position through one of his most potent weapons, humor, announcing that

> I have never had the least apprehension that I or my friends would marry negroes if there was no law to keep them from it, but as Judge Douglas and his friends seem to be in great apprehension that they might, if there were no law to keep them from it, I give him the most solemn pledge that I will to the very last stand by the law of this State, which forbids the marrying of white people with negroes. I will add one further word, which is this, that I do not understand there is any place where an alteration of the social and political relations of the negro and the white man can be made except in the State Legislature—not in the Congress of the United States—and as I do not really apprehend the approach of any such thing myself, and as Judge Douglas seems to be in constant horror that some such danger is rapidly approaching, I propose as the best means to prevent it that the Judge be kept at home and placed in the State Legislature to fight the measure. I do not propose dwelling longer at this time on this subject.[42]

In response, all Douglas could muster was "I am glad that I have at last succeeded in getting an answer out of him upon this question of negro citizenship and eligibility to office."[43] Despite all of this, Douglas would later return to his original argument that Lincoln was in favor of complete equality. Over the course of the next three debates, Douglas continued his strategy of linking Republicans with radical abolition, while Lincoln concentrated upon the immorality of slavery.

---

40. *Chicago Press and Tribune*, September 21, 1858.

41. Lincoln, "Fourth Debate with Stephen A. Douglas at Charleston, Illinois, September 18, 1858," in *Collected Works*, "First Debate with Stephen A. Douglas at Ottawa, Illinois, August 21, 1858," 3:1–37.

42. Ibid. "First Debate with Stephen A. Douglas at Ottawa, Illinois, August 21, 1858," 3:1–37.

43. Ibid.

Stephen Douglas (1813–61), Abraham Lincoln's political rival in Illinois and in the 1860 presidential race. The Lincoln-Douglas debates made Lincoln well known in the North and helped secure him the Republican nomination.

Lincoln's statements in Charleston, though considered heinous today, should be taken as they were intended, those of a political candidate appealing to an electorate. Lincoln was being advised by Republican associates that he needed to refute Douglas' charges, and so he did. As a career politician, he understood that a rigid adherence to a personal philosophy would limit his appeal to voters. In October 1845, Lincoln himself questioned the advisability of his philosophical adherence when he wrote to a friend, Williamson Durley. In the letter, Lincoln expressed surprise that despite the fact that Durley and others like him had been against the annexation of Texas because of the slavery issue, they had refused to vote for Henry Clay (who also rejected annexation) because Clay was a slave owner. Lincoln chided his friend, asking, "By the fruit the tree is known. . . . If the fruit of electing Mr. Clay would have been to prevent the extension of slavery, could the act of electing [have] been evil?"[44] By refusing to support Clay in 1844, the Democrats were able to elect James K. Polk, who annexed Texas and led the nation into the Mexican War.

Remarkably, throughout the seven debates, the fact that Lincoln believed that "there is no reason in the world why the negro is not entitled to all the rights enumerated in the Declaration of Independence—the right of life, liberty and the pursuit of happiness" was continually reaffirmed by *both* candidates.[45] At Ottawa, Galesburg,

44. Ibid., Lincoln to Williamson Durley, October 3, 1845, 1:347–48.

45. Ibid., "First Debate with Stephen A. Douglas at Ottawa," 3:16. Lincoln's remarks at Ottawa and Quincy are nearly identical, whereas his remarks at Galesburg and Alton embody the same sentiment of equality.

Quincy, and Alton, Lincoln proudly proclaimed these beliefs. While at Freeport, Jonesboro, and Charleston, Douglas mockingly accused him of "reading that part of the Declaration of Independence to prove that the negro was endowed by the Almighty with the inalienable right of equality with white men."[46]

In the end, Douglas would win the contest and return to the Senate for a third term, yet Lincoln's efforts were not a total failure. These debates helped move Lincoln from a regional candidate to a more national platform and proved critical as stepping-stones to the White House. In one of the great ironies of history, in the final debate at Alton, Senator Douglas referred to Lincoln and his associates as abolitionist "agitators" for his remarks during the debates.[47] Today some consider Lincoln a racist for the exact same remarks.

Lincoln's Inauguration

If Lincoln hated slavery, why at his inauguration did he endorse the Corwin Amendment guaranteeing slavery? Why did he announce that he would not harm slavery where it existed? Why didn't he simply abolish slavery?

As strange as it may seem, a number of people point to Lincoln's First Inaugural Address as proof that the president cared little for the plight of slaves. They claim that he was no longer a candidate on the campaign trail but was now the elected leader and should have immediately advocated for the total abolition of slavery. They ask why he reiterated that he had "no purpose . . . to interfere with the institution of slavery in the States where it exists."[48] They wonder why he made reference to the Corwin Amendment that would guarantee slavery in perpetuity, which had passed through Congress and was awaiting ratification by the states, when he said, "I have no objection to its being made express and irrevocable."[49]

When Lincoln took the oath of office on March 4, 1861, the country was coming apart. His election the previous November had prompted seven Southern states (South Carolina, Mississippi, Florida, Alabama, Georgia, Louisiana, and Texas) to withdraw their congressional delegations from Washington and form a new nation, the Confederate States of America. Swept up in both the excitement and fear elicited by secession, prominent citizens and statesmen on both sides began hurling invectives against each other, claiming that their opponents were timid and weak and that they were fulfilling

---

46. Ibid., "Third Debate with Stephen A. Douglas at Jonesboro, Illinois, September 15, 1858," 3:113. Douglas' statements at Freeport, Jonesboro, and Charleston are all similar in tone and critical of Lincoln's arguments regarding equality and the Declaration of Independence.

47. Ibid., "Seventh and Last Debate with Stephen A. Douglas at Alton, Illinois, October 15, 1858," 3:283–325.

48. Ibid., "First Inaugural Address, March 4, 1861," 4:262–271.

49. Ibid. 270.

the true destiny laid down by the Founding Fathers. When word began to filter in that the Southerners had begun seizing federal property within their borders, most of it taken without firing a shot, tensions were ratcheted up even further. Newspapers in the North began tracking the Southern takeovers as they were happening. Each day Northerners could read how a customhouse in Georgia or a fort in Louisiana had been seized by state authorities. This meant that public outrage in the North, with demands for action, never subsided since each new day seemed to bring more evidence of "Southern treachery."[50] In a speech given on the floor of the House in January 1861, Virginia congressman Roger Pryor opined that "no compromise which can be made will have any effect in averting the present difficulty."[51] Pennsylvania congressman Thaddeus Stevens angrily responded the following day that "when I see these States in open and declared rebellion against the Union, seizing upon her public forts and arsenals, and robbing her of millions of the public property . . . I have no hope that concession, humiliation, and compromise, can have any effect whatever."[52]

Between the election and the inauguration, Lincoln was receiving advice daily, both solicited and unsolicited, about how he should deal with the South. Some claimed that the South was simply posturing, hoping to improve its position and possibly barter concessions from the new administration. Others argued that the South should be allowed to stand on its own, that it had been a burden to the government, and that its deficiency in up-to-date forms of infrastructure, such as railroads, industry, and shipping, would force it to plead for readmission in the near future. Lincoln along with many others believed that Union sentiment in the South was strong, and if left alone, eventually the unionists' love of country would drown out the secessionists who had temporarily seized the spotlight. This was the environment in which Lincoln would deliver his first public remarks as president.

So why didn't Lincoln abolish slavery in his inaugural address? Because even as president of the United States, he did not have the power to do so. The power to either maintain or abolish slavery had always been delegated to the individual states. While it had existed in every colony prior to the Revolutionary War, by 1861 eight states had taken the steps necessary to abolish it.

Slavery had been a part of the American landscape since long before there was even a Lincoln family in America. Slavery is believed to have existed in Spanish Florida as early as 1539 and was found in the colony of Virginia by 1619; Samuel Lincoln did not arrive until 1637. When the colonies declared their independence from Great Britain and formed the United States, they made sure that slavery would be maintained, and it was written into the Constitution in three different locations. Article I, Section 2—the famous three-fifths compromise—stipulated that for purposes of representation in

---

50. *New York Times*, March 14, 1861.

51. Cong. Globe, 36th Cong., 2d Sess. (1861), 601–3.

52. Hans Trefousse, *Thaddeus Stevens: Nineteenth-Century Egalitarian* (Chapel Hill: University of North Carolina Press, 1997), 106; Cong. Globe, 36th Cong., 2d Sess. (1861), 621–24.

Congress each slave would be counted as three-fifths of a free citizen. Article I, Section 9, guaranteed that the importation of slaves could not be prohibited until 1808. Article IV, Section 2—the fugitive slave clause—guaranteed that runaway slaves would be returned to their owners even if they escaped to a free state. Lincoln knew that these rules collectively guaranteed that slavery, as it existed at that time, could not be eradicated by the federal government without first amending the Constitution.

That did not mean that slavery could expand unchecked. Article IV, Section 3, of the Constitution specifically gave Congress the "Power to make all needful Rules and Regulations respecting the Territory." This clause had allowed the Founding Fathers to ensure that slavery would be excluded from the Northwest Territory (what became the states of Ohio, Indiana, Michigan, Illinois, Wisconsin, and part of Minnesota). Lincoln also knew that he would have a fight on his hands because the Supreme Court's ruling in the 1857 *Dred Scott* decision rejected the original interpretation of that clause. The court had ruled that a prohibition placed upon a citizen in "holding and owning" of property (slaves) in the territories "is not warranted by the Constitution, and is therefore void."

Lincoln countered by acknowledging on several occasions that while the court might be the ultimate arbitrator of individual cases brought before it, "the United States Constitution is the supreme law of the land."[53] This in Lincoln's mind meant that decisions by the court that ran counter to the Constitution, such as the power to expand slavery where the Constitution had prohibited it, could be reversed, overturned, or in extreme cases ignored. For the president believed that if governmental policy was to be "irrevocably fixed by decisions of the Supreme Court . . . the people will have ceased to be their own rulers." The following summer a Republican Congress would defy the court's ruling in the *Dred Scott* case by passing free-soil legislation, namely the Homestead Act of 1862, specifically restricting slavery from the western territories.

We tend to forget that when Lincoln averred that he had "no purpose . . . to interfere with the institution of slavery . . . where it exists," he was specifically addressing several very different groups. First and foremost, he was attempting to conciliate the seceded states in hope of getting them to rejoin the Union, but was also speaking to the eight slave states that had not yet departed. The president's remarks also served a subtler purpose as well; his statement "where it exists" was clear affirmation to his supporters that slavery's expansion would not be tolerated during his administration. After the firing on Fort Sumter and the president's call for volunteers to put down the rebellion, it would be revealed that his efforts had been only partially successful. The states of Virginia, Tennessee, Arkansas, and North Carolina chose to join their Southern secessionist sisters. But the Border States of Missouri, Kentucky, Maryland, and Delaware, and the future state of West Virginia, chose to stay loyal to the Union. All would make important contributions to the Union's success in the Civil War, but the

---

53. Lincoln, "Fragment: Notes for Speeches" [c. September 15, 1858], in *Collected Works*, 3:100. See also ibid., "Fifth Debate with Stephen A. Douglas at Galesburg, Illinois, October 7, 1858," 3:207–44; ibid., "Speech at Columbus, Ohio, September 16, 1859," 3:400–425.

large population numbers and agricultural resources of Missouri and Kentucky were critical to the Union's efforts. No less vital was Maryland, with the key port city of Baltimore and the strategic advantage of bordering Washington, D.C., on three sides. Its departure would have likely required the abandonment of the nation's capital.

On addressing the Corwin Amendment to the Constitution, which had passed through Congress and was awaiting ratification by the states, Lincoln was again staying true to his principles about stopping slavery's expansion. In the weeks leading up to the inauguration, President-elect Lincoln in private correspondence with allies in Washington, D.C., continually stressed, "Let there be no compromise on the question of extending slavery."[54] He was concerned that the fear gripping the nation would lead some elected officials to offer virtually anything to stave off secession. In Washington, in a last-ditch effort to avoid conflict, three different plans were presented by various officials to try to head off secession: the Crittenden Compromise, the Washington Peace Convention, and the Corwin Amendment. Of these, both the Crittenden proposal and the Peace Convention not only guaranteed slavery in perpetuity but also guaranteed its expansion into the western territories. The Corwin Amendment, while certainly not ideal, simply guaranteed that the government would not interfere with slavery where it already existed; it made no concessions for its expansion. Staying true to his ideals, he picked the best of three bad choices.

The Corwin Amendment passed through a depleted Congress; the seven Southern states that had seceded had already withdrawn their delegations two days before Lincoln's inauguration. Its chances of receiving ratification by 75 percent of the states and becoming law were nearly nonexistent, since nearly half of the states that would benefit from it had already departed. Lincoln could use the proposed amendment, however, as an opportunity to remind the nation that legal and peaceful procedures were already in place, so that when the citizens "grow weary of the existing government, they can exercise their *constitutional* right of amending it, or their *revolutionary* right to dismember, or overthrow it."[55]

Every word spoken by the president that day had been carefully weighed and considered not just by Lincoln but also by future Secretary of State William Seward, Senator Orville Browning, of Illinois, and a host of others. Lincoln and his advisors came up with nearly one hundred suggested revisions from the first draft, and while many were accepted, others were discarded. While seven Southern states had already departed, this first official statement by the new administration was eagerly awaited by many in both the North and South, as it would set the tone for Lincoln's first term. Lincoln and his advisors knew that they must be conciliatory but not weak; they needed to remain firm on their principles without antagonizing the South and to appeal to all Americans:

---

54. Ibid., Lincoln to Lyman Trumbull, December 10, 1860, 4:149–50.
55. Ibid., "First Inaugural Address," 4:262–71.

Though passion may have strained, it must not break our bonds of affection. The mystic chords of memory, stretching from every battle-field, and patriot grave, to every living heart and hearthstone, all over this broad land, will yet swell the chorus of the Union, when again touched, as surely they will be, by the better angels of our nature.[56]

Colonization

If Lincoln was not a racist, why did he push for the removal of African Americans from the United States?

In the summer of 1862, President Lincoln met with a delegation of five African American ministers and community leaders to seek their input and support on the voluntary emigration of free African Americans across the Atlantic Ocean to the African colony of Liberia. In a speech that shifted back and forth from sympathy to condescension, the president declared that "your race are suffering . . . the greatest wrong inflicted on any people."[57] He quickly added, however, that "without the institution of slavery and the colored race as a basis, the war could not have an existence."[58] At the close of the meeting, the likely shocked delegation informed the president that they would hold a consultation and provide him in a short time with an answer.

The movement to colonize African Americans grew out of efforts in the late eighteenth century to abolish slavery and return the emancipated slaves to their homeland. This movement, frequently touted as humanitarian in nature—a chance to return those who had been kidnapped back to their birthplace—was also considered by many to be a safety measure. The horrors both real and imagined accompanying the slave uprisings in Haiti and the ever-present menace of threatened insurrections in the United States led some to argue that to offer emancipation and integration would be "not only fruitless, but injurious."[59] When the American Colonization Society was founded in 1816, it was rapidly endorsed by such influential figures as Daniel Webster, Francis Scott Key, and President James Monroe. One of its earliest supporters, Henry Clay, even believed that funds collected from the sale of western lands "should be applied to the objects of internal improvement and colonization of free blacks."[60] While support for colonization came from many prominent Northerners and Border State leaders, its reception in the Deep South, where the largest slave populations resided, was tepid at best. Over the years, as more and more African

---

56. Ibid. 271.

57. Ibid., "Address on Colonization to a Deputation of Negroes, August 14, 1862," 5:370–75.

58. Ibid.

59. Wilbur Fisk, *Substance of an Address Delivered before the Middletown Colonization Society . . . July 4, 1835* (Middletown, CT: G. F. Olmsted, 1835), 15.

60. *Sangamo Journal* (Springfield, IL), May 17, 1832.

Americans rejected the notion, support began to wane and became confined mostly to the Border State regions.

For Lincoln, the first close contact with colonization efforts likely came from his future law partner John Todd Stuart, who in August 1833 was named secretary of the Sangamon County Colonization Society.[61] Stuart and Lincoln, who had served together briefly during the Black Hawk War, would both be elected to the Illinois legislature in 1834, and by 1837 become law partners. It seems likely that during their many hours together working and traveling, when the subject of slavery arose, colonization was discussed; yet Lincoln seems to have resisted this idea for some time. There is no mention of his taking an active role in colonization meetings, nor did he advocate it in public speeches or personal correspondence during this time. His first recorded support of colonization came on July 6, 1852, when he delivered his eulogy on Henry Clay. In it, Lincoln endorsed Clay's policies of emancipation and colonization, quoting from Clay that "there is a moral fitness in the idea of returning to Africa her children, whose ancestors have been torn from her by the ruthless hand of fraud and violence."[62]

Over the next few years, Lincoln would be asked to address the Illinois Colonization Society on several occasions; he obliged it in 1853 and 1855. In a speech at Peoria in 1854, he admitted the impossibility of full-scale colonization, remarking that "if they were all landed there in a day, they would all perish in the next ten days."[63] In the lead-up to and during his campaign for the Senate, he touched on the issue of colonization a total of four times, including during the fifth debate at Galesburg. As president, Lincoln's first official endorsement of colonization occurred in December 1861 in his first annual message to Congress, reflecting the views of a large number of Republicans and Democrats alike.

General Benjamin Butler astutely observed in May 1861 that Virginia's secession from the Union meant that it could no longer claim the benefits of the Fugitive Slave Act of 1850; runaway slaves could now be held as "contraband" instead of being returned. This opened the floodgates, and as the number of fugitive slaves streaming into the Northern military camps began to swell, so did a concern by many in the North about who would bear the responsibility of caring for these runaways. While later in the war General Butler's actions would result in his being removed from command, Lincoln believed it needed to be studied further.[64] The president suggested that Congress should appropriate funds for a voluntary colonization effort that would be available to emancipated slaves as well as "free colored people" who "may desire [to]

---

61. *Sangamo Journal* (Springfield, IL), August 31, 1833.

62. Lincoln, "Eulogy on Henry Clay, July 6, 1852," in *Collected Works*, 2:121–32.

63. Ibid., "Speech at Peoria, Illinois, October 16, 1854," 2:247–83.

64. Burlingame, *Abraham Lincoln*, 2:351; Blair to Butler, May 29, 1861, in *Private and Official Correspondence of Gen. Benjamin F. Butler, During the Period of the Civil War*, ed. Blanche Butler Ames (Norwood, MA: Plimpton Press, 1917), 1:116.

be included in such colonization."[65] Over the next few months, Congress debated whether colonization should be voluntary or mandatory and had by July 1862 appropriated a total of $600,000 for the president to use at his discretion to subsidize colonization. In an appeal to the Border State representatives on July 12, 1862, he again returned to the topic of colonization to assuage fears of what was to become of the freedmen when the issue of gradual emancipation arose. Lincoln assured his guests that "room in South America for colonization, can be obtained cheaply, and in abundance; and when numbers shall be large enough to be company and encouragement for one another, the freed people will not be so reluctant to go."[66]

In his annual message to Congress in December 1862, Lincoln mentioned that he had received applications by many "free Americans of African descent" requesting the opportunity to emigrate.[67] This speech, given on December 1, 1862, would be his last public address advocating colonization. A single effort in April 1863 to voluntarily relocate almost five hundred African American men, women, and children to Île à Vache (Cow Island) off the coast of Haiti would be a complete failure, with substantial numbers succumbing to disease and starvation, much to the president's stated dismay. The remnants of the colonists were returned to the United States in March of the following year. Earlier, in 1862, a contract to set up a colony in Chiriquí in Central America had to be suspended due to outrage from government officials in that region over a failure to secure treaties to set up the colony. The matter seemed to be closed entirely when in a diary entry on July 1, 1864, Lincoln's personal assistant John Hay wrote "the President has sloughed off that idea of colonization."[68]

Historians have long debated whether Lincoln's advocacy of colonization constituted a genuine desire to see an ethnic cleansing of America or was simply a political tool to calm public fears over abolition. Unlike his advocacy of the abolition of slavery, which can be found in numerous public and private documents throughout his entire life, his support of colonization lasted from 1852 to 1864. When he could have positioned himself as a promoter of it during his four terms in the Illinois legislature and his single term in Congress, we find no mention of it whatsoever. When he did begin to address it in 1852, it was only in a professional capacity through speeches or communications with government officials; there are no private letters endorsing it.

His revival of the notion as president and its mention in two addresses to Congress would draw outrage from many prominent African Americans, who clearly demonstrated their unwillingness to support it. During his meeting with the African American leaders at the White House in 1862, he included among his guests a *New York*

---

65. Lincoln, "Annual Message to Congress, December 3, 1861," in *Collected Works*, 5:35–53.

66. Ibid., "Appeal to Border State Representatives to Favor Compensated Emancipation, July 12, 1862," 5:318–19.

67. Ibid., "Annual Message to Congress, December 1, 1862," 5:518–37.

68. Tyler Dennett, ed., *Lincoln and the Civil War in the Diaries and Letters of John Hay* (New York: Dodd, Mead, 1939), 203.

Tribune reporter who ran the story the following day. This story, while welcomed by some, further outraged many white supporters who felt that the president had laid the fault for the war on the slaves themselves. Not mentioned to Lincoln's guests that day was his plan to issue the still-secret Emancipation Proclamation, which he had presented to his cabinet three weeks earlier. And finally, when Congress decided to end the colonization program in 1864 and withdraw any remaining sums of the original $600,000 appropriation, it was found that less than $40,000 had been expended.

His public support for the program beginning in the 1850s and lasting until the issuing of the Emancipation Proclamation coincides neatly with public fears regarding what was to become of newly freed slaves. As president, it would have been practical for him to keep the option of overseas colonization open to those few who might seek to take advantage of it. But Lincoln, despite having funds at his disposal, always stressed that any relocations "must be voluntary and without expense to themselves."[69]

Colonization efforts by private citizens would continue in a minor way into the early part of the twentieth century. Indeed, the American Colonization Society was revived in the 1870s by several African American leaders as a response to the failure of Reconstruction. While its focus would later shift to educational and missionary efforts, it would remain active until 1964, when the society was dissolved and its records were donated to the Library of Congress.

Lincoln's exact motives behind supporting colonization will never be known. His support while in Illinois might have stemmed from a firm belief that blacks would be forever denied by whites any opportunity to succeed. When Lincoln spoke in Springfield in June 1857, he noted that Republicans believed "that the negro is a man; that his bondage is cruelly wrong," while Democrats "deny his manhood . . . crush all sympathy for him, and cultivate and excite hatred and disgust against him."[70] His support of it in Washington might have been a political ruse to tamp down opposition to emancipation, since it was frequently argued that abolition would unleash a tidal wave of four million newly freed slaves that would overwhelm society and cripple the economy. Without a doubt, by January 1863 the president had fully shifted his efforts from turning blacks into colonists to turning blacks into soldiers.

The Emancipation Proclamation

The Emancipation Proclamation was simply a political trick that didn't free anyone.

---

69. William E. Gienapp and Erica L. Gienapp, eds., *The Civil War Diary of Gideon Welles* (Urbana: University of Illinois Press, 2014), 60.

70. Lincoln, "Speech at Springfield, Illinois, June 26, 1857," in *Collected Works*, 2:398–410; Lincoln would return to this theme of fear and loathing that many white citizens had toward African Americans on numerous occasions, including the Lincoln-Douglas debates and his 1862 speech to African American religious leaders.

On January 1, 1863, President Abraham Lincoln, along with Secretary of State William Seward and Seward's son Frederick, retired to the president's private office on the second floor of the Executive Mansion. The president had originally intended to begin his day by signing the Emancipation Proclamation, but upon discovering a minor error, he asked that the document be sent back to the State Department to be corrected. In the interim, the president attended the annual New Year's Day reception, which commenced with an audience with all the foreign ministers and dignitaries in the city before being opened to the general public. The Washington *Daily National Republican* noted that "the reception at the Executive mansion was numerously attended—noticeably more so than in former years."[71]

Later, as he reviewed the corrected document and prepared to affix his signature, his arm began to tremble uncontrollably. The president turned to Seward and his son and remarked:

> I never, in my life, felt more certain that I was doing right, than I do in signing this paper. But I have been receiving calls, and shaking hands since nine o'clock this morning, till my arm is stiff and numb. Now, this signature is one that will be closely examined, and if they find my hand trembled, they will say "he had some compunctions." But any way, it is going to be done![72]

The president regained his composure and with a steady and clear hand signed his full name at the bottom of the document. Immediately, Secretary Seward took the document to be placed within the archives, and copies were presented to the press.

For many abolitionists and radical Republicans this represented the first step to healing a nation that had been for too long infected with slavery. At the Cooper Union in New York one month later, Frederick Douglass decreed that "we are all liberated by this proclamation . . . the amazing approximation toward the sacred truth of human liberty."[73] Moderates were more conservative, with one editorialist commenting that if it aided in restoring the Union, "we care little about the means necessary . . . being willing to sacrifice slavery . . . as we are certainly willing to sacrifice anti-slavery."[74] For Democrats the president's actions were not only unwarrantable in military or civil law but a gigantic usurpation of the government's original goal when entering the conflict. In a meeting attended by Lincoln's former law partner John Todd Stuart held in the Illinois legislature, a delegation resolved that the war that had "commenced . . . for the vindication of the authority of the Constitution" was now

---

71. *Daily National Republican* (Washington, D.C.), January 2, 1863.

72. Frederick W. Seward, *Seward at Washington as Senator and Secretary of State: A Memoir of His Life, with Selections from His Letters, 1861–1872* (New York: Derby and Miller, 1891), 150–51.

73. Philip S. Foner, ed., *The Life and Writings of Frederick Douglass* (New York: International Publishers, 1975), 3:326.

74. *Evening Star* (Washington, D.C.), January 1, 1863.

"a crusade for the sudden, unconditional and violent liberation of three millions of negro slaves . . . with far-reaching consequences of the most dismal forebodings of horror and dismay."[75]

The decision to issue the Emancipation Proclamation was not made hastily or without great reflection, as some today might claim. It was one step in a process that had commenced in April 1861 with the firing on Fort Sumter and culminated in the passage of the Thirteenth Amendment, four years later in 1865. When it became apparent in the fall of 1861 that the government would not quickly put down the rebellion through military action, both the president and Congress began to consider other options. After learning in the summer of that year that some slave owners were loaning or hiring out their slaves to actively assist the Southern war effort, some Republicans in Congress decided to act by seizing these slaves. Democrats and Border State representatives who feared this was the first step to a complete emancipation initially resisted the measure. They were eventually swayed, however, by stories of slaves handling the routine daily tasks of an army, thereby rendering all Southern white men available for combat. In an attempt to limit the measure to apply only to those slave owners who aggressively supported the rebellion, it was decided that only slaves who actively aided the Southern war effort could be removed. To further ensure that only those slave owners who openly supported the rebellion were punished and that loyal slave owners would not be molested, each individual case would be reviewed by the federal district or circuit courts.

Fearful that secessionist elements within the Border States would eventually push Kentucky, Missouri, Maryland, and Delaware into the Confederacy, the president began exploring separate plans of gradual emancipation. In none of these states did slaves constitute more than 20 percent of the state's entire population, and gradual emancipation there would have the twin effects of preserving these vital regions for the country while simultaneously demonstrating that slavery was not necessary for their future.

In November 1861, the president set his sights on Delaware. With a slave population of just under eighteen hundred, it had by far the smallest number of slaves, who represented a mere 2 percent of the state's total population. The president offered a plan whereby the federal government would compensate slave owners in the form of bonds after the state had abolished slavery. Unlike the Confiscation Acts (1861–64), which were designed to liberate slaves in the secessionist states and required determination of whether the slave owner had remained loyal to the Union, this plan would assure the slaves' freedom without violating the Fifth Amendment, which guarantees that private property cannot be seized without just compensation. The plan was quietly circulated through the Delaware legislature in February 1862 but failed to garner enough support and was never submitted for a vote. In a stinging rebuke, the state's

---

75. *Illinois Journal* (Springfield), January 7, 1863.

General Assembly asserted that "when the people of Delaware desire to abolish slavery within her borders, they will do so in their own way."[76]

Hoping fruitlessly to gain support for the plan in Washington, Lincoln sent a letter to Senator James A. McDougall, of California, a noted "war Democrat." The president argued that at $400 per slave, it would cost the government less than $720,000 to free all the slaves in Delaware. With the daily cost of prosecuting the war already at $2,000,000, less than one day's fighting would pay for all the slaves in Delaware, and "less than eighty seven [sic] days cost of this war" would pay for the slaves in all four Border States and the District of Columbia.[77] While rejected by all the Border States, the effort was not a total failure. On April 16, 1862, the president signed the District of Columbia Emancipation Act, purchasing the freedom of nearly three thousand slaves in the nation's capital.

On July 12, 1862, President Lincoln made one last effort to persuade the Border State congressmen to accept compensated emancipation. In a meeting at the White House, he implored his guests to accept his proposal, which "shortens the war, and secures substantial compensation."[78] The president's pleas, however, would be ignored, and it came time to shift his focus in a different direction. The following day, July 13, the president, while on a carriage ride with Secretary of State Seward and Secretary of the Navy Gideon Welles, began discussing the Emancipation Proclamation. In his diary, Secretary Welles would later recall that "he dwelt earnestly on the gravity, importance, and delicacy of the movement . . . [adding] we must free the slaves or be ourselves subdued."[79] Nine days later, on July 22, 1862, the president presented the first draft of the Proclamation to the entire cabinet. The reaction from his cabinet members was mixed, with some thinking it went too far while others believed that it didn't go far enough. Secretary Seward advised holding off issuing it until there was a major military victory, so that it did not appear to the European powers as a desperate act. Heeding Seward's advice, Lincoln shelved the announcement until after the Battle of Antietam in September of that year; the president then issued the Proclamation, declaring that it would go into effect on January 1, 1863.

Only one day after the first anniversary of the Battle of Bull Run (fought July 21, 1861), President Lincoln had committed himself and his cabinet to a plan of emancipation, although few outside the president's cabinet were aware. Nearly one month later in August, unaware of the president's plan and angered at what he considered a failure to "execute the laws" of the country, Horace Greeley, the influential editor of the *New York Tribune*, penned an editorial entitled "The Prayer of Twenty Millions."[80]

---

76. *Delaware House Journal*, special session (1861–62), 269.

77. Lincoln to James A. McDougall, March 4, 1862, in *Collected Works*, 5:160.

78. Ibid., "Appeal to Border State Representatives to Favor Compensated Emancipation, July 12, 1862," 5:317–319.

79. Gienapp and Gienapp, *Diary of Gideon Welles*, 3.

80. *New York Tribune*, August 20, 1862.

In it Greeley accused Lincoln of being "unduly influenced by . . . certain fossil politicians hailing from the Border Slave States" and that attempting to put down the rebellion while simultaneously upholding slavery was "preposterous and futile."[81] Lincoln responded two days later that

> I would save the Union. I would save it in the shortest way under the Constitution. . . . My paramount object in this struggle is to save the Union and is not either to save or destroy slavery. If I could save the Union without freeing any slave I would do it, and if I could save it by freeing all the slaves I would do it; and if I could save it by freeing some and leaving others alone, I would also do that. . . . I have here stated my purpose according to my view of official duty; and I intend no modification of my oft-expressed personal wish that all men everywhere could be free.[82]

The president's remarks in that letter are frequently misinterpreted by those who either fail to read it in its entirety or simply choose to select single passages to fit their arguments. It is claimed as proof that Lincoln cared nothing for the plight of slaves, since he did not endorse complete and immediate emancipation. The president's message is more nuanced and begins by stating that it is his obligation to save the Union in the quickest manner possible "under the Constitution." His declaration regarding freeing all the slaves, none of the slaves, or only some of the slaves simply reiterates that his focus, first and foremost, was to preserve the Union and end the war as quickly as possible. This announcement, however, also presents a subtler secondary message: the abolition of slavery on either a limited or national scale *might be required* in order to save the Union. Since the president and his cabinet had already decided on issuing the Emancipation Proclamation, this statement and its implications become much clearer. The president concludes his remarks by noting that these views are in accordance with his "official duty" but that his personal wish was "that all men everywhere could be free."

It is also worth noting that Lincoln wasn't the only individual in the North who was considering how slavery should be dealt with in the face of secession and the Civil War. As previously mentioned, General Benjamin Butler in May 1861 took a unique perspective on the issue. The former attorney turned general decided that, rather than returning three runaway slaves who had turned up at Fort Monroe, Virginia, as he was bound to do under the 1850 Fugitive Slave Act, he would use his authority as a military commander to seize them like "any other property of a private citizen," especially property "that was to be used against the United States."[83] Butler would argue that

---

81. Ibid.

82. Lincoln to Horace Greeley, August 22, 1862, in *Collected Works*, 5:388–89.

83. War Department, *The War of the Rebellion: A Compilation of the Official Records of the Union and Confederate Armies* (Washington, D.C.: Government Printing Office, 1880–1901), ser. 2, 1:752. The three slaves in question had been constructing nearby Confederate fortifications when they slipped away from their overseer.

the military's right to seize property that was necessary for the prosecution of the war superseded the rights and privileges granted to slave owners in the Constitution. The removal of human property, or slaves, was no different than seizing food or weapons or any item that benefited the Confederacy. While little is known about Lincoln's approval of this measure, it is clear that he did not ban it immediately; this was not always the case, however, when one of Lincoln's generals attempted to use military authority to circumvent civilian laws.

On August 30, 1861, in response to attacks by Confederate guerrillas, General John Frémont placed the state of Missouri under martial law and issued his own emancipation proclamation. Frémont declared that all rebels would face court-martial and execution and that those assisting secessionists would have their property confiscated and slaves emancipated. This declaration significantly increased tensions in Missouri, which was a slave state but remained loyal to the Union, and set other Border State representatives on edge. Lincoln ordered Frémont to revise his proclamation in two ways. The first was that that no man was to be shot without the "approbation or consent" of the president.[84] The second was that in regard to the liberation of slaves, Frémont's order would conform to the recently approved Confiscation Act. Three weeks earlier, Congress had passed the First Confiscation Act, which allowed for the seizure of slaves who were "employed in or upon any fort, navy yard, dock, armory, ship, entrenchment, or in any military or naval service whatsoever."[85] Frémont's proclamation significantly expanded the scope of the seizures, from those actively assisting the Southern war effort to those "giving or procuring aid to the enemy."[86] This meant that the removal of slaves was no longer limited only to those owners who specifically loaned their slaves out to assist the Confederate war effort; now essentially anyone who supported the rebellion in any way could lose their property. It also eliminated the civilian oversight of these cases by moving them from the federal district or circuit courts to a military tribunal. When Frémont refused, the president revoked Frémont's proclamation and quickly removed him from command in Missouri. Lincoln later defended this move when he wrote,

> The Kentucky Legislature would not budge till that proclamation was modified . . . I think to lose Kentucky is nearly the same as to lose the whole game. Kentucky gone, we can not hold Missouri, nor as I think, Maryland. These all against us, and the job on our hands is too large for us.[87]

The following May in 1862, when General David Hunter issued a proclamation similar to Frémont's, Lincoln was again forced to revoke one of his commander's

---

84. Lincoln to John C. Frémont, September 2, 1861, in *Collected Works*, 4:506–7.

85. *Statutes at Large, Treaties, and Proclamations of the United States of America* (Boston: Little, Brown, 1863), 12:319.

86. *New York Times*, September 1, 1861.

87. Lincoln to Orville H. Browning, September 22, 1861, in *Collected Works*, 4:531–33.

"I'm sorry to have to drop you, Sambo, but this concern won't carry us both!" Lincoln is portrayed in this cartoon from Frank Leslie's *Illustrated News* as uncaring because of his response to Frémont's emancipation proclamation. Image courtesy of the Library of Congress.

orders. Hunter, however, had gone even further than his colleague in Missouri by declaring that all slaves within his military district were free, regardless of whether their owners supported or rejected secession. He also quickly instituted a draft among "persons of color as are able-bodied and may be required" to augment his own forces that he mistakenly feared were outnumbered.[88] This overreach of the congressional Confiscation Acts by General Hunter and the president's own plans for emancipation required the president to rescind Hunter's decree.

88. War Department, *The War of the Rebellion*, ser. 1, 26:333.

Understanding that the First Confiscation Act contained certain flaws (such as a lack of clarity about the status of the slaves after they had been seized by the government), Congress had spent the spring of 1862 crafting revised and expanded legislation. Passed on July 17, the Confiscation Act of 1862 allowed for the seizure of all real and personal property, including slaves, by anyone supporting the rebellion, yet exempted loyal slaveholders and, like earlier legislation, required that each case be decided by the courts. Lincoln would reluctantly sign the legislation, fearing that the courts would eventually overturn the permanent forfeiture of property, offering that "with great respect, I am constrained to say I think this feature of the act is unconstitutional—It would not be difficult to modify it."[89]

A mere five days after Congress had passed the 1862 Confiscation Act, Lincoln unveiled his plan for emancipation to his cabinet. The reason why the president had decided to break with his First Inaugural vow to not "interfere with the institution of slavery in the States where it exists" grew from a combination of both political and military events.[90] On the political front, both the first and second Confiscation Acts offered by Congress in the fall of 1861 and summer of 1862 were limited in their scope because they required individual judicial proceedings to determine the loyalty of the individual slaveholders. This meant that the court system would have been clogged for years, possibly decades, as most slaveholders, in an effort to retain their slaves, would have argued that they had never renounced their loyalty to the Union, but had been unfairly entangled by secession. While the Confiscation Acts might have been flawed, they weren't useless; some slaves escaping to federal lines were able to gain their freedom by virtue of these acts. Just as important was that their passage demonstrated to the president that both the public and Congress' views on the power of the government vis-à-vis the rights of property owners were evolving.

The failure of the Border State representatives to agree to compensated emancipation further reinforced the necessity of freedom by military edict. As he would later explain to Albert Hodges, this refusal left him "the alternative of either surrendering the Union, and with it, the Constitution, or of laying strong hand upon the colored element."[91] From the military perspective, Lincoln's decision is best summed up by his Secretary of the Navy Gideon Welles, who remarked that:

> the [military] reverses before Richmond, and the formidable power and dimensions of the insurrections which extended through all the Slave States, and had combined most of them in a confederacy to destroy the union impelled the administration to adopt extraordinary measures to preserve the National existence.[92]

---

89. Lincoln to the Senate and House of Representatives, July 17, 1862, in *Collected Works*, 5:328–31.

90. Ibid., "First Inaugural Address," 4:262–271.

91. Ibid., Lincoln to Albert G. Hodges, April 4, 1864, 7:281–83.

92. Gienapp and Gienapp, *Diary of Gideon Welles*, 4.

Using the Second Confiscation Act as a framework, Lincoln bypassed Congress and instead relied upon the war powers that were vested in him by the Constitution as commander in chief when issuing the Emancipation Proclamation. Like the Second Confiscation Act, the Emancipation Proclamation ensured that slaves who came under the control of the United States government would be forever free and could be employed by the Union in various capacities. However, the Emancipation Proclamation went much further by declaring that all slaves held in rebel territory would be freed regardless of the slaveholders' loyalties. By limiting the Proclamation to only those regions in rebellion, Lincoln at least partially relieved any apprehensions that his declaration would later be declared unconstitutional by the courts because it was employed "as a fit and necessary military measure."[93] As he would later justify it, secession created a danger to the Constitution, which meant "that measures, otherwise unconstitutional, might become lawful, by becoming indispensable to the preservation of the Constitution."[94]

While individuals such as Lerone Bennett, Jr., and Thomas DiLorenzo might argue that Lincoln's Proclamation freed no one and that it was a political gimmick, the reality was far different. Beginning on January 1, 1863, every mile of territory that the Union army covered resulted in the freedom of the local slave population. Perhaps just as important was the clause in the Proclamation that allowed for the enlistment of African American soldiers, which further inspired slaves to flee their plantations and make their way into the Union lines. This confounded Southern slave owners so much that occasionally some of them appealed to Union military commanders by complaining that conditions on their plantations that had fallen under federal control had become deplorable. They argued that it was the responsibility of the U.S. government to require "obedience & work from our slaves" to "save the country & especially the poor negroes."[95] Within five months of the issuance of the Proclamation, the superintendent of contrabands at Fort Monroe, Virginia, testified that as many as ten thousand escaped slaves had arrived there.[96]

Those who might believe that emancipation was simply a political trick to garner support are sorely mistaken. The preliminary proclamation was so unpopular that after the president announced it in September 1862, the Democrats gained twenty-eight seats in the House of Representatives during the congressional elections

---

93. Lincoln, "Emancipation Proclamation—First Draft, July 22, 1862," in *Collected Works*, 5:336–38.

94. Ibid., Lincoln to Hodges, April 4, 1864, 7:281–283.

95. Louisiana planters to Major Genl. Banks, January 14, 1863, M-108 1863, Letters Received, ser. 1920, Civil Affairs, Department of the Gulf, U.S. Army Continental Commands, Record Group 393, pt. 1, National Archives.

96. "Testimony of Capt. C. B. Wilder before American Freedmen's Inquiry Commission, May 9, 1863," O-328 1863, Letters Received, ser. 12, Record Group 94, Adjutant General's Office, National Archives.

in November. Despite this electoral backlash against abolishing slavery on even a limited scale, in 1864 the president pushed forward his support for the Thirteenth Amendment, which would permanently abolish slavery. After the amendment passed through the House of Representatives on January 31, 1865, the president declared that it was "a King's cure for all the evils."[97]

On April 11, 1865, two days after Robert E. Lee's surrender of the Army of Northern Virginia, Lincoln addressed a euphoric crowd that had gathered at the White House. In his speech, which congratulated the army and navy on their victories, he spoke of the future and how best to reunite the nation. In the course of his remarks, the president stated that the opportunity for African Americans to vote should be conferred upon the literate and those who had served in the military. In the crowd was a young Shakespearean actor named John Wilkes Booth, who upon hearing the president's statement turned to his companion and announced "that is the last speech he will ever make."[98] Three nights later, Booth shot the president in the back of the head with a .44-caliber Derringer; the president died the following morning.

On June 1, 1865, exactly six weeks after the president's death, Frederick Douglass stood before a capacity crowd of "equal proportions of white and colored people" at the Cooper Institute in New York.[99] This event had been organized, in part, after authorities in New York City had refused to allow all but a small handful of African Americans to march in the president's funeral procession through the city on April 25. Douglass eulogized the late president by noting that "no people or class of people in the country . . . have a better reason for lamenting the death of Abraham Lincoln, and for desiring to honor and perpetuate his memory, than have the colored people." Indeed, Lincoln's record was remarkable when compared "with the long line of his predecessors, many of whom were merely the facile and servile instruments of the slave power." Douglass further declared that "while unsurpassed in his devotion, to the welfare of the white race, [Lincoln] was also in a sense . . . emphatically, the black man's President: the first to show any respect for their rights as men. . . . He was the first American President who . . . rose above the prejudice of his times, and country."[100]

Once, in the 1850s, while preparing remarks to refute some of the traditional arguments made by pro-slavery advocates, Lincoln warned that enslaving individuals simply because of their color meant that "by this rule, you are to be slave to the first man you meet, with a fairer skin than your own."[101] He advised those who believed that intelligence was the great separator, "You are to be a slave to the first man you

---

97. Lincoln, "Response to a Serenade, February 1, 1865," in *Collected Works*, 8:254–55.

98. "Testimony of Thomas T. Eckert regarding Interrogations of Lewis Payne, 30 May 1867," "Impeachment of the President," House Report no. 7, 40th Cong., 1st sess. (1867), 671–74.

99. *New York Herald*, June 2, 1865

100. Burlingame, *Abraham Lincoln*, 2:829–30.

101. Lincoln, "Fragment on Slavery" [c. April 1, 1854], in *Collected Works*, 2:222–23.

meet, with an intellect superior to your own."[102] And finally, he cautioned those who believed that it was in their self-interest to enslave others that "if he can make it his interest, he has the right to enslave you."[103] Unmindful of those words, individuals accusing Lincoln of racism have suggested that because he failed to rise to the level of men like William Lloyd Garrison or John Brown he must have cared little for the plight of slaves. In fact, Abraham Lincoln throughout his life despised the institution of slavery but also understood that the Constitution made certain provisions that guaranteed citizens the right to own slaves in states where slavery was legal. Rather than casting aside this seminal document that was the legal basis for the nation, as many abolitionists demanded, he attempted to work within its legal framework while moving the country away from slavery. Prior to his election, slavery had existed for nearly 250 years, infested half of the nation, and represented the second-largest investment in capital behind only real estate. Four short years later the nation was emerging from the Civil War, and the Thirteenth Amendment had forever abolished slavery as a legal institution. As a young man, he might not have adopted the language or the tactics of the radical abolitionists, but his desire to see slavery abolished was no less sincere. His experiences with African Americans from all walks of life pushed him as president to move beyond the abolition of slavery and to seek equality for all. In the words of Frederick Douglass, "I never met with a man, who, on the first blush, impressed me more entirely with his sincerity, with his devotion to his country, and with his determination to save it at all hazards."[104]

---

102. Ibid.

103. Ibid.

104. Frederick Douglass, *Proceedings of the American Anti-Slavery Society . . . December 3 & 4, 1863* (New York: American Anti-Slavery Society, 1864), 117.

3. African Americans in Confederate Military Service: Myth and Reality

Brooks D. Simpson

It is understandable that a student of the American Civil War might be astonished to hear claims that African Americans served in the ranks of the Confederate army, especially if they are termed "soldiers." After all, why would African Americans voluntarily serve in an army whose mission was to secure independence for a nation-state founded, as its vice president proclaimed, on the cornerstone of slavery? Were blacks really willing to fight to keep their kinfolk enslaved? Or, just maybe, the thought might cross your mind that if African Americans were willing to fight for the Confederacy, then perhaps the war was not over the preservation and protection of slavery. That, after all, is what many Confederate heritage groups want you to believe: that the Civil War had next to nothing to do with slavery, and the "fact" that African Americans were in Confederate military service is incontrovertible evidence supporting that argument.

Like most myths, this tale has a slight foundation in fact, but it is very slight. Much depends on one's definition of "soldier," which is normally understood as an individual who formally enlists in an army. Much also depends on which African Americans are under discussion. Are we talking about free blacks or slaves? Or maybe Creoles and other people of color who do not easily fit into the traditional "black/white" dichotomy of defining Americans by race? Much also depends upon one's analysis and interpretation of the evidence usually presented to substantiate claims of black military service in the Confederacy, including photographs and pension records as well as newspaper reports and recollections. Evidence matters, as do definitions and terminology. One needs to examine all of these considerations carefully to winnow out fact from fiction and fantasy.

The secession crisis of 1860–61 presented a challenge to blacks, enslaved and free, in the Deep South. For years, the same white Southerners who celebrated the concept of the happy slave who was part of the family also shared rumors and whispers about the potential for an uprising by slaves, assisted by their free black allies, that would shake Southern society to its core. Advocates of secession raised the specter of slave rebellion as a reason to leave the Union before Abraham Lincoln and his black Republicans, whom they were convinced were intent upon destroying slavery, took over the national government. Although secessionists offered their list of grievances and infractions committed by Northerners in the past, at the heart of their movement was the need to create a climate of fear and foreboding about what might happen down the road once the Republicans were in power.

White Southerners, worried about slave uprisings, carefully scrutinized the behavior of free blacks. Usually congregated in urban centers, free blacks took advantage of their surroundings to carve out lives that did not always come under white supervision. Some, in fact, had amassed significant property, including slaves. Both New Orleans and Mobile, Alabama, had substantial Creole populations that challenged traditional conceptions of Southern race relations, then and now. How would these free blacks respond to the secession crisis? How would they address white suspicions about their loyalty during such an emergency?

Some of New Orleans' free men of color knew that the best way to protect themselves and preserve their property was to demonstrate their allegiance to the standing order in their city, and so they did just that. They volunteered to defend New Orleans from invading forces. In April 1861, some fifteen hundred free men of color offered their services to Louisiana's governor, Thomas O. Moore, ten days after the attack on Fort Sumter.[1]

Before long the 1st Louisiana Native Guards were ready to serve, and on May 29, 1861, Moore appointed three white officers to command the regiment. Free blacks filled out the roster of line officers (captains and lieutenants); members were responsible for securing uniforms and armaments. Although the unit marched through the streets of New Orleans several times, their service, such as it was, proved ornamental and short-lived. The Louisiana state legislature passed legislation at the beginning of 1862 that limited membership in the state militia forces to "free white males capable of bearing arms." In response, the unit disbanded in February 1862, but the following month, in response to the appearance of U.S. naval forces under the command of David G. Farragut at the mouth of the Mississippi River, Governor Moore took it upon himself to revive the organization. After U.S. forces approached New Orleans itself, the Native Guards were left as the Crescent City's only defenders, as white forces fled to avoid combat and capture. Nor did the Native Guards offer any resistance to the city's captors. On April 25, the day New Orleans was occupied by Farragut's command, General John L. Lewis of the Louisiana state militia ordered that the Native Guards be disbanded and its members return to their homes—although a number of them would see service later that year, wearing blue uniforms as members of the U.S. Corps d'Afrique, organized by Benjamin Butler that September.[2]

As the Native Guards disappeared, Creoles in Mobile, Alabama, sought military service. On April 23, 1862, G. Huggins Cleveland wrote to Secretary of War George W. Randolph to inquire whether the Confederacy would accept into service a battalion

---

1. James G. Hollingsworth, Jr., *The Louisiana Native Guards: The Black Military Experience during the Civil War* (Baton Rouge: Louisiana State University Press, 1995), 1–2.

2. Ibid., 3–10.

and perhaps even a regiment of Creoles. Endorsing the application, Congressman Edmund S. Dargon, who hailed from Mobile, testified that the men in question "will render as efficient aid as any class we have." Nevertheless, Richmond rejected the offer, but advocates for Creole Confederates persisted. That November, Alabama's General Assembly passed legislation authorizing the enrollment of Creoles in the state militia, although requiring that a white officer command any such units. In response to this opportunity, a single company of a hundred men, the Creole Guards, was raised and assigned to guard warehouses containing government property.[3]

In November 1863 General Dabney H. Maury, in command of Mobile's defenses, requested that the War Department accept companies of Creole state militia into Confederate service, with the idea of using them as heavy artillerists to man the city's shore batteries. Secretary of War James A. Seddon rejected Maury's proposal. Blacks, he reminded Maury, could serve as laborers or in other military tasks, but could never be enlisted as soldiers: "Our position with the North and before the world will not allow the employment as armed soldiers of negroes."[4]

As Farragut's ships and eventually Union soldiers approached Mobile once more in August 1864, Confederate commanders called upon the Creole population for help to defend the city from capture. Some free blacks might have made their way into a cavalry unit; as the city was about to capitulate, authorities raised a single company of Creoles (now called the Native Guards) that had once been a group of firefighters, but the company disappeared with the city's occupation by U.S. forces. Perhaps some members of the unit were among the Confederates who surrendered in May 1865, when General Richard Taylor capitulated.[5]

By the time the Native Guards appeared, Confederate policy toward the enlistment of African Americans (in this case slaves) had changed. Earlier, Confederate regulations had barred the enlistment of African Americans as soldiers; Confederate authorities had discharged several men who, upon investigation, were defined as black in Southern law and practice.[6] To be sure, Confederate policy provided for the impressment of slaves as laborers and to perform other functions (teamster or cook, for example) in support of Confederate military operations, but it drew a clear and unmistakable line at enlistment. Some Confederate leaders questioned that line. The

---

3. Arthur W. Bergeron, Jr., *Confederate Mobile* (Jackson: University Press of Mississippi, 1991), 105.

4. Ibid., 105–6.

5. See "The Confederate 'Creoles of Color' of Mobile, Alabama," *La Costa Latina Newspaper*, http://www.latinomediainc.com/, accessed July 7, 2016; for evidence of continuing Creole support for the Confederacy in Mobile, see Hilary N. Green, "African Americans' Struggle for Education, Citizenship, and Freedom, in Mobile, Alabama, 1865–1868," in *Confederate Cities: The Urban South during the Civil War Era*, ed. Andrew L. Slap and Frank Towers (Chicago: University of Chicago Press, 2015), 229.

6. For an example, see Arthur W. Bergeron, Jr., "Free Men of Color in Grey," *Civil War History* 32 (September 1986): 250.

most famous challenge to the enlistment policy before the winter of 1864–65 came from General Patrick Cleburne. In December 1863 Cleburne advanced the idea of enlisting blacks into Confederate military service as soldiers in a memo addressed to his fellow generals in the Army of Tennessee. All those slaves who enlisted would be freed and their families protected from sale. Given what Cleburne judged to be the Confederacy's dire military situation, he reasoned that "as between the loss of independence and the loss of slavery, we assume that every patriot will freely give up the latter—give up the negro slave rather than be a slave himself."[7]

Most of Cleburne's colleagues as well as his superiors denounced him and his proposal. Critics claimed it smacked of abolition: it was, depending on the source, "infamous," "hideous and objectionable," or a "monstrous proposition" that was "revolting to Southern sentiment, Southern pride, and Southern honor." General Joseph E. Johnston attempted to stifle the discussion, but a copy of Cleburne's proposal made its way to Richmond, where Jefferson Davis and his cabinet denounced it, with Davis ordering an end to discussions of the idea. Yet by the time Cleburne fell dead at Franklin, Tennessee, later that year, Davis himself was moving toward recommending what he had once rejected.[8]

During the winter of 1864–65 the Confederate Congress debated proposals that would have provided for the enlistment of African Americans in the Confederate army as soldiers. Proponents claimed that necessity justified this measure; what remained unclear was whether black soldiers would remain slaves or be granted their freedom as a reward for their service. Some people quietly added that slavery was on its last legs because of the impact of the war, so it was pointless to preserve that which was disappearing in any case. Critics countered that if the Confederacy enlisted slaves, it lost its rationale for existence. "The day you make soldiers of them is the beginning of the end of the revolution," cried Congressman Howell Cobb of Georgia. "If slaves will make good soldiers our whole theory of slavery is wrong."[9]

By the time the Confederate Congress adopted a bill that would allow Davis to solicit masters for permission to have their slaves serve in the ranks of the army as soldiers while remaining the property of their masters, Appomattox was less than a month away. Davis and Robert E. Lee went one step further in saying that the Confederate army would accept into service only those blacks who had consented to such service and who were given their freedom by their masters. However, only a few dozen free blacks answered the call for service, and not many more enslaved blacks followed

---

7. Bruce C. Levine, *Confederate Emancipation: Southern Plans to Free and Arm Slaves during the Civil War* (New York: Oxford University Press, 2006), 27.

8. Ibid., 28.

9. Howell Cobb to James A. Seddon, January 8, 1865, in *The War of the Rebellion: A Compilation of the Official Records of the Union and Confederate Armies*, War Department (Washington, D.C.: Government Printing Office, 1880–1901), ser. 4, 3:1009–10.

suit. At most two companies were organized, and even that process was interrupted when Richmond was captured.[10]

So much for organized efforts to recruit African Americans systematically. It is an inconvenient truth to point out to people who believe that large numbers of enslaved men willingly served in Confederate ranks as soldiers that the generals supposedly in command of those men knew nothing of these black soldiers. Moreover, during the debate over enrolling slaves as Confederate soldiers, no one mentioned that there was no need for legislation or that it would simply confirm prevailing practice. Nor does one uncover letters from white Confederate soldiers describing the activities of their fellow black soldiers, because of the simple fact that they were not present in significant numbers. Moreover, had black Confederate soldiers existed in any significant number, we would expect to find many reports of them killed, wounded, or missing, although a handful of African American servants and laborers were scooped up by U.S. forces after Gettysburg.

This is not to say that slaves were not present with Confederate armies. They were. In fact, the Confederate government took steps to impress slaves into military service—but not as soldiers. They came to dig trenches, build forts, cook, and drive wagon trains. Alongside them were African American servants of officers and some enlisted men—although these men, too, were not soldiers. Indeed, the entire notion of a slave volunteering for military service avoids the plain fact that slaves could not act without the permission of their owners.[11]

There are occasional stories of African American men working for the Confederate army or individual Confederates engaged in combat. Take the case of John Parker, who claimed that he was forced to work as part of an artillery crew of four black men at First Manassas. He's not someone that advocates of black Confederate military service mention too often. Why? Because Parker later admitted that the men working the cannon "wish[ed] to our hearts that the Yankees would whip, and we would have run over to their side but our officers would have shot us if we had made the attempt." In the months to come, Parker would make various statements about other blacks being forced to fight at First Manassas, which fit Frederick Douglass' claim that the time had come for the United States to welcome blacks into military service in order to level the playing field—and to open the path to emancipation and equality.[12]

---

10. Levine, *Confederate Emancipation*, 119–28.

11. See, for example, Ervin L. Jordan, Jr., *Black Confederates and Afro-Yankees in Civil War Virginia* (Charlottesville: University of Virginia Press, 1995); and James H. Brewer, *The Confederate Negro: Virginia's Craftsmen and Military Laborers, 1861–1865* (Durham, NC: Duke University Press, 1969).

12. Andy Hall, "Frederick Douglass' Black Confederate," *Dead Confederates: A Civil War Era Blog*, February 20, 2015, https://deadconfederates.com, accessed July 7, 2016; Kate Masur, "Slavery and Freedom at Bull Run," *New York Times*, *Disunion* (blog), July 27, 2011, http://opinionator.blogs.nytimes.com, accessed July 7, 2016.

Over the years, people have identified and researched a handful of African Americans who were associated in some way with the Confederate army. For example, there was Holt Collier, who accompanied his master to the front and later served as a scout and a sharpshooter but who never actually enlisted (he is better known elsewhere as the fellow who took Theodore Roosevelt bear hunting in Mississippi).[13] Then there's Dick Poplar, who was captured at Gettysburg: one prisoner of war record actually listed him as a private, but Poplar's 1886 obituary says that he "attached himself to a Virginia cavalry unit as a servant, not as a soldier."[14] You might come across the fantastic tale of Turner Hall, Jr., a supposed black Confederate who served as an orderly for Robert E. Lee and was Nathan Bedford Forrest's slave, thus bringing together two of the Confederate heritage's most beloved heroes. According to Al Arnold, who is Hall's descendant, all this is true, although the documentation for it is scarce and questionable, relying on twentieth-century newspaper reports.[15] Not all that different are the claims made by Nelson W. Winbush that his ancestor, Louis Napoleon Nelson, fought under Forrest, although Nelson's own pension records rest content with classifying him as a cook and a servant.[16] Finally, there's William Mack Lee, who claimed after the war that he had served alongside none other than Robert E. Lee himself (as a cook), but even Confederate veterans scoffed at that tale.[17] As already noted, there are instances of Confederate soldiers being dismissed from the service when someone discovered that they were defined as African Americans attempting to pass for white. On the whole, however, it has proven extraordinarily difficult for proponents of the position that significant numbers of African Americans served as soldiers in the Confederate army to document such service, although it shouldn't seem so hard if there were anywhere near the number of black Confederate soldiers that they claim.

So what do we know? First, although it is easy to recognize the efforts of free people of color to organize military units in New Orleans and Mobile during the Confederacy's lifetime, one should not make too much of these efforts. Students of Creole

---

13. "Holt Collier," United States Fish and Wildlife Service, https://www.fws.gov, accessed July 8, 2016.

14. "Black CSA POWs," Descendants of Point Lookout POW Organization, http://www.plpow.com/, accessed July 8, 2016. Note that this Internet site, despite the evidence it cites, nevertheless claims Poplar served as a private. See also Kevin Levin, "Happy Richard Poplar Day," *Civil War Memory* (blog), September 18, 2010, http://cwmemory.com/, accessed July 8, 2016.

15. Al Arnold, *Robert E. Lee's Orderly: A Modern Black Man's Confederate Journey*, http://www.orderlyforlee.com, accessed July 8, 2016; Brooks D. Simpson, "On Al Arnold, Turner Hall, Jr., and 'Black Confederates,'" *Crossroads* (blog), March 19, 2016, https://cwcrossroads.wordpress.com/, accessed July 8, 2016.

16. Stephanie Garry, "In Defense of His Confederate Pride," *Tampa Bay Times*, October 7, 2007, http://www.sptimes.com, accessed July 8, 2016; Andy Hall, "Pension Records for Louis Napoleon Nelson," *Dead Confederates*, December 16, 2012, https://deadconfederates.com/, accessed July 8, 2016.

17. Kevin Levin, "William Mack Lee Outed in *Confederate Veteran*," *Civil War Memory*, May 27, 2016, http://cwmemory.com/, accessed July 8, 2016.

populations in these cities suggest that their interests were not identical with those of the enslaved or free black population there or elsewhere. To group Creoles with free African Americans under binary notions of racial identity distorts reality and obscures very real differences. In fact, there are serious differences between what happened in New Orleans and Mobile. Whereas a good number of the Louisiana Native Guards eventually found their way into U.S. military service—in the Corps d'Afrique and the 73rd and 74th Regiments of the U.S. Colored Troops, or as members of Louisiana's Unionist militia—Mobile's Confederate Creoles, although far fewer in number, continued to view themselves as apart from the African American community of that city. In neither case, however, can one claim that these groups were representative of anyone other than themselves.

Perhaps it is better to divide our analysis into four parts. The first issue someone exploring this issue will inevitably consider concerns presence. Many people spend a great deal of time trying to arrive at a determination of just how many enslaved blacks accompanied Confederate armies in camp and campaign. No responsible historian would claim that black labor did not assist Confederate military operations: indeed, one cannot explain the passage of the First Confiscation Act in August 1861 without acknowledging that the act targeted Confederate use of black labor. On the other hand, to claim that there were thousands of black Confederate soldiers who marched and fought alongside their fellow white soldiers in the struggle for Southern independence is to make an assertion that lacks a basis in evidence.

The second issue one needs to consider concerns status. Just because enslaved black laborers and servants accompanied Confederate forces does not make them soldiers, who enlisted or were drafted into Confederate military service. Nor does it make any sense to claim that because in modern military forces enlisted personnel perform many of the same tasks as enslaved black laborers performed in the Civil War, such people were de facto soldiers. That would be engaging in the ahistorical (and some would say unhistorical) practice of "presentism," in which one imposes present views and opinions on past actions, regardless of whether they are historically appropriate. Ironically, many of the same people who engage in presentism in this instance—including a rather healthy number of Confederate heritage activists—reject presentism when it comes to assessing white racial attitudes, insisting that people in the past must be understood and interpreted according to the standards of their era. Why one would make an exception for the legal status of a soldier remains a puzzle, unless one believes that Confederate heritage advocates who make the claim that status does not really matter have a larger point to pursue.

One must then contemplate a third and far more elusive issue: motivation. Were the enslaved blacks who accompanied the Confederate armies there by choice? That would seem difficult to argue in most cases, since they were impressed laborers. However, one can well imagine a slave preferring to be at the front and away from home for many reasons. Some of those reasons will sound familiar to people who examine why white men left home to go to war. Home might be boring. War is an adventure, and it can be exciting, especially for those who have yet to experience its horrors. For the handful of men classified as black who attempted to pass as white (and doubtless for those who were never discovered by the authorities), actual enlistment provided a means of escape and a chance to reforge one's identity by denying one's actual racial heritage. For enslaved blacks, proximity to Union lines opened up the prospect of freedom if they were able to escape and survive—an opportunity they were far less likely to have while they remained back home, far from the battlefront, where escape was problematic, risky, and often deadly. We have little evidence about motivation: the John Parkers are few. We have even less evidence that a significant number of African Americans either enlisted in or accompanied Confederate armies because they endorsed the Confederate cause. If there was any loyalty to anyone other than to themselves, their family, or their race, it might well be to their master and his family. It would not be until the war was well over that any enslaved blacks praised a cause that pledged to keep them enslaved, and they usually did so because they were seeking pensions or support from Confederate veteran groups.

Finally, one must consider the question of significance. What impact does one's conclusions about the first three points—presence, status, and motivation—have on one's understanding of secession, war, and the role of slavery in the coming of the conflict and the creation of the Confederacy? The mere presence of enslaved blacks within Confederate military forces does not make that army integrated in any meaningful sense, any more than a white homeowner in an all-white locality who chooses to hire black servants or workers to landscape the grounds or build an addition to the house is integrating a neighborhood or a family. Indeed, as several participants in the debate over enlisting slaves knew, that act would challenge one of the basic reasons for establishing the Confederacy in the first place: to protect slavery and black subordination. Point to the Confederate civil or military leader who claimed during the war that the presence of blacks within Confederate ranks demonstrated that neither the conflict nor the creation of the Confederacy had anything to do with slavery. Try it: it is very challenging.

It is, in fact the Creole exceptions in New Orleans and Mobile that prove the rule that the vast majority of African Americans did not harbor love for the Confederacy. When U.S. forces approached, most blacks sought their freedom, and understandably so; for all the stories of loyal house servants, one can find far more accounts in which masters and plantation mistresses deplore the ingratitude of the former slave. Nor do we find the Ku Klux Klan or other white supremacist terrorist organizations, composed largely of white Confederate veterans, seeking to have their alleged black comrades join in the crusade to restore home rule and white supremacy. Only once those goals were achieved did some blacks, either down on their luck or seeking to exploit an opportunity, rise up to declare that they, too, had served the Confederacy, although the nature of that service was sometimes concealed when they donned gray uniforms or posed for pictures alongside white Confederate veterans, most of whom made clear that the black man in the picture was not a fellow soldier.

This brings us to a rather interesting misuse of evidence: pension records. After the Civil War, former Confederate states eventually arranged to provide pensions to Confederate veterans. At first, African Americans who had served as servants or in other noncombatant capacities with the Confederate army were excluded from such pension programs, except in Mississippi. However, following World War I, the other former Confederate states followed suit. An African American filing for such a pension was not evidence that he had served in the Confederate military as a soldier. More likely than not, he had been an enslaved servant or a laborer. Nevertheless, some people insist that the pension files prove the existence of many black Confederate veterans.[18]

In short, the evidentiary record in support of claims that significant numbers of African Americans, enslaved or free, fought as soldiers in the Confederate army is rather slim and problematic and does not withstand scrutiny. But that does not mean that people do not believe it.

In the last half century, certain advocates of Confederate heritage have embraced a new history of African American participation in the Confederate war effort. They have claimed that large numbers of African Americans—sometimes numbering over 100,000, and occasionally reaching seven digits—were soldiers in the Confederate army.[19] The four steps of analysis outlined earlier help one understand the argument. Citing large numbers establishes presence, as if the mere presence of these men in such numbers makes an open-and-shut argument by itself. Proponents of this view then pursue one of several lines of argument when it comes to status (sometimes endorsing contradictory positions in the process). One claim is that these African Americans were, indeed, enlisted soldiers because they were listed on regimental rosters (or have a combined service record entry in the National Archives) or received pensions after the war (rarely is the type of pension or other detail given much scrutiny—the existence of a pension, of whatever sort, is cited as conclusive evidence). Another claim is that records that would have revealed a far more extensive number of black Confederate soldiers were destroyed at the end of the war, either in the chaos that attended the evacuation of Richmond or as a deliberate act of sabotage to conceal the presence of black soldiers in Confederate ranks. Finally, advocates assert that status is irrelevant: that service in whatever capacity with Confederate armies qualifies

---

18. James G. Hollandsworth, Jr., "Black Confederate Pensioners after the Civil War," *Mississippi History Now*, http://mshistorynow.mdah.state.ms.us/, accessed July 8, 2016.

19. See Brooks D. Simpson, "Confederate Heritage Salutes Veterans," *Crossroads*, May 29, 2016, https://cwcrossroads.wordpress.com/, quoting a May 29, 2016, tweet by Sea Raven Press that a million blacks "took up arms against tyrant Lincoln's regime"; Charles Kelly Barrow, J. H. Segars, and R. B. Rosenburg, eds., *Black Confederates* (Gretna, LA: Pelican, 2004), 3; H. K. Edgerton, "Black Confederates," SouthernHeritage411.com, http://www.southernheritage411.com/, accessed September 1, 2016; Andy Hall, "Do the Guinness People Know about This?" *Dead Confederates*, February 10, 2016, https://deadconfederates.com/, accessed September 1, 2016; and Andy Hall, "'Black Confederates' Jumps the Shark," *Dead Confederates*, December 20, 2014, https://deadconfederates.com/, accessed September 1, 2016.

an African American as a soldier, especially if those functions are now performed by military personnel.[20] That this is ahistorical, indeed presentist, apparently presents no problem to people who believe what they want to believe.

Proponents of the existence of a significant number of African American soldiers in Confederate ranks spend little time discussing motivation based on actual evidence. Instead, they assert that service in support of a cause is the same as support of a cause. Some advocates remind critics that conscripted soldiers are honored for their service, even if it was not voluntarily given, and so the same privilege should be extended to blacks in Confederate service, even if they were not soldiers. However, these proponents rarely address the policies of impressment or the presence of servants who serve their master and not a broader cause. That involuntary service is not the same as voluntary support is of little account in this argument.

That lapse in logic is easily explained when one turns to understanding why proponents of this position believe it is significant. They declare that the presence of African Americans in large numbers in Confederate ranks demonstrates that the Civil War was not about slavery (why else would blacks support the Confederacy?); that the vast majority of enslaved African Americans were loyal to their owners, to their homeland, and to the cause of Confederate independence; and that the Confederacy was in fact far more tolerant and far less racist than its Yankee counterpart. Confederate armies, so the argument goes, were integrated, not segregated, unlike their blue-belly foes. The Civil War was simply a war for independence or an act of self-defense against an invading foe bent on conquest and submission of the South. If the war was truly about slavery, why did Lincoln wait so long to issue the Emancipation Proclamation, and why didn't he free the slaves in areas under U.S. control? In short, proponents of the position that large numbers of blacks served in Confederate ranks see that argument as a means to the end that they have always sought: that of detaching the cause of the Civil War from the growing challenges slavery presented to the maintenance of the Union and asserting that the Confederacy had nothing to do with slavery. If anything, white Southerners always had the best interests of black Southerners in mind, and their concern was repaid with the loyalty of the enslaved and the free blacks.

Critics of this interpretation have sometimes termed it the "myth of Black Confederates" (or the "Black Confederate Myth," or BCM) to distinguish it from a discussion of the actual historical record.[21] Yet the term "Black Confederate Myth" is in itself

---

20. Bruce Levine, "In Search of a Usable Past: Neo-Confederates and Black Confederates," in *Slavery and Public History: The Tough Stuff of American Memory*, ed. James Oliver Horton and Lois E. Horton (Chapel Hill: University of North Carolina Press, 2006), 188–91; Eric Richardson, foreword to *Virginia's Black Confederates: Essays and Rosters*, by Greg Eanes (Crewe, VA: Eanes Group, 2014), iii–iv; and Andy Hall, "Soldiers All," *Dead Confederates*, July 6, 2011, https://deadconfederates. com/, accessed September 1, 2016.

21. See, for example, Glenn Brasher, "What Should Historians Make of 'Black Confederates?'" *The Civil War Monitor*, May 5, 2014, http://www.civilwarmonitor.com, accessed September 1, 2016; Brooks D. Simpson, "Professional Historians and the Black Confederate Myth: Part One,"

problematic: after all, if one can demonstrate that some African Americans served the Confederate cause, including as soldiers, then what is claimed to be myth is actually fact, and the evidence presented is but the tip of the iceberg. Indeed, proponents of this position sometimes proceed by proclaiming that critics of their position deny that any blacks served as Confederate soldiers, evidence to the contrary notwithstanding. That other scholars who enter this debate unprepared and misinformed sometimes make this same mistaken claim is unfortunate, as all their assertions do is fuel the attack.[22] At times scholarly debate makes strange bedfellows.

In pursuit of these claims, proponents of the Black Confederate Myth are not above misinterpreting, mishandling, or even fabricating evidence. Such behavior persists despite research that documents such distortion and deceit, in part because the Internet proves elusive to correction for those who are unskilled wielders of search engines or are determined to stand by their preferred accounts. One need only reject accountability to the rules of evidence and historical interpretation to make a claim that soon spreads across the Internet into either unsuspecting or determined hands.

A few examples illustrate the problem.

The Confederate Memorial at Arlington National Cemetery is sometimes cited by Confederate heritage advocates as offering evidence that blacks served as Confederate soldiers. They point to the fact that a black man wearing military headgear is indeed portrayed on the monument. Of course, one could argue that the monument, dedicated in 1914 (the year before the release of *Birth of a Nation*), presents how Confederate heritage organizations at the time wanted to portray the role of enslaved blacks in the Confederate war effort—and one would be right. Here is the description of the memorial at the time of its dedication: "On the right is a faithful negro body-servant following his young master. . . ." Not a soldier, but a personal servant, one used to illustrate "the kindly relations that existed all over the South between the master and the slave. . . . The astonishing fidelity of the slaves everywhere during the war to the wives and children of those who were absent in the army was convincing proof of the kindly relations between master and slave in the old South."[23] Thus, recent efforts to identify the image as that of a black soldier run afoul of evidence that it was included for a different reason, although in both cases the general argument is the same—that enslaved blacks willingly supported the Confederacy. Current Confederate heritage advocates are simply seeking to replace one myth with another.

Crossroads, June 18, 2011, https://cwcrossroads.wordpress.com/, accessed August 4, 2016; and Brooks D. Simpson, "Professional Historians and the Black Confederate Myth, Part Two," *Crossroads*, June 20, 2011, https://cwcrossroads.wordpress.com/, accessed August 4, 2016.

22. See, for example, John Stauffer, "Yes, There Were Black Confederates. Here's Why," *The Root* (blog), January 20, 2015, http://www.theroot.com/, accessed August 4, 2016.

23. Hilary A. Herbert, *History of the Arlington Confederate Monument* (n.p.: United Daughters of the Confederacy, 1914), 77.

Andrew Chandler and his slave Silas Chandler served in the 44th Mississippi Infantry. This image and the fact Silas is heavily armed are often erroneously used as evidence that African Americans fought for the Confederacy. Image courtesy of the Library of Congress.

Also frequently cited as evidence of black Confederates is an image of one Silas next to his owner Andrew Chandler. Both men are brandishing rather large knives; Silas holds a rifle, Andrew a revolver, with each man carrying a second handgun in his uniform, thus bristling with weaponry. One might interpret from this that Silas was actually a Confederate soldier, but he remained a slave in the Chandler family throughout the Civil War, first following Andrew in the 44th Mississippi Infantry before Andrew's wounding at Chickamauga in 1863. Much has been made of how Silas rescued his owner and brought him home; several months later Silas returned to the front, this time as the servant of Benjamin Chandler, Andrew's younger brother.[24]

Engaging in a search for images available on the Internet might bring the user to what purports to be a photograph of the 1st Louisiana Native Guards in 1861.

24. See Myra Chandler Sampson and Kevin M. Levin, "The Loyalty of Silas Chandler," *Civil War Times* 51 (February 2012): 30–35.

This picture, titled "1st Louisiana Native Guards in 1861," is offered as proof that organized African American units existed in the Confederate army.

The original, undoctored image of an unknown group of Union troops with their white officer. This photograph was taken in a studio in Philadelphia and was eventually used as a recruiting poster for the U.S. Army. Images courtesy of Jerome S. Handler.

That image is a fabrication, however. It is based upon an actual photograph of African American Union soldiers taken in 1864, one used as the basis for a color lithograph portraying black soldiers in camp. Removing the (white) U.S. officer is perhaps the most visible sign of what two researchers called "a rather amateurish digital manipulation" of the 1864 photograph (the "U.S." on one soldier's belt buckle remains visible).[25]

Much has been made of a report by Dr. Lewis Steiner, an inspector with the U.S. Sanitary Commission, of what he observed during Lee's invasion of Maryland in September 1862. Observing Stonewall Jackson's army moving through Frederick, Maryland, on September 10, Steiner estimated that of the 64,000 men he saw (a number far larger than Jackson's actual strength), some 3,000 blacks were present, clad in various sorts of uniforms (including U.S. uniforms) and carrying weapons: "They were manifestly an integral portion of the Southern Confederacy." Steiner thought this was interesting in light of Confederate outrage at the notion that perhaps the U.S. Army should recruit and employ African Americans.[26] However, one cannot find mention of any such black soldiers in Confederate records (let alone any mention of formal black Confederate units). That blacks moving with a Confederate army would soon don various uniforms is no surprise, given the lack of alternative clothing; they did not appear to be moving in formation, and in any case Steiner had wildly overestimated Confederate strength. No one observed these men fighting at Harpers Ferry or Antietam within the following week. As for his report that they carried weapons (he does not report how many did so), nineteenth-century soldiers could reasonably be expected to hand off a heavy unloaded musket to an available "bearer."

Another highlighted report came from none other than Frederick Douglass, who stated in his monthly magazine in September 1861 the following:

> It is now pretty well established, that there are at the present moment many colored men in the Confederate army doing duty not only as cooks, servants and laborers, but as real soldiers, having muskets on their shoulders, and bullets in their pockets, ready to shoot down loyal troops, and do all that soldiers may to destroy the Federal Government and build up that of the traitors and rebels. There were such soldiers at Manassas, and they are probably there still. There is a Negro in the army as well as in the fence, and our Government is likely to find it out before the war comes to an end. That the Negroes are numerous in the rebel army, and do for that army its heaviest work, is beyond question. They have been the chief laborers upon those temporary defences in which the rebels have been able to mow down our men. Negroes helped to build the batteries at

---

25. Jerome S. Handler and Michael L. Tuite, Jr., "Retouching History, The Modern Falsification of a Civil War Photograph," http://people.virginia.edu, accessed July 8, 2016.

26. Lewis H. Steiner, *Report of Dr. Lewis H. Steiner, M. D., Inspector of the Sanitary Commission* (New York: Anson D. F. Randolph, 1862), 19–20.

Charleston. They relieve their gentlemanly and military masters from the stiffening drudgery of the camp, and devote them to the nimble and dexterous use of arms. Rising above vulgar prejudice, the slaveholding rebel accepts the aid of the black man as readily as that of any other. If a bad cause can do this, why should a good cause be less wisely conducted?[27]

Powerful words, these, but proof of very little that cannot easily be explained. By September 1861 everyone knew that the Confederacy was employing blacks as military laborers: the First Confiscation Act of the previous month addressed how U.S. forces were to treat captured blacks who had been acting in that capacity. As for reports of black soldiers at First Manassas, as we have seen, some men (such as John Parker) were indeed forced to fight, but notions that there were actual infantry regiments and artillery batteries composed of black recruits was utter nonsense. Nevertheless, Douglass used what stories he could amass in pursuit of a larger purpose: inducing U.S. authorities to recruit and deploy black men in uniform, a policy that would justify their emancipation. Early the next year, Douglass offered a different take: "There are English rebels, Scotch rebels, Irish rebels, but I believe there are no black rebels. The black man at heart, even if found in the rebel camp, is a loyal man, forced out of his place by circumstances beyond his control."[28]

Finally, there has been an assortment of claims that reflect a willingness to distort what someone has said. Ed Bearss, former chief historian for the National Park Service, once opined, "I don't want to call it a conspiracy to ignore the role of Blacks both above and below the Mason-Dixon line, but it was definitely a tendency that began around 1910." This unexceptional assertion has been twisted into a statement that Bearss was claiming that there had been an effort to conceal the presence of black Confederate soldiers, but one might note that there was no widespread claim of such service before 1910, either.[29]

Yet the tale of enslaved and free African Americans swarming in large numbers to serve as soldiers in the Confederate army persists. Why? Well, listen to what one representative of the Sons of Confederate Veterans (SCV) has to say: "I think probably only a few people would say there were no black soldiers in the Confederate Army—there were." According to Marc Allen, a public affairs officer for the SCV's Mississippi Division, "You have to ask yourself a question: Why would they do that? Why would they fight in a war so that slavery could be maintained, so that they could continue being a slave? Well, the easy answer is, that wasn't what the war was fought

---

27. Frederick Douglass, "Fighting Rebels with Only One Hand," *Douglass' Monthly*, September 1861, reprinted in *The Life and Writings of Frederick Douglass*, ed. Philip S. Foner (New York: International, 1952), 3:153–54.

28. Frederick Douglass, "The Reasons for Our Troubles," January 14, 1862, in *Douglass' Monthly*, February 1862; my thanks to Kenneth Noe for bringing this to my attention.

29. Brooks D. Simpson, "Keeping It Honest: What Did Ed Bearss Say?" *Crossroads*, February 1, 2011, https://cwcrossroads.wordpress.com/, accessed July 8, 2016.

about chiefly."[30] What Allen thinks is the "easy answer" might not be the right answer, of course, and the so-called easy answer ducks the question of why enslaved blacks would willingly fight to remain enslaved. Even Allen concedes that.

Allen's claim, however, points to what is behind the assertion that there were large numbers of African Americans who willingly took up arms as soldiers in the Confederate army. Simply put, it is another attempt to deny the centrality of slavery in the coming of the Civil War and as the fundamental reason why the Confederacy came to be—to protect, defend, and even expand the peculiar institution. At one time, part of this defense rested upon the notion that slavery was a benign, even civilizing institution that benefited the enslaved—an argument that echoed nineteenth-century proslavery claims that the peculiar institution was a positive good. As that argument grew less acceptable, Confederate heritage advocates, having gained little traction in the popular mind with claims that white Northerners and their leaders were no more inclined to embrace black equality on its merits than did their Confederate counterparts, sought to get with the times by portraying the Confederacy as a diverse, multicultural, tolerant experience, complete with an integrated army—embracing the very values they decried elsewhere as a sign of political correctness. Surely such an endeavor was not designed to defend the enslavement of fellow human beings. Rather, it must have been a quest for self-determination, using the constitutionally sanctioned process called secession, which sought to defend home, hearth, and Southern society from the advent of a crass American empire featuring centralized government and Yankee values.

Historian Kevin Levin has concluded that one can identify the origins of this approach in the aftermath of the televising of *Roots*, a series depicting Alex Haley's novel of the same name, in 1977, followed over a decade later by the release of the 1989 movie *Glory*, which told the tale of the 54th Massachusetts Regiment.[31] Dean Boggs, then commander in chief of the Sons of Confederate Veterans, knew that the message offered by *Roots* was powerful. "Politics often ignores the truth, and the truth is that the majority of Southern Negroes, slave and free, sided [with] the Confederate effort tremendously," Boggs declared. "Some were under arms and in combat."[32] More recently, in 2014 the SCV elected as its commander in chief Charles Kelly Barrow of Georgia, author of two books on black Confederates, suggesting the persistence of these claims as a hallmark of Confederate heritage advocacy.

For some advocates of this interpretation, the mere presence of some (and one hoped more) men of color in Confederate military service was sufficient to make the case that the struggle for Confederate independence had nothing to do with slavery. Obscuring the differences between noncombatants and combatants simply increased

---

30. Adam Serwer, "The Secret History of the Photo at the Center of the Black Confederate Myth," *BuzzFeed*, April 17, 2016, https://www.buzzfeed.com/, accessed July 8, 2016.

31. Kevin M. Levin, "The Myth of the Black Confederate Soldier," *The Daily Beast*, August 7, 2015, http://www.thedailybeast.com/, accessed July 8, 2016.

32. Ibid.

the number of blacks that could be said to have served the Confederacy, with the assumption that they did so willingly.

The Georgia Division of the SCV assembled a website purporting to be a "curriculum"—in truth, a gathering of undigested material—designed to promote (among other things) the notion that African Americans fought for the Confederacy.[33] Other Confederate heritage advocates followed suit, some offering rather attractively illustrated if thinly documented presentations.[34] Sometimes the creators of these websites have found themselves embarrassed by their poor historical research skills. Ann DeWitt, creator of a website that now focuses on genealogical research to identify black Confederate ancestors, found herself in just such a situation.[35] She misread a document detailing rations for a Texas heavy artillery regiment under the command of Colonel Joseph J. Cook as evidence that there was a regiment of African American cooks in the Confederate army.[36]

It is important to note that mishandling and misinterpreting evidence of black participation in the Confederate military is not limited to Confederate heritage advocates. Indeed, starting in 2011, Professor John Stauffer of Harvard University, who had written on John Brown as well as black abolitionists, began turning his attention to the subject of black Confederates. In 2015, he argued that between three thousand and six thousand blacks served as Confederate soldiers, although he was painfully vague as to how he arrived at such an estimate. Admitting that this number was "statistically insignificant," he nevertheless claimed that their mere presence "explode[d] the myth that a slave wouldn't fight on behalf of masters"—an argument that used presence to assign motivation, without a scintilla of proof to support it.[37]

In his argument, Stauffer ignored a great deal of work that had been done to examine the documents he cited in support of his claim, and gave readers no reason to trust the rest, from Frederick Douglass' claims about black Confederates at Manassas to the story of John Parker. Indeed, Stauffer claimed that Douglass' statement, made in the summer of 1861, was based on testimony that in fact was not shared until the following February.[38] Stauffer repeats unsupported reports that three regiments of blacks fought at First Manassas but fails to identify them (it's interesting that no Confederate

33. John K. McNeill, "A Southern View of History: The War for Southern Independence; Part IX. Confederate Allies and Northern Political Intervention," Sons of Confederate Veterans, http://www.scv.org/, accessed July 8, 2016.

34. Skid Billeaudeaux, "Black Confederates," *The Politically Incorrect Illustrated South*, http://www.greyriderfordixienet.com/, accessed July 8, 2016.

35. Ann DeWitt, Black Confederates Soldiers Website, http://blackconfederatesoldiers.com/home.html, accessed July 8, 2016.

36. Andy Hall, "Famous 'Negro Cooks Regiment' Found—In My Own Backyard!" *Dead Confederates*, August 8, 2011, https://deadconfederates.com/, accessed July 8, 2016.

37. Stauffer, "Yes, There Were Black Confederates."

38. Andy Hall, "Frederick Douglass, Time Traveler?" *Dead Confederates*, January 20, 2015, https://deadconfederates.com, accessed July 7, 2016.

report mentions them). Elsewhere Stauffer asserts that "most black soldiers, at First Manassas and elsewhere, were free blacks," again without any supporting evidence. In fact, Stauffer was not sure-handed in his own treatment of evidence, implying that one historian's highlighting of the ways in which proponents mishandled, deliberately distorted, or fabricated evidence of black Confederate soldiers constituted an outright denial of the existence of any such men, while he seemed unable to take advantage of that work as he fell victim to many of the traps set by such problematic handling of the evidentiary record.[39]

Several historians immediately contested Stauffer's argument and use of evidence: he declined to engage them in discussion, which struck some observers as surprising given his reputation as being somewhat contentious in challenging other scholars.[40] But others, notably Confederate heritage advocates who read and cited Stauffer selectively, took heart that a Harvard professor had agreed with them. Stauffer also failed to engage their interpretations of his claims. Nor did he respond to evidence that he had misrepresented the scholarship of others in constructing a straw man of scholarly consensus to attack.

Nor is Stauffer alone. Take Earl L. Ijames, curator of African American history at the N.C. Museum of History, who has made the study of "colored Confederates" his personal mission. Like Stauffer, Ijames fumbles with evidence, especially pension records and rosters, in blurring the lines between noncombatant and combatant roles, rendering the status of "soldier" nearly meaningless. Yet advocates of Confederate heritage rushed to publish Ijames' rather sloppily assembled summary in a book entitled *Understanding the War Between the States* as well as to share it on the website of the Abbeville Institute, a group that claims that its purpose "is to critically explore what is true and valuable in the Southern tradition" and to challenge what its founders claim is the corruption of that tradition, a tradition that celebrates the Confederacy.[41]

What, then, are we to make of what some call the Black Confederate Myth, and how do we address it? First, historians should delve into researching the question of

---

39. Stauffer, "Yes, There Were Black Confederates." In a misguided effort to come to Stauffer's support, Jim Downs managed to confuse the issues at stake still more. See Downs, "'Do You See What I See': The Debate over Black Confederates," *Huffington Post*, January 23, 2015, updated March 25, 2015, http://www.huffingtonpost.com/, accessed August 10, 2016; Kevin Levin, "Jim Downs Comes to the Defense of John Stauffer," *Civil War Memory*, January 23, 2016, http://cwmemory.com, accessed August 10, 2016.

40. For example, Kevin Levin, "John Stauffer Goes Looking For Black Confederates and Comes Up Empty . . . Again," *Civil War Memory*, January 20, 2015, http://cwmemory.com/, accessed August 4, 2016; Brooks D. Simpson, "John Stauffer and Black Confederates Redux," *Crossroads*, January 20, 2015, https://cwcrossroads.wordpress.com/, accessed August 4, 2016; and Brooks D. Simpson, "Just the Facts, Please," *Crossroads*, January 24, 2015, https://cwcrossroads.wordpress.com/, accessed August 4, 2016.

41. Earl L. Ijames, "Black Soldiers, North and South, 1861–1865," *Abbeville Blog*, January 8, 2016, http://www.abbevilleinstitute.org/-, accessed July 8, 2016.

how African Americans were involved in the Confederate war effort. It is true that the involuntary labor of enslaved African Americans enabled the Confederacy to mobilize a rather high percentage of Southern white adult males for military service; it is also true that Confederate policy called for the impressment of slave labor in direct support of the Confederate war effort. One must draw a distinction between the use of enslaved labor in support of the Southern quest for independence and the notion that African Americans themselves supported the Confederacy. One should also understand that the free men of color who formed units in New Orleans and Mobile were not representative of much other than themselves and their peculiar circumstances. To confuse them with tales of the loyal slave is to do great violence to the historical record.

Abraham Lincoln once explained that African Americans had their own interests during the war. "I thought that whatever negroes can be got to do as soldiers, leaves just so much less for white soldiers to do, in saving the Union," he explained. "Does it appear otherwise to you? But negroes, like other people, act upon motives. Why should they do anything for us, if we will do nothing for them? If they stake our lives for us, they must be prompted by the strongest motive—even the promise of freedom."[42] If, for Lincoln, freeing and arming black men was a means to the end of preserving the Union, then it is logical to reason that African Americans, enslaved and free, viewed the American Civil War as a means to secure their interests of freedom and security. Preserving the Union or securing Confederate independence was not their objective: how they would respond in those circumstances, including the chaos, destruction, and opportunity offered by war and the path of events, would reflect how they thought such events served as means to achieve what was most important to them. Frederick Douglass, for example, cared little for a war waged merely to reunite the nation, but when the war to save the Union required that it also become the war to destroy slavery, he was ready to support it. Thus it is a mistake to suggest that black men and women shared the same interests and objectives as did their white counterparts.

Moreover, all this fuss about whether African Americans served in large numbers as Confederate soldiers and the supposed significance of such service risks overshadowing the fact that upwards of 200,000 African Americans, free as well as formerly enslaved, served in the armed forces of the United States. By 1864 they formed a significant portion of the U.S. Army, and their presence played an important role in subduing the Confederacy. Escaped slaves became Union soldiers, enlisted, paid, armed, and recognized as veterans after the war. These men might have fought to save the Union, but they did so primarily to secure their own freedom and the freedom of their fellow African Americans.

Freedom and security, of course, did not always go hand in hand. The rebellious slave seeking freedom placed the security of his family at risk. A slave uprising far behind the lines would be extinguished by whites, whether they were left at home due

---

42. Abraham Lincoln to James C. Conkling, August 26, 1863, in *The Collected Works of Abraham Lincoln*, ed. Roy Basler et al. (New Brunswick, NJ: Rutgers University Press, 1953), 6:409.

to the workings of Confederate conscription legislation (which provided for limited service exemptions) or served in the home guard, which aimed to preserve law and order. Appearing loyal, regardless of one's true sentiments, could be a matter of life or death, and one would be foolish, indeed, to place one's family and kin at risk unless one believed that a quest for freedom would succeed. Sometimes one waited for an opportunity as the Yankees came closer and closer; at other times one could best serve one's family's interest by going off to war with the owner, as Silas Chandler did. Certainly he knew that while he might seek his freedom in the disorder and chaos of the battlefield, his wife back home might suffer the consequences. Loyalty meant self-preservation, regardless of whether it was sincere or feigned or dwelled someplace in between.

In short, for all the talk of Confederate heritage advocates that there were significant numbers of African Americans serving as soldiers in the ranks of the Confederate armies, such is not the case. Moreover, to assume that black slaves willingly supported the cause of Confederate independence is an argument advanced without proof. If anything, a close examination of the small numbers of men of color who served—or sought to serve—in the Confederate army in any capacity argues against the notion that their presence signified support for the Confederate cause. To decry these findings as an example of political correctness, when in fact, it is continuing to argue in favor of the Black Confederate Myth in the face of the documentary record, which is an exercise in what one could call "heritage correctness." And it has little to do with historical accuracy. The real story is far more interesting: it helps to demonstrate that a war fought to preserve and protect slavery could only be waged with the use of slave labor but that the result was a conflict that destroyed the very institution it was supposed to protect and defend.

4. The Myth of the "Great" Conventional Battlefield War

Barton A. Myers

The war began when the Confederates bombarded Union soldiers at Fort Sumter, South Carolina on April 12, 1861. The war ended in Spring, 1865. Robert E. Lee surrendered the last major Confederate army to Ulysses S. Grant at Appomattox Courthouse on April 9, 1865. The last battle was fought at Palmito Ranch, Texas, on May 13, 1865.[1]

—Civil War Trust

For the past 150 years, many, if not most, readers have viewed the essential military events of the American Civil War as taking place on large, conventional battlefields away from civilian populations. The great battles at Shiloh, Antietam, Chancellorsville, Gettysburg, and Spotsylvania Court House were fought by citizen-soldiers recruited, trained, and disciplined in the use of linear tactics by some of our nation's most famous generals. Lee, Grant, Hood, Hooker, Hancock, Longstreet, Thomas, and Jackson planned the strategy behind these bloody battles and executed campaigns that dominated the countryside for four years. Furthermore, conventional battles and well-executed military strategy culminated with the clear, formal surrenders of the Confederate armies in 1865. That is the story that we, as Americans, tell ourselves. Moreover, in the imagination of many Americans, the conventional regular armies of blue and gray that marched and fought on the fields of northern Virginia, middle Tennessee, and the Trans-Mississippi were hermetically sealed away from civilian populations. That is, it was the norm until, in 1864, General William Tecumseh Sherman arrived at the head of hordes of blue-clad Yankee vandals to terrorize the population of the Deep South and help General Ulysses S. Grant bring about the ultimate defeat of the regular Confederate armies, especially General Robert E. Lee's resolute Army of Northern Virginia.

Despite a death toll that claimed more than 750,000 Americans, approximately 2.5 percent of the U.S. population (the equivalent loss in 2017 would be eight million people),[2] it was a war that somehow becomes easier to accept when the story

---

1. "Civil War Facts," Civil War Trust, http://www.civilwar.org/, accessed February 14, 2017.

2. J. David Hacker, "A Census-Based Count of the Civil War Dead," *Civil War History* 57 (2011): 307–48. Hacker uses an actuarial analysis of the U.S. census to reject the conventional figure of 620,000 military deaths from 1861 to 1865. He replaces this lower figure with an estimated range of between 752,000 and 851,000 out of a total population of about thirty-one million.

is told like that: a war that had a clear beginning at Fort Sumter, South Carolina, in April 1861 and a certain end at Appomattox Courthouse in April 1865 with a number of epic battles interspersed between the two bookend events. Given this perception, the debate over military history for many readers of Civil War histories centers on finding the potential military turning points on these great battlefields and connecting those moments to the ultimate defeat of the Confederacy.

Contrary to this notion are two other realities. The thunder in Charleston Bay and the stillness that shrouded Appomattox did not respectively signal the beginning and cessation of military activity. So also, the Civil War was fought in thousands of locations away from the "great battlefields" and involved a significant percentage of the two nations' civilian populations.

While conventional battlefield engagements between large armies were a vital component of the American Civil War, they were far from the only type of battle or the only role played by the military, either citizen-soldiers or other warriors in the conflict, and the outcomes of great battles were not the only military reasons that the Confederacy found its defeat in four years. As the Confederate cause waned, the war aims of the Confederates mutated from establishing a separate nation based on racial supremacy to securing a racial caste system, in spite of military failure on the conventional battlefield. A closer examination of this other war of the 1860s demonstrates that there was no clear end to armed hostilities in 1865 over some of the Confederacy's central war aims, in particular white home rule and racial control. The reasons for the perpetuation of the myth that the Civil War was fought solely on vast, distant battlefields by regular armies are manifold, and present an opportunity for deeper discussion of other types of military activity and irregular military engagements that also had a concurrent and deep impact on the course of military conflict in the 1860s.[3]

Popular and Academic Mythmakers

Hollywood filmmakers, Civil War re-enactors, and scholars alike have perpetuated this myth of conventional battlefields constituting the entire military history of the American Civil War. According to this view, during the Civil War long lines of blue and gray clashed in remote places, where civilians were safely behind the lines living on a home front distant from the fields where the war was won and lost. Several of the most historically important and financially successful films about the era, including *Gone with the Wind, Glory, Gettysburg, Gods and Generals, The Red Badge of Courage*, and the TV mini-series *North and South*, encourage parts of this myth. With a few

3. On the continuation of warfare by other means post-1865, see Douglas R. Egerton, *The Wars of Reconstruction: The Brief, Violent History of America's Most Progressive Era* (New York: Bloomsbury Press, 2014); George C. Rable, *But There Was No Peace: The Role of Violence in the Politics of Reconstruction* (Athens: University of Georgia Press, 1984); and Carole Emberton, *Beyond Redemption: Race, Violence, and the American South after the Civil War* (Chicago: University of Chicago Press, 2013).

exceptions, Civil War films have emphasized large-scale battles between armies that were mustered, led, and employed in traditional ways. Notable films like *The Horse Soldiers, Shenandoah, The Outlaw Josey Wales, Cold Mountain, Ride with the Devil*, and most recently *The Free State of Jones* have helped to push back against this myth, but they are rare exceptions in the realm of popular culture.[4]

Some popular mid-twentieth-century Civil War historians, searching for a coherent military narrative, helped create the myth, whereas other historians worked to integrate into the broad story military events off the conventional field of battle. Yet even many of the historians who helped create a narrative history of military events rooted solely in large battlefields seemed uncomfortable with that narrow focus. In 1953 historian Bruce Catton published the final volume in his Army of the Potomac trilogy. That book, *A Stillness at Appomattox*, was a grand, magisterial work of narrative military history and garnered him commercial success as well as the Pulitzer Prize in History and a National Book Award for Nonfiction. Catton went on to become the founding editor of *American Heritage* magazine, which inspired generations of readers. Through this publication his views on the war influenced a generation of young historians coming of age in the 1960s and 1970s. It was Catton, however, who built a fire under Virgil Carrington Jones, a newspaperman living in Richmond, Virginia, who had already published a first-rate biography of Confederate Partisan Ranger John Singleton Mosby in 1944.[5] Catton walked into V. C. Jones' office and demanded, "Why in the hell doesn't someone write a history of the guerrillas?" Jones' subsequent book, *Gray Ghosts and Rebel Raiders*, addressed the broader border war of northern Virginia, Maryland, and West Virginia but fell short of the fuller treatment of Civil War irregular warfare and activities that Catton had sought.[6]

Even James McPherson's 1988 Pulitzer Prize–winning narrative history, *Battle Cry of Freedom: The Civil War Era*, which is widely considered the most important one-volume narrative of the war published in the last fifty years, relegated the topic of guerrilla warfare to a discussion of regional conflicts primarily in Missouri, West Virginia, Virginia, and Tennessee. McPherson's analysis of the topic covered fewer than sixteen pages in his 862-page tome. Esteemed British military historian John Keegan offered even less analysis of the topic in his book *The American Civil War: A Military History*, limiting his keen analytical mind to only the problems of guerrilla conflict in Missouri.[7]

In other studies, it was not absence of analysis but a conceptualization of the argument related to irregular warfare and activity during the American Civil War that was

---

4. "Greatest Civil War Films," IMDb, January 13, 2011, http://www.imdb.com/list/ls000038854/, accessed January 25, 2016.

5. Virgil Carrington Jones, *Ranger Mosby* (Chapel Hill: University of North Carolina Press, 1944).

6. Virgil Carrington Jones, *Gray Ghosts and Rebel Raiders* (New York: Holt, Rinehart, and Winston, 1956), xvi.

7. James M. McPherson, *Battle Cry of Freedom: The Civil War Era* (New York: Oxford University Press, 1988); John Keegan, *The American Civil War: A Military History* (New York: Vintage, 2009).

and is a problem for rectifying the myth. In his widely read history *The Confederate War: How Popular Will, Nationalism, and Military Strategy Could Not Stave Off Defeat* (1997), University of Virginia professor Gary W. Gallagher argued that "guerrilla war was not a viable option within the Confederate context and thus should not be put forward in retrospect as the most desirable national strategy for the South." While Gallagher was examining the feasibility of guerrilla warfare as a military strategy for Confederates to win the war, especially in early 1865, his argument mischaracterized and poorly framed a valuable dimension of the entire issue. Confederates not only made widespread use of guerrilla warfare in its many forms throughout the conflict, they adopted it as part of their military policy, debated it in their Congress, and deployed it in the form of the Partisan Ranger service in every seceding and Border South slave state, save Delaware. This policy and strategy ultimately failed and also planted many of the seeds of the Confederacy's destruction in the process of failing. Confederates also encountered widespread armed resistance by warriors who deployed irregular warfare tactics and techniques to resist the establishment of a Southern nation.[8]

The myth of the great regular battlefield war of 1861–65 is just that: a convenient construction of historical narration that leaves out the Civil War military experience of a large number of Americans. While it is quite alluring to believe the myth, good campaign strategy and proficient use of linear tactics on symmetrical battlefields alone did not, in the span of four years, lead to a clear conclusion, for all Americans, of violence waged over the broad range of issues at stake in the war. In the face of the last fifty years of U.S. military history, which have rarely seen decisive warfare on the pitched conventional field of battle lead to clear ends to conflicts, the myth that conventional battles alone can solve the nation's problems in a swift stroke of military genius offers comfort to readers plagued with a world of complex military problems. A twenty-first-century world of irregular warriors, improvised weapons, heinously visible and invisible enemies, a dearth of conventional battlefield victories, and the absence of clear military ends to wars causes many Americans to long for the supposedly tidy battlefields of blue clashing with gray away from civilian populations.[9]

Both U.S. and Confederate leaders, with a few notable exceptions like U.S. General-in-Chief Winfield Scott, expected a short, conventional war in 1861, culminating in a momentous, climactic battle. Scott, a Virginian and a hero of both the War of

---

8. Gary W. Gallagher, *The Confederate War: How Popular Will, Nationalism, and Military Strategy Could Not Stave Off Defeat* (Cambridge: Harvard University Press, 1997), 127. On the geographic extent and strategic role of the guerrilla wars of the American South, see Brian D. McKnight and Barton A. Myers, "'Lightning around the Edge of a Cloud': Guerrilla Warfare's Place in the History of the American Civil War," and Barton A. Myers, "'Of Incalculable Benefit to Our Cause': Partisan Ranger Petitions and the Confederacy's Authorized Guerrilla Service," in *The Guerrilla Hunters: Irregular Conflicts during the Civil War*, ed. Brian D. McKnight and Barton A. Myers (Baton Rouge: Louisiana State University Press, 2017).

9. On the absence of decisive conventional battles in recent wars, see Victor Davis Hanson, *The Father of Us All: War and History, Ancient and Modern* (New York: Bloomsbury Press, 2010), chap. 8.

1812 and the Mexican-American War, proposed a strategic plan for conquering the rebellious South by blockading its ports with warships, severing it in two by projecting an amphibious operation down the Mississippi River, and ultimately launching a large invasion force into the South to defeat resistance and occupy the land. It was a strategic plan rooted in the expectation that the Southern population would eventually pressure the leadership of the Confederacy into surrender as a result of invasion and military occupation. It was also a plan based on the idea of fighting a long and sustained national war against a domestic insurrection, not one punctuated only by brief, large-scale conventional battles that would end the war quickly. It was also the population-focused military strategy that, in part, ultimately helped the Union armies defeat Confederate forces in 1865. Yet, like their leaders, most Northerners and Southerners in 1861 expected a short war that would end the crisis within a matter of weeks or months and derisively referred to Scott's strategy as the "Anaconda Plan," a reference to Scott's scheme of slowly strangling the South, much as an anaconda crushes to death its victims.[10]

Most Americans of the 1860s also expected their war to be fought on battlefields remote from civilian populations and between large armies of disciplined but volunteer, uniformed soldiers, organized by competent officers and responsive to civilian governmental authority. The war of 1861–65, however, was immediately and throughout a war characterized by a wide spectrum of violence and combat: riots, sabotage, kidnapping, espionage, raids, militant resistance to conscription, guerrilla warfare (sanctioned and unsanctioned), irregular naval warfare, military occupation, forced depopulation, violent self-emancipation, assassination, and atrocity. And each of these areas created a need for new military thinking to address a wider range of military operations and behavior. Not all American civil warriors fought in regular armies as citizen volunteers. Tens of thousands of men were combatants of a different type, fighting personally directed wars in self-constituted groups, or were reluctant conscripts and deserters, who bolted from the armies at first opportunity, fighting back against home guards sent to return them to the ranks.[11]

Irregular Wars

Irregular warfare took many forms in the American Civil War, from riot and sabotage to well-planned cavalry raids to officially authorized guerrilla units to new naval technology designed for surprise underwater attack. It occurred on land and sea, and it

---

10. Russell F. Weigley, *The American Way of War: A History of United States Military Strategy and Policy* (Bloomington: Indiana University Press, 1973), 93–95.

11. The historiography on these issues is now extensive; for a good introduction, see Daniel E. Sutherland, *A Savage Conflict: The Decisive Role of Guerrillas in the American Civil War* (Chapel Hill: University of North Carolina Press, 2009).

was the American Civil War experience for thousands upon thousands of people. Both sides went off to war using a version of the U.S. Articles of War originally adopted by Congress in 1806. This document provided guidelines for the treatment of soldiers guilty of crimes and placed firm limits on the appropriate conduct of soldiers interacting with enemy civilians in a time of war. Under the articles, democratic-citizen armies were expected to treat civilians respectfully, even as private property might be impressed for reasons of military necessity. The clear lines of treatment and conduct for soldiers in the Articles of War would be consistently challenged and crossed by warriors, regular and irregular, from 1861 through 1865. As more Americans interacted with soldiers and other combatants of diverse loyalties than ever before, the question arose for many civilians and military leaders about what actually constituted the battlefield and what the battlefield's defined parameters were. Even the concept of military necessity itself was debated by Northern and Southern legal minds during the war. Neither the articles nor any of the important works on the laws of war dealt with the many varied problems of an expansive civil war.[12]

The problems presented by Civil War irregular warfare were not confined to one region or state and began even before the Battle of Bull Run (First Manassas) in July 1861. Americans have always deployed street violence in their major political struggles, and the Civil War was no exception. Riot was an integral part of the American Civil War, and at many moments during the conflict, soldiers of both armies acted as police waging a war against a civilian population to maintain control. American soldiers had on occasion been summoned for the purpose of crowd control or putting down a domestic insurrection in the peacetime years of the antebellum Republic. Most notably, George Washington led troops to put down the Whiskey Rebellion in 1791, but the consistent use of troops to quell riots was a departure from what many expected the war to be or what mythologizers created in the aftermath of the conflict.[13]

In Baltimore, Maryland, in the heady days of April 1861, militia troops sent from Massachusetts to secure Washington, D.C., encountered angry Southern sympathizers bent on preventing them from protecting the president and the seat of the U.S. government. The resulting brawl ended with deaths on both sides—the first mortal casualties in what was to be a bitter conflict fought in many different ways in a wide variety of arenas. In March 1863, the wives and mothers of Confederate soldiers rioted in Salisbury, North Carolina, over the high price of flour, molasses, and salt. Many Confederates blamed the ineffectiveness of their state and federal governments in dealing with the shortages. In early April 1863, the high cost of food and skyrocketing inflation collided with poverty in Richmond when another bread riot broke out, which ultimately

---

12. U.S. War Department, *Revised United States Army Regulations of 1861, with an Appendix Containing the Changed and Laws Affecting Army Regulations and Articles of War to June 25, 1863* (Washington, D.C.: Government Printing Office, 1863); Confederate States War Department, *Articles of War, for the Government of the Army of the Confederate States* (Montgomery, AL: Barrett, Wimbish, 1861).

13. Joseph J. Ellis, *His Excellency: George Washington* (New York: Vintage, 2004), 224–26.

UNITED STATES VOLUNTEERS ATTACKED BY THE MOB, CORNER OF FIFTH AND WALNUT STREETS, ST. LOUIS, MISSOURI.—[SKETCHED BY M. HASTINGS, ESQ.]

Union troops attacked by a rioting mob in the streets of St. Louis. Image courtesy of the Library of Congress.

required troops to suppress the insurrection. Confederate President Jefferson Davis himself came out to speak to the rioters, many of them women, in order to quell the violence: "You say you are hungry and have not money. Here is all I have; it is not much, but take it." Davis emptied his pockets, tossed the money into the crowd, and then pulled his pocket watch out. "We do not desire to injure any one, but this lawlessness must stop. I will give you five minutes to disperse, otherwise you will be fired upon."[14]

Riot control by uniformed troops on an unprecedented level was only one of many roles given soldiers on both sides of the war. Northern and Southern military minds were inventive as they pushed the boundaries of warfare. To both promote and regulate guerrilla warfare, the Confederates developed their own official policy for deploying *petite guerre* units alongside their conventional war effort. In April 1862 as they debated national conscription, the Confederate Congress also implemented the Confederate Partisan Ranger Act, which sanctioned and authorized such "asymmetrical" units. Widespread Confederate use of irregular tactics also challenged the old army

14. Haskell M. Monroe et al., eds., *The Papers of Jefferson Davis*, 14 vols. (Baton Rouge: Louisiana State University Press, 1971–2015), 9:146; William Kauffman Scarborough, ed., *The Diary of Edmund Ruffin* (Baton Rouge: Louisiana State University Press, 1976), 2:28, 612–13.

apparatus. Both U.S. and Confederate commanders came to understand that making sense of guerrilla warfare and the definition of various types of combatants was vital for protecting the line between soldiers and civilians in a time of war.

In 1862, the frustrated Union army high command asked renowned legal scholar Dr. Francis Lieber, a Columbia College professor of history and political science, to address a myriad of new issues emerging during the war related to irregulars. Eventually he would lead a committee that developed in 1863 the Lieber Code, officially known as *Instructions for the Government of Armies of the United States in the Field*, or General Orders No. 100. This became a seminal document for the modern international law of war, which subsequently governed U.S. troops down through the Philippine-American Conflict (1899–1902) and was a foundation for the Hague Conventions of 1899 and 1907. In his document Lieber banned torture, though he did not define it. He would allow for hostage taking, though for reasons of controlling the violence of armies. Lieber even attempted to clearly define the nuanced levels of irregular warfare and activity for general officers, who went off to war expecting conventional battlefields to be their area of primary operation.[15]

Citizens and military personnel who engaged in deception and sabotage during the war tested the boundaries of accepted military practice. The Civil War saw the use of land mines in America. In May 1862, Confederate ordnance and torpedo specialist Gabriel Rains, a veteran of the Second Seminole Indian War, planted mines at Yorktown, Virginia, during the Peninsula Campaign, killing several soldiers. Deceptive tactics appalled citizen-soldiers from both armies, but it did not prevent inventors from further employing technologically innovative deception. Both Northern and Southern soldiers deployed explosives regularly throughout the war to disrupt communications by destroying railroad bridges and rail lines as well. Confederate cavalry raiders frequently cut telegraph lines to prevent communication from one town to the next in order to prevent the Union army from being alerted to their raids on communities in the Border South and Lower North. Occasionally, more unorthodox types of warfare were used, as in the case of Godfrey J. Hyams, a displaced Arkansan shoemaker, who, in 1864, was allegedly paid $100 by a Confederate spy to auction off yellow fever–contaminated bedding and clothes in Washington, D.C., in the hope of creating an epidemic. Although the plot proved unsuccessful because yellow fever cannot be transmitted in this manner, it is stark evidence that some were willing to resort to what today would be termed "bioterrorism" in the quest for revenge and national survival.[16]

---

15. Francis Lieber, *Instructions for the Government of Armies of the United States in the Field, Originally Issued as General Orders No. 100, Adjutant General's Office, 1863* (Washington, D.C.: Government Printing Office, 1898).

16. W. Davis Waters, "'Deception Is the Art of War': Gabriel J. Rains, Torpedo Specialist of the Confederacy," *North Carolina Historical Review* 66 (1989): 29–60; Monroe, *The Papers of Jefferson Davis*, 11:217, 512; Jacob Roberts, "Yellow Fever Fiend," Chemical Heritage Foundation, Spring 2014, https://www.chemheritage.org/, accessed February 2, 2016; United States War Department, *The War*

Even when the Confederacy's sanctioned *petite guerre* forces worked well, their operations frequently departed from the character of the regular regimental operations of cavalry and infantry that most considered standard practice prior to the Civil War. Confederate Partisan Ranger John Singleton Mosby's famed Fairfax Court House raid of March 1863, when Mosby's Rangers slipped into Union-occupied territory and captured U.S. General Edwin Stoughton asleep at his own headquarters, presents a notable example of the change in military encounters brought on by the Civil War. The high-profile success of the behind-the-lines raid and capture of a Union general in his own bed was meant to intimidate Union soldiers, capture valuable horses, and gather information on the activities of the Union army in northern Vir-

Famous Confederate partisan John S. Mosby's attack on a supply train depicted on the cover of *Harper's Weekly.* Image courtesy of the Library of Congress.

ginia. According to the Pulitzer Prize–winning historian Douglas Southall Freeman, who contributed to the promotion of many myths of the Civil War, "this was the performance that first brought Mosby to the attention of the army."[17] Clearly, while many wartime operations of great renown occurred on the conventional fields where Joseph E. Johnston or Robert E. Lee's armies fought, the irregular wars of the Civil War also saw impressive exploits.

---

of the Rebellion: A Compilation of the Official Records of the Union and Confederate Armies (Washington, D.C.: Government Printing Office, 1880–1901), ser. 1, 49:1213 (hereinafter cited as *Official Records*). 17. *Official Records*, ser. 1, 25:43–44; Douglas Southall Freeman, *Lee's Lieutenants: A Study in Command* (New York: Charles Scribner's Sons, 1943), 2:455.

In an effort to hunt down Confederates like Mosby, the Union army also turned to the development and recruitment of specialized unconventional units that used guerrilla warfare to target their wily foe. One of these units, Blazer's Independent Union Scouts, commanded by Captain Richard Blazer, used the same skills of topographical awareness and knowledge of the local loyalties in western Virginia's Shenandoah Valley and in West Virginia's mountain passes to defeat elements of Mosby's command on several occasions in the fall of 1864 as both sides vied for an advantage in supplies and intelligence.[18]

Indeed, for hundreds of communities and neighborhoods across the South, the conventional battles of the war were not what dominated their everyday military experience. By early 1863, Confederate guerrillas were becoming a multi-pronged problem for Northern and Southern leadership.

On March 21, 1863, Confederate President Jefferson Davis wrote to his Secretary of War James A. Seddon about a thorny issue regarding the anti-Union "partisan corps" operating along the interior rivers of the Confederacy. Union Admiral David D. Porter had ordered his men to give no quarter to individuals caught firing upon unarmed ships and other vessels on the Mississippi River, and he released a threatening letter to Confederates operating in the region, which made it all the way to Jefferson Davis' desk. The notice declared, "If this savage and a barbarous Confederate custom cannot be put a stop to, we will try what virtue there is in hanging." It also threatened individuals who were ransacking houses, forcing contributions from locals, and destroying cotton bales.[19] The obviously irritated Confederate president diagnosed the situation in light of his own understanding of the existing laws of war:

> When the river banks are marked by burned houses and devastated estates, it is mockery to proclaim a purpose to abstain from injury to private property; and when the river is the enemy's line of communication upon which both his supplies and troops are transported; it was worse than idle to prevent [proclaim] the use of unarmed boats as dedicated to humane and charitable purposes. The enemy have no plausible pretext for objecting to the dress of our troops. They may not be in uniform, may have not other than citizens dress; without in any degree subjecting themselves to the charge of being disguised. To avail themselves of cover, and thus to effect a surprise, it is the ordinary and recognized practice of war.

Davis, who had graduated from West Point, performed with distinction in the Mexican-American War, and later served as U.S. secretary of war, further argued,

---

18. Darl L. Stephenson, *Headquarters in the Brush: Blazer's Independent Union Scouts* (Athens: Ohio University Press, 2001).

19. U.S. Naval War Records Office, *Official Records of the Union and Confederate Navies in the War of the Rebellion* (Washington, D.C.: Government Printing Office, 1894–1922), ser. 1, 24:364–67, 369.

"To destroy their transportation and capture their foraging parties is the fit service of the partisan corps; and the enemy's epithets cannot deprive them of the rights of prisoners of war, if captured, or change the nature of their acts." The Confederate president, therefore, sanctioned and gave political cover within the South to irregular warfare.[20]

Two similar incidents from the southwestern corner of Tennessee and northern Mississippi border region highlight this different type of war that Union commanders and soldiers were increasingly pulled into at the hands of Confederate irregulars. On March 30, 1863, Major General Stephen A. Hurlbut, commanding the Union's 16th Army Corps at Memphis and responsible for the security of the Memphis and Charleston Railroad, described the capture of a train filled with twenty-five armed Union soldiers and several officers at the hands of only twelve Confederate guerrillas near Moscow, Tennessee: "Yet [the soldiers] made no attempt to defend themselves & the public property." However, as he further reported, "The Engineer started his engine when he discovered the Guerillas with such suddenness as to break the coupling[,] ran up to Moscow[,] took down 100 Soldiers and saved the train." The frustrated commander continued by describing how, while waiting for rescue, "passengers were robbed & the officers & soldiers carried off North. If they are returned under parole I do not intend to receive them. Pursuant to directions received in Jany [January] from Genl. Grant I am now preparing a list of ten families of secessionists to be sent outside the lines selecting the most wealthy & prominent in position."[21]

Later, on April 18, 1863, Hurlbut described the same incident in this way: "An attack was made by a party of Guerillas living North of the Road, of the most gross & cowardly nature. This band of 20 or 25 are . . . simply plunderers who when caught claim organization but are not enrolled or subject to any military authority." Consequently, Hurlbut exiled eight families of "prominent secessionists" in accordance with Grant's orders regarding measures to be taken in response to this interference with the railroad. Grant's expulsion was calibrated as a measured punishment to target families that might have been harboring the guerrillas. The precise manner by which to respond to the Confederate guerrilla threat led directly to harsher Union military policies against a civilian population that was viewed as harboring, supporting, and protecting the irregulars and their activities. The regular attacks by irregular guerrillas on vital rail lines were a frequent problem for Union soldiers.[22]

In both the major eastern and western theaters of the war, a Confederate strategy of border raids launched by regular and irregular cavalry played a critical role of garnering supplies, intimidating Unionists, gathering intelligence, and bolstering Confederate morale. Union officers simultaneously struggled to develop a counter-irregular policy

---

20. Monroe, *The Papers of Jefferson Davis*, 9:110–11.

21. John Y. Simon, ed., *The Papers of Ulysses S. Grant* (Carbondale: Southern Illinois University Press, 1979), 8:17.

22. Ibid., 8:44.

A *Harper's Weekly* drawing of the destruction of the city of Lawrence, Kansas, and the massacre of its inhabitants by the Rebel guerrillas led by William Clarke Quantrill, August 21, 1863. More than 150 residents were killed. Image courtesy of the Library of Congress.

and tactics to defeat highly mobile and adept practitioners of raiding warfare. One of the most effective masters of the Confederate raiding strategy was Kentuckian John Hunt Morgan, "the Thunderbolt of the Confederacy." Morgan's July 1863 raid into Indiana and Ohio terrified citizens living in the Lower North and caused Ohio Governor David Tod to deploy thousands of troops to track Morgan. Eventually Union cavalry captured Morgan near Salineville, Ohio, and imprisoned him at Ohio State Penitentiary in Columbus. He later escaped to the South, only to be hunted down and killed in September 1864.[23]

The irregular wars waged by the South during the 1860s also led to brutal and dark moments. In August 1863, William Clarke Quantrill assembled a collection of roughly 450 Confederate bushwhackers to launch what became one of the most infamous events of the American Civil War. Quantrill's raid on the Unionist stronghold of Lawrence, Kansas, developed into a combination of personal revenge and massacre. Quantrill's guerrillas killed more than 150 men and boys, leaving many of their bodies burned and mangled, as they ransacked the town. The Union army's response was perhaps the most draconian Union military policy implemented during the war,

---

23. James A. Ramage, *Rebel Raider: The Life of General John Hunt Morgan* (Lexington: University Press of Kentucky, 1986), 170–82.

General Orders No. 11, the forced depopulation of four counties in western Missouri to directly target the families of Quantrill's raiders.[24]

Another moment from the western theater of the war also challenges the myth of the glorious conventional battlefield conflict. In the aftermath of the September 27, 1864, massacre of more than two dozen unarmed U.S. soldiers at Centralia, Missouri, the bushwhackers commanded by William "Bloody Bill" Anderson met a U.S. Army counter-irregular force of over 150 Union soldiers in battle near the scene of the morning's executions. The soldiers of the 39th Missouri Militia under Major A.V. E. Johnston were armed with Enfield rifle muskets and when ordered to dismount in line of battle, they were able to fire one volley before being charged by Anderson's men, who were armed with revolvers. Anderson's guerrillas gave no quarter as they moved among Johnston's surrendering force. Johnston himself may have been shot to death by famed post–Civil War outlaw Jesse James during this action.

It was in the aftermath of these engagements, however, when perhaps the most disturbing events took place. According to Union Brigadier General Clinton B. Fisk in his official report of the incident, Anderson's men "subjected [Major Johnston and his soldiers] to the most inhuman butchery and barbarities that blacken the pages of history. Major Johnston was murdered and scalped. One hundred and thirty of his officers and men shared his fate. Most of them were shot through the head, then scalped, bayonets thrust through them, ears and noses cut oft [sic] and privates torn off and thrust in the mouths of the dying."[25] According to Union Lieutenant W. T. Clarke, who visited the scene of the engagement shortly afterward, 115 bodies were found. Clarke went on to describe the scene: "This should be washed out with the blood of the friends of these demons. Ears were cut off and all commissioned officers were scalped. One wounded man reports the privates cut from one wounded soldier while living and thrust in his mouth. Other shameful indignities upon the corpses are mentioned."[26]

Clearly, many of these soldiers sought revenge. In Anderson's case it might have been for the death of his sister in a jail that collapsed after Union soldiers took his family hostage to try to stop his activities. Yet this kind of killing of prisoners, corpse desecration, mutilation, and body part collecting goes beyond simple revenge killing. Other reports on Anderson and his men attest to their using hair or body parts as decoration for their saddles and bridles. Anderson also carried a silk sash on which he tied a knot for every soldier he killed. This is another form of grotesque but gratifying

---

24. Thomas Goodrich, *Bloody Dawn: The Story of the Lawrence Massacre* (Kent, OH: Kent State University Press, 1991); Edward E. Leslie, *The Devil Knows How to Ride: The True Story of William Clarke Quantrill and His Confederate Raiders* (New York: Random House, 1996), 200, 237, 258.

25. Clinton B. Fisk Report, September 29, 1864, in *Official Records*, ser. 1, vol. 41, pt. 3, 488.

26. W. T. Clarke Report, September 29, 1864, in *Official Records*, ser. 1, vol. 41, pt. 3, 489. On the psychological costs of atrocity, see Dave Grossman, *On Killing: The Psychological Cost of Learning to Kill in War and Society* (New York: Back Bay Books, 2009), 197–232.

remembrance, what some anthropologists have called "trophies of dominance." Now it is easy to chalk this up to mental illness, posttraumatic stress, or perhaps a psychopathic personality. War might have allowed some psychopaths to flourish and even led others into the path of murder, mutilation, and war crimes. But consider the sheer, sick entertainment value of what these young men were doing. Killing and mutilating the enemy was not only exciting, as battle is for many immature young soldiers, but the murder of unarmed men and playing with their body parts was also amusing for these men. In other moments, Anderson and his men decapitated Federal soldiers and rearranged their heads, another form of entertainment through corpse desecration. Castration, and rearrangement of enemy identities, emasculated fallen Union soldiers, a form of primal, predatory dominance. If Bill Anderson and his boys had had iPhones or Canon PowerShot cameras, Americans might remember the Civil War in a somewhat different way. In place of this, Americans are left with the often-posed images captured by famed photographers Mathew Brady and Alexander Gardner, giving deceptively quiet dignity to the bodies of the dead.[27]

The Irregular Naval Struggle

While waging a war of national survival, Confederate and Union naval forces used irregular tactics and technologies as well. The Confederacy began the war with very few warships and little capacity to outfit new vessels that could directly challenge the U.S. Navy in open, symmetrical battle on the high seas. C.S. Naval Secretary Stephen Mallory, one of Confederate President Jefferson Davis' most able cabinet members, invented a Confederate navy from the South's scattered industrial plants (159 in the 1860 census), private dockyards (several score were in use by Confederates during the war), and a small number of naval facilities seized early in the war. Despite the

---

27. On William T. Anderson and his guerrillas' scalping, ear collecting, and rearranging heads on dead Union soldiers' bodies, see Larry Wood, *The Civil War Story of Bloody Bill Anderson* (New York: Eakin Press, 2003); and Albert Castel and Thomas Goodrich, *Bloody Bill Anderson: The Short, Savage Life of a Civil War Guerrilla* (Mechanicsburg, PA: Stackpole Books, 1998). Other examples of Civil War "trophy hunting" are examined in anthropological and sociological literature; see Simon Harrison, *Dark Trophies: Hunting and the Enemy Body in Modern War* (New York: Berghahn Books, 2012), 2, 93–106. Harrison notes in his work that there is a recurring pattern in modern conflict of corpse desecration and that it has an impact on the long-term mental trauma of soldiers. In 2003, the U.S. Army made an official statement about the issue of mutilation as a result of rising numbers of incidents. In interviews recorded shortly before his execution in 1989, convicted serial killer Ted Bundy described mutilation, body part collecting, necrophilia, and collecting mementos of his crimes as a way of remembering and reliving the acts of violence; see Stephen G. Michaud and Hugh Aynesworth, *Ted Bundy: Conversations with a Killer* (Irving, TX: Authorlink Press, 2000). Bundy also described these acts in his final death row interview with Dr. James Dobson in January 1989, in which Bundy blamed his exposure to violent pornography as the root of his murders of at least thirty women.

loss of naval yards at Norfolk and Pensacola and private shipyards at Memphis and New Orleans, the Southerners still managed to develop plans, contract for, or build 150 warships between 1861 and 1865. Many of these ships were used in irregular commerce raids, inland brown-water warfare, and unorthodox or illicit defensive operations. While this was only a fraction of the six hundred warships built by the U.S. Navy, it is, nonetheless, remarkable evidence of the ingenuity and efficiency of Mallory and his department's engaging in a naval conflict that challenged an ever-tightening Union blockade of Confederate port cities.[28]

On the high seas Confederates deployed commerce raiders like the C.S.S. *Shenandoah*, which during its twelve months in Confederate service sailed 58,000 miles around the entire globe and sank or captured thirty-eight U.S. ships. The *Shenandoah*, under the command of North Carolinian James Waddell, a twenty-year veteran of the U.S. Navy prior to the Civil War, hunted merchant vessels, primarily whaling ships in the Arctic and Pacific Oceans. The *Shenandoah*'s attack on whaling ships in the Bering Sea near the Aleutian Islands was the final hostile act of the Confederate navy during the American Civil War and occurred in late June 1865, two months after the surrender of Robert E. Lee's army. The *Shenandoah*'s crew eventually sailed to England and turned its ship over to the British government in November 1865.[29]

Perhaps the most famous military invention of the Confederates was the C.S.S. *Hunley*, which used subterfuge to attack a surface ship, the U.S.S. *Housatonic*, with a barbed torpedo in February 1864. The *Housatonic* has the ignominious status of being the first surface ship sunk by a submarine in world history.

Far from being a war fought solely on conventional fields of battle, the Civil War revolutionized the very nature of warfare and pushed Americans to develop new, unconventional technologies and tactics on both land and sea.[30]

Conscription Resistance North and South

Both the Confederacy and the United States in 1862 and 1863, respectively, would be forced by flagging volunteerism to pass conscription laws compelling citizens to serve as soldiers in the war. In both the North and South, riots and resistance occurred, but in the Confederate states, which could ill afford militant dissent, the problem was acute. Albert Burton Moore has estimated that the Confederacy's Conscription Bureau, a huge military apparatus that stretched its tentacles deeply into the neighborhoods and

---

28. Raimondo Luraghi, *A History of the Confederate Navy* (Annapolis, MD: Naval Institute Press, 1996), 34–35.

29. Ibid., 341–44; Tom Chaffin, *Sea of Gray: The Around-the-World Odyssey of the Confederate Raider Shenandoah* (New York: Hill and Wang, 2006), chaps. 16 and 17.

30. Tom Chaffin, *The H.L. Hunley* (New York: Hill and Wang, 2008), 11.

communities of the South, directly placed 81,993 men into the army. Additionally, an indeterminate number of men went into the Confederate army out of fear of the social stigma of conscription once the Confederacy enacted compulsory military service. Other men ran to the mountains, woods, and caves of the southern Appalachian highlands to resist the long arm of the Confederate state.[31]

The combination of anti-conscription, Southern Unionist, and other dissident elements, including slaves seeking freedom and willing to fight for it, was a deadly cocktail for the Confederacy. It also led to a very different kind of warfare than the one fought on the fields of northern Virginia and middle Tennessee, but it was the Civil War experience for a significant percentage of white and black Southerners during the 1860s. For Southerners, some of the dissent came from the dysfunctional nature of conscription at the local level. In Georgia, William M. Browne of Atlanta complained about the limited value of conscription in the state and wrote President Jefferson Davis to complain that he believed twenty thousand additional men could be recruited from the state if the conscription officers were replaced with "men of more sense, zeal, and discretion," because many of the current enrolling officers "cruelly insulted & oppressed the people." Browne criticized Major Charles J. Harris, the commandant of conscripts for Georgia, for being "entirely incompetent to the task imposed on him" and called for his replacement as head of the office in charge of enforcing the draft in the state.[32] The conduct of enrolling officers, in particular, became a problem leading to conflict. "A Citizen of Hinds County," Mississippi, also wrote Davis, angry about several draft issues and alerted the president that if more troops were needed from Mississippi, they could enlist at least one regiment of conscript-enrolling officers "and their places could be admirably supplied by the Old maids that are circulating around," a rather weak endorsement of the efficiency of conscription officers in the Magnolia State.[33]

The Southern Unionists' war against the Confederacy stretched across every seceding state and Border South slave state. Tens of thousands of Unionists from Virginia and North Carolina to Louisiana and Arkansas openly and illicitly sought the downfall of the Confederate government and liberation at the hands of Union armies. Many Unionists ran to Union lines to join the new United States Colored Troops and white Union regiments recruited in the occupied areas of the South. In North Carolina, an interior Southern state that became the number-four overall producer of Confederate manpower (and the number-two producer by percentage of its white male population in the ranks), the problems presented by opposition to Confederate policies boiled out of the political cauldron and onto an unconventional battlefield. North Carolina's home guard consisted of only four thousand men backed by a small

---

31. Albert Burton Moore, *Conscription and Conflict in the Confederacy* (New York: Macmillan, 1924), 356.

32. Monroe, *The Papers of Jefferson Davis*, 10:221.

33. Ibid., 10:271, 612.

number of Confederate military-veteran invalids and volunteers periodically released from service to aid in the enforcement of slave laws. Eventually, the combination of resistance to Confederate conscription, the loyalties of Unionists, and the sentiments of other anti-Confederate elements in the population would embroil thirty-two of the eighty-six counties in the state in irregular conflicts—warfare that was never contained by the Confederates. Irregular wars, battlefield deaths, conscription, and inflation left the North Carolina population war weary by 1864, and many were ready for peace. North Carolina's peace advocate, candidate for governor, and Raleigh newspaperman William Woods Holden was physically threatened, and his press was burned by Georgia troops in the state's capital. Though Holden had little chance of winning a statewide vote in North Carolina, voter intimidation, including Confederate troops stationed at the polling places in many locales, led to poor voter turnout for the opposition peace candidate, who was soundly defeated in 1864.[34]

Conscription resistance in the North, while not as deep or critical to the Union war effort, given the Union's enormous manpower advantage at the beginning of the war, was also a problem. In the North, 168,649 men were provided to the Union armies in the field by the draft law. But 117,986 of these were hired substitutes with only 50,663 actually drafted directly by the Bureau of Conscription. The draft was unpopular in both rural and urban environments, but in the ethnic salad bowl of mid-nineteenth-century American cities, high levels of immigration made it a dangerously combustible policy.[35]

The largest incident of resistance to the draft in the Northern states came with the New York City draft riots of July 1863, when five days of bloody insurrection caused more than one hundred deaths and one hundred buildings were burned. This included rioters attacking a Brooks Brothers men's clothing store, which was known to the rioters as a government contractor for military uniforms, producing tens of thousands for the war effort. Impoverished Irish immigrants in the city were targeted with draft calls under the new Union conscription law, sparking their involvement in the violence. Many of those immigrants connected the war to Abraham Lincoln's Emancipation Proclamation, issued earlier that January. As a result, angry men hanged and beat free blacks on the streets of New York. At one point, the rioters even burned to the ground the Colored Orphan Asylum, home to many small children. Only Union troops arriving from the battlefield of Gettysburg restored order on the urban battlefield of New York City's streets.[36]

---

34. Carl N. Degler, *The Other South: Southern Dissenters in the Nineteenth Century* (New York: Harper and Row, 1974), 158–87; Barton A. Myers, *Rebels against the Confederacy: North Carolina's Unionists* (New York: Cambridge University Press, 2014), 116–17, 125.

35. William C. Kashatus, *Abraham Lincoln, the Quakers, and the Civil War: "A Trial of Principle and Faith"* (Santa Barbara, CA: Praeger, 2014), 76.

36. Iver Bernstein, *The New York City Draft Riots: Their Significance for American Society and Politics in the Age of the Civil War* (New York: Oxford University Press, 1990), 3, 5, 27, 298.

The Fire in the Confederate Rear

Another war of great ferocity and intensity raged behind the lines in the South over the issues of service in the Confederate army. Secessionists could ill afford resistance, given their already steep deficit in population (9 million in the Confederate South, including 3.5 million enslaved African Americans, to 22 million in the non-seceding United States) and the strategic problem of defending over 750,000 square miles of Confederate territory.[37] The enforcement of the unpopular conscription law in the Confederacy led to even greater and violent dissent on the home front than in the North. This produced a very different kind of battle characterized by ambushes, the deployment of bloodhounds, hit-and-run assaults, robbery, and murder. It became a peoples' war of resistance that spread throughout large sections of the Confederate countryside as more and more individuals faced contact with a Confederate state demanding compulsory military service.

The American South never truly united behind the cause of the Confederate government. Establishing a nation rooted in the cornerstone belief "that the negro was not equal to the white man" was tenuous, given the large number of slaves who were left at home when hundreds of thousands of white Confederate men (estimates range between 800,000 and 1.2 million total enlistments over the course of the war) left for service in the regular armies.[38] Three and one half million inhabitants of the South were enslaved (40 percent of the total population of the Confederacy), and of the 5.5 million whites living in the Confederacy in 1861, there were enough Southern Unionists and anti-Confederates to eventually provide 100,000 white troops to the Union army. Eventually, black men from the Border South and seceding states would contribute 150,000 of their number to the Union ranks. As a byproduct of this large dissident group, during the four years of war a major military struggle erupted behind the lines in the Confederacy that threatened Confederate control in counties and neighborhoods across the South. It took many forms at the local level, and some of it manifested as a widespread collection of guerrilla wars spread across every state of the Confederacy.[39]

In East Tennessee, Southern Unionists consistently challenged Confederate military authorities as occupiers within their home communities. Bridge burnings, hangings, and farmyard executions characterized a desperate struggle against local Unionists to hold on to an important Confederate supply and communication hub at Knoxville and the eventual gateway to Chattanooga and the Deep South as the Union armies approached. In northeastern Texas, Confederates arrested more than two hundred Unionist men for their sympathies in October 1862 and hanged at least

---

37. U.S. Bureau of the Census, *Population Schedule of the 8th Census of the United States*, 1860.

38. Charles B. Dew, *Apostles of Disunion: Southern Secession Commissioners and the Causes of the Civil War* (Charlottesville: University of Press of Virginia, 2001), 14.

39. William W. Freehling, *The South vs. the South: How Anti-Confederate Southerners Shaped the Course of the Civil War* (New York: Oxford University Press, 2001), xii–xiii.

forty-four at Gainesville in one of the largest mass executions of the war. A similar incident in Kinston, North Carolina, in February 1864 directed by Confederate General George E. Pickett saw twenty-two Unionists and deserters from the Confederate army executed for their resistance.[40]

The expansion of violence and battle, symmetrical and asymmetrical, to civilian areas was coupled with another dynamic development, the involvement of African American men on conventional and irregular battlefields. This opened another behind-the-lines battlefront against the Confederacy. Both armies enlisted and mustered in 1861 believing that the war would be fought on battlefields away from the civilian population, but few could have predicted in 1861 that the war would become an interracial conflict in which the U.S. government would draw upon both Southern and Northern blacks to fill the ranks of its battlefield regiments. Between 1862 and 1865, Lincoln's administration recruited nearly 180,000 black men for the Union land armies, which included 120 infantry regiments, eventually making up roughly 12 percent of the Union forces on land. These men fought in more than 449 engagements, including the major battles of Ulysses S. Grant's pivotal Overland Campaign, engaged in the siege of Petersburg in 1864, and battled Confederate guerrillas in locations across the South. While black men had served in every major war of the American Republic, they had never seen line service on this scale or been recruited in such large numbers for a war effort. Retaining social and racial control over these men and their families during the war was a principal struggle for white Confederates. This racial control was a Confederate war aim, and the armed struggle over this issue would continue long after 1865.[41]

The vast range of military problems that the Confederate War Department dealt with demonstrates the inaccuracy of the myth of a narrowly conventional military effort. In January 1863, James A. Seddon, the Virginia-born Confederate secretary of war, submitted his annual report to the president's office and highlighted just a small fraction of the issues he was administering and for which he was trying to find solutions. After optimistically praising Confederate citizens for contributing what he believed "would in all probability be the largest [army] in proportion to population ever maintained in actual service by any nation," he went on to defend the military necessity of conscription. He provided an overview of the selection of enrolling officers and the establishment of camps of instruction, argued for a revision to exemption provisions in the "twenty-slave law," and discussed numerous other issues related specifically to manpower control and procurement in the Confederacy. The twenty-slave law

---

40. Noel C. Fisher, *War at Every Door: Partisan Politics and Guerrilla Violence in East Tennessee, 1860–1869* (Chapel Hill: University of North Carolina Press, 1997), 62–101; Richard B. McCaslin, *Tainted Breeze: The Great Hanging at Gainesville, Texas, 1862* (Baton Rouge: Louisiana State University Press, 1994), 1; Daniel E. Sutherland, ed., *Guerrillas, Unionists, and Violence on the Confederate Home Front* (Fayetteville: University of Arkansas Press, 1999), 45–46.

41. Dudley Taylor Cornish, *The Sable Arm: Black Troops in the Union Army, 1861–1865* (Lawrence: University Press of Kansas, 1987), ix.

shielded the wealthiest of the Confederacy from conscription by allowing one white male for every twenty slaves (and later every fifteen slaves) to remain at home to police the slave population, but it led to class resentment and unrest, as the Confederate conscription sought ever-greater numbers of soldiers from among the poor white and yeoman farmers of the South. Seddon, whose role was critical to both the conventional and unconventional military efforts of Confederates, was also responsible for appointments and overseeing organizational efforts for a host of "special units," which included "Signal Corps, partisan rangers, and sharpshooters."[42]

Beyond conscription, the tax in kind and military impressment of private property also riled a primarily rural, agricultural, poor white and yeoman population in the South. By 1864 many in the Confederacy, one of the wealthiest agricultural regions in the world in 1860, were starving. Difficulty in moving crops around the South, because of railroad disruption, the U.S. Navy and Army's seizure of the Mississippi River, and the inability to harvest crops in some areas made shortages acute. The Confederate military policy of impressing crops, animals, and other supplies necessary for the war also created military problems. The military was at citizens' doorsteps demanding the very sustenance of life and did it with a pistol in hand. In December 1864, P. A. Lawson of Griffin, Georgia, wrote to President Davis, "Unless something is done, and that speedily too, there will be thousands of the best citizens of this/ State/ [sic] and heretofore as loyal as any men in the Confederacy, that will not care one cent which army are victorious in Ga. I say this with heartfelt sorrow, and deep regret." General Joseph Wheeler's soldiers destroyed "all the corn & fodder, [drove] off all the stock of the farmers on each side of the Rail Road," and as a consequence "there [would] be thousands upon thousands of acres of lands uncultivated the next year for the want of plow stock which has been stolen . . . by men claiming to act under orders from those high in authority." Many men who are presently quartermasters in the state "four years ago [were] not worth the clothes upon their backs, [yet] are now *large dealers in lands negroes and real estates*." "There are hundreds of families that have not one ear of corn left," Lawson wrote, "whose husbands are now in the Army, and have been for the last three years, and now we are notified that our tithing must be paid." For many Southerners, therefore, the war at home was a battle not just against the invading Union army but by late 1864 also against a combination of Confederate army abuses, inefficiencies, and excesses.[43]

A Wider War

The Civil War's violence stretched far beyond the rolling fields of Virginia and Pennsylvania to the deserts of Arizona and New Mexico. The Far West of America became

---

42. Monroe, *The Papers of Jefferson Davis*, 9:6–7.
43. Ibid., 11:255; *Official Records*, ser. 4, 3:967.

a battleground for many smaller cavalry engagements over resources and territorial control as Confederates attempted to establish a formal Confederate Territory of Arizona under Kentucky-born colonel and military governor John Baylor. Baylor, a ruthless commander, was eventually removed from his command and governorship by Jefferson Davis for his intentions to massacre resisting Apaches. In early 1862, Confederate General Henry Sibley, seeking to establish control over the gold and silver mines of Colorado and eventually the ports of California, launched a military campaign to secure the Southwest as possible future slave territory for the Confederacy. Sibley's 1862 New Mexico Campaign was eventually defeated at the Battle of Glorieta Pass along the strategically important Santa Fe Trail in March and his small army forced to retreat back to Texas. On November 29, 1864, southeastern Colorado became the scene of the Sand Creek Massacre, as Colonel John Chivington led part of the U.S. First and Third Colorado Cavalry regiments in an attack on roughly five hundred Cheyenne and Arapaho camping under a white flag. His soldiers eventually killed or mutilated more than 150 Native Americans, primarily women and children. The incident rates as one the worst wartime massacres of the 1860s.[44]

Wartime Atrocities

Wartime atrocity on both conventional and irregular fields of battle shocked Americans in the 1860s and challenge the idea of a controlled military conflict fought narrowly on regular battlefields by disciplined soldiers and officers. While the exact number of those innocents killed, raped, and tortured during the American Civil War is difficult to estimate, individual and mass atrocities occurred consistently from 1861 through 1865. Individuals and groups motivated by revenge, frustration, battle weariness, desensitization to death, racial hostility, psychopathic tendencies, and politicized hatred participated. The killing of unarmed or surrendering soldiers and civilians was perpetrated by Americans of virtually every stripe of political loyalty during the conflict and by some whose loyalties were difficult to define.

In his classic work *Gray Ghosts and Rebel Raiders* (1956), Virgil Carrington Jones includes a chapter entitled "The Dead Behead Easily," which focuses on the case of Major Sullivan Ballou. Ballou, the Rhode Island soldier killed at First Bull Run in July 1861 and made famous in 1990 by Ken Burns in his documentary *The Civil War*, was beheaded, denuded, and burned by a Georgia regiment after the battle. The Georgians were almost certainly searching for the body of his commanding officer Colonel John Slocum. Differing accounts have either the 8th or 21st Georgia Infantry

---

44. Jerry D. Thompson, *Colonel John Robert Baylor: Texas Indian Fighter and Confederate Soldier* (Hillsboro, TX: Hill Junior College Press, 1971); Jerry D. Thompson, *Henry Hopkins Sibley: Confederate General of the West* (Natchitoches, LA: Northwestern State University Press, 1987); Ari Kelman, *A Misplaced Massacre: Struggling over the Memory of Sand Creek* (Cambridge, MA: Harvard University Press, 2013).

Regiment responsible for the exhumation and beheading because of either Slocum's abolitionist views or his bravery in leading his Rhode Islanders in battle against the Georgians. Regardless, the acts seem to have been motivated by personal revenge. These chilling moments of the American Civil War are rarely discussed and have never been collectively examined.[45]

Union soldiers also desecrated corpses and mutilated the bodies of their Confederate enemies. After the Battle of Antietam in September 1862, an exhausted burial party of Union soldiers demonstrated their callous attitude and hatred for the enemy by dumping a group of fifty-eight Confederate bodies into a local farmer's well as opposed to digging proper resting places for the dead. During a conflict when a "good death" meant having a body, whole and intact for a family to mourn, these acts of brutality were especially powerful political and social statements of hatred.[46]

The killing of unarmed or surrendering black soldiers and civilians by Confederate soldiers at Plymouth, North Carolina; Fort Pillow, Tennessee; and the Petersburg "Crater" in the spring and summer of 1864 demonstrates the translation of Confederate racial attitudes that were not expected by most Americans in 1861 directly into the experience of combat. The introduction of black soldiers to the battlefields increased Confederate fears of losing racial control in the South. The scale of civilian involvement in the war in direct contact with the military was also borne out by the murder of unarmed black men and women as well.

Fort Pillow, the relatively insignificant west Tennessee stronghold, was manned by a mixed force of loyal Unionists from Tennessee and United States Colored Heavy Artillery soldiers numbering roughly 580 men. Famed Confederate cavalry commander Nathan Bedford Forrest struck the fort on June 12, 1864, with a force of more than fifteen hundred Confederates. What ensued was one of the darkest moments in American military history. Forrest's men, who "did not recognize negroes as United States soldiers . . . would . . . show them no quarter."[47] The black units at the fort suffered 68 percent killed and lost 93 percent in total casualties in a battle that turned into a massacre as Forrest's men drove many off a cliff to drown in the river below. Forrest's soldiers claimed to have buried 450 bodies after the engagement but suffered fewer than 6 percent total casualties.[48]

---

45. Jones, *Gray Ghosts and Rebel Raiders*, 66–73; Ted Nesi, "Revisiting Headless Ballou and RI's Civil War Years," WPRI blog, April 18, 2011, http://blogs.wpri.com/, accessed January 25, 2016. Frederic Denison, a First Rhode Island Cavalry veteran, pointed to the 8th Georgia Infantry as the unit responsible for Ballou's mistaken beheading.

46. Drew Gilpin Faust, *This Republic of Suffering: Death and the American Civil War* (New York: Alfred A. Knopf, 2008), 69.

47. George S. Burkhardt, *Confederate Rage, Yankee Wrath: No Quarter in the Civil War* (Carbondale: Southern Illinois University Press, 2007), 116.

48. Ibid., 105–17.

Even the Confederate Army of Northern Virginia, fighting for its survival while defending Petersburg and Richmond from Ulysses Grant's encircling army along a thirty-mile front, employed racial atrocity in its war of maneuver and siege. On the morning of July 30, 1864, Union coal miners from the 48th Pennsylvania Infantry finished placing four tons of explosives underneath Confederate entrenchments. After scurrying out of their 510-foot-long tunnel, the Union soldiers detonated the explosives, having planned an infantry assault on the confused Confederates. Roughly 350 Confederates were killed or wounded in the initial blast, which created a massive crater. The blast was quickly followed by a failed Union infantry attack. Black soldiers sent in as part of the assault were shown no mercy as they attempted to surrender. Colonel William Ransom Johnson Pegram, one of Lee's finest young artillery officers, described to his sister, "It seems cruel to murder them in cold blood, but I think the men who did it had very good cause. . . . I have always said that I wished the enemy would bring some negroes against this army . . . it has a splendid effect on our men."[49] Between 900 and 950 black Union soldiers were killed in the Battle of the Crater out of the 4,400 total U.S. casualties in the assault. One estimate places half of those deaths as part of the massacre.[50]

While few have viewed these atrocities as central to the Civil War's course or outcome, these events highlight the fact that a war broadly fought by Confederates to defend slavery and racial control as part of a national economic and political strategy was concurrently a conflict in which this was also a central war aim of the Confederate military on both conventional and unconventional fields of battle. It was a war aim that continued in the hands of nominally ex-Confederate white terrorist organizations long after Joseph Johnston, Kirby Smith, and Robert E. Lee surrendered their major armies in 1865.[51]

As the war moved deep into 1864, the scale of economic destruction on the home front escalated at the hands of the major field armies. William Tecumseh Sherman's campaign in Georgia after the fall of Atlanta was a primary example of this. His seizure of Atlanta in September 1864 had ensured President Abraham Lincoln's reelection and, as a result, the vigorous prosecution of the war by the Union armies to its conclusion. Sherman's March from Atlanta to Savannah beginning in September waged psychological and economic warfare against the Southern population by using "hard war" tactics. With sixty thousand Union soldiers, he left a wide path (twenty to sixty miles) of economic destruction in his wake. Barns, factories, crops, livestock, and some houses

---

49. Michael Fellman, *In the Name of God and Country: Reconsidering Terrorism in American History* (New Haven, CT: Yale University Press, 2010), 68.

50. Ibid., 159–74; for another careful scholarly treatment of the Petersburg "Crater" engagement, see Kevin M. Levin, *Remembering The Battle of the Crater: War as Murder* (Lexington: University Press of Kentucky, 2012).

51. Gregory J. W. Urwin, ed., *Black Flag over Dixie: Racial Atrocities and Reprisals in the Civil War* (Carbondale: Southern Illinois University Press, 2004).

were destroyed. Yet even though Sherman sought to "demonstrate the vulnerability of the South, and make its inhabitants feel that war and individual ruin are synonymous terms" and plainly stated that he would enter "the very bowels of the Confederacy . . . [and] leave a trail that will be recognized fifty years hence," his campaign was not "total war" or genocide.[52] Very few civilians were killed in the campaign.[53]

The Union army operations of General Philip Sheridan in the Shenandoah Valley of Virginia in the fall of 1864 also escalated the war waged against the civilian population base, including the targeted destruction of food, homes, and barns that might support the Confederate war effort. Many Confederates called this war simply "the Burning." While killing, sexual violence, and physical abuse of Southern civilians was limited by the strenuous efforts of Union officers, economic warfare focused on the civilian population was widespread. The invasion of homes, the confiscation and destruction of property by both armies in the South, and the widespread devastation to the prewar agricultural economy wrought by the war significantly weakened the Confederacy.

Another element weakening the Confederacy from within by 1864 was irregular conflict on many fronts. Retaliation by Union soldiers and violence perpetrated by unscrupulous pro-Confederate guerrillas against the Southern civilian population were taking their toll. One historian has estimated the civilian death toll during the war as at least fifty thousand, almost certainly a low estimate in light of other recent scholarly analysis.[54]

The deadly meat grinder of the conventional battlefields of the war eventually drove approximately 103,400 Confederate deserters (estimates range between 8 and 13 percent of the total recruits) from the ranks and more than 200,000 U.S. soldiers (10 percent) from the Union armies.[55] As the Confederate armies fell apart, the problems of regular soldiers returning from the home front added to the existing warfare behind the lines. In Pennsylvania's lumber-producing Appalachian region, one of the most important centers of deserter resistance emerged. It paralleled draft resistance to the Confederate cause in the southern Appalachian Mountains, especially in northern Alabama, western North Carolina, and in the new U.S. state of West Virginia. Lumbermen exploited by firms projected their alienation onto the Federal government as it pressed for greater numbers of men to fill the Union ranks in the aftermath of bloody battles. Eventually, by late 1864, resistance became so acute in Columbia and

---

52. Fellman, *In the Name of God and Country*, 60.

53. Mark Grimsley, *The Hard Hand of War: Union Military Policy toward Southern Civilians* (New York: Cambridge University Press, 1995), 190–204.

54. McPherson, *Battle Cry of Freedom*, 619n.

55. Ella Lonn, *Desertion during the Civil War* (New York: Century, 1928); Lesley J. Gordon, Michael Fellman, and Daniel E. Sutherland, *This Terrible War: The Civil War and Aftermath* (New York: Longman, 2003), 256; Mark Weitz, *More Damning Than Slaughter: Desertion in the Confederate Army* (Lincoln: University of Nebraska Press, 2005), 303.

Clearfield Counties that the Union Provost Marshall's Bureau in Pennsylvania sent an expedition to round up the between twelve hundred and eighteen hundred resistors.[56]

For Confederates, however, the desertions were felt even more acutely as they faced mounting losses, growing internal resistance by dissidents, and the byproducts of widespread guerrilla warfare. "Public opinion must make it a shame and disgrace for a man to skulk from his duty, or to enquire not what he is able to do, but what the law will make him do! Our women must take broomsticks and drive absentees and stragglers to their duty," Jefferson Davis proclaimed in February 1865.

> We have one cause to sustain, one country to defend. He who falls on the soil of Louisiana, or sheds his blood on the soil of North Carolina or Virginia, is alike an honored martyr. The inquiry among us must be, not what service we can escape, but instead of that a generous rivalry among citizens and States which shall do most, and give most to the cause.[57]

It was a forlorn hope for Davis' government.

The End of the Confederate War?

The war had transformed many soldiers of the conventional battlefield by 1865. Even some of the staunchest members of the regular armies were now willing to consider completely changing the nature of their military struggle for the Confederate nation to survive. Though Southerners had engaged in the widespread use of guerrilla warfare from 1861 through 1865, some were now proposing to shift Lee's army to a wider guerrilla struggle, including Lee's trusted artillery commander Brigadier General Edward Porter Alexander. According to Alexander, he and Lee had a conversation about the issue shortly before the surrender. "If I took your suggestion & ordered the army to disperse," Lee asked, "how many do you suppose would get away?" "Two thirds of us, I think would get away," Alexander answered. "We would scatter like rabbits & partridges in the woods, & they could not scatter so to catch us." "There are here only about 15,000 men with muskets," Lee responded sardonically. "Suppose two thirds, say 10,000, got away. Divided among the states their numbers would be too insignificant to accomplish the least good. Yes! The surrender of this army is the end of the Confederacy. Suppose I should take your suggestion & order the army to disperse & make their way to their homes," Lee continued. "The men would have no rations & they would be under no discipline. . . . They would have to plunder and rob to procure subsistence. The country would be full of lawless bands in every part, & a state of society would ensue from which it would take the country years to recover,"

---

56. Robert Sandow, *Deserter Country: Civil War Opposition in the Pennsylvania Appalachians* (Bronx, NY: Fordham University Press, 2011), chap. 6.

57. Monroe, *The Papers of Jefferson Davis*, 11:386.

Lee argued. "Then the enemy's cavalry would pursue in the hopes of catching the principal officers, & wherever they went there would be fresh rapine & destruction. And as for myself, while you young men might afford to go to bushwhacking, the only proper & dignified course for me would be to surrender myself & take the consequences of my actions."[58]

On April 20, 1865, Robert E. Lee, having already surrendered the vaunted Army of Northern Virginia to Grant at Appomattox eleven days earlier, wrote to Jefferson Davis on the subject of his army's performance in the final campaigns around Richmond and the future of the Confederacy. "The apprehensions I expressed during the winter, of the moral condition of the Army of Northern Virginia, have been realized. The operations which occurred while the troops were in the entrenchments in front of Richmond and Petersburg were not marked by the boldness and decision which formerly characterized them," the general wrote. Lee continued by acknowledging the problems of the home front:

> Except in particular instances, they were feeble; a want of confidence seemed to possess officers and men. This condition, I think, was produced by the state of feeling in the country, and the communications received by the men from their homes, urging their return and the abandonment of the field.

"A partisan war may be continued, and hostilities protracted, causing individual suffering and the devastation of the country," Lee suggested, "but I see no prospect by that means of achieving a separate independence." Lee's comments and example proved important in bringing an end to conventional battlefield hostilities in the spring of 1865 for the large Confederate field armies that once hoped to establish a separate Southern nation.[59]

Estimates now place the human cost of the American Civil War at 750,000 or more dead, and while the war decided the fate of slavery and Southern secession, other issues of the war remained unresolved by the regular battlefield conflict. One war ended in 1865, and another continued. The conventional battlefield war over the establishment of the Confederacy as a separate nation concluded. The major, regular Confederate armies furled their banners, surrendered their cannon, stacked their arms, and were paroled to the home front. Other warriors fought on in another kind of war that also began as part of the Confederate project between 1861 and 1865. A Reconstruction-era irregular war of terrorism and vigilante violence waged to maintain white political and social control over poor white and black labor, mobility, and economic opportunity commenced in earnest long before Confederate armies

---

58. Gary W. Gallagher, ed., *Fighting for the Confederacy: The Personal Recollections of General Edward Porter Alexander* (Chapel Hill: University of North Carolina Press, 1989), 532.

59. Clifford Dowdey and Louis H. Manarin, eds., *The Wartime Papers of Robert E. Lee* (Boston: Little, Brown, 1961), 938–39.

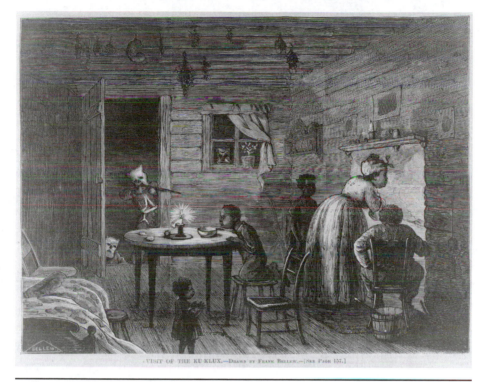

VISIT OF THE KU KLUX.—Drawn by Frank Bellew.—[See Page 157.]

An illustration from *Harper's Weekly* showing the continued violence in the occupied South carried out by groups like the Ku Klux Klan. Image courtesy of the Library of Congress.

surrendered in 1865. Confederates waged this war between 1861 and 1865 as they faced militant dissent from white and black Unionists, recusant conscripts, escaped slaves, and deserters, but after the defeat of their main political cause in the spring of 1865, this irregular conflict of local and regional racial and political control within the South emerged as the primary military threat to the Union army as it continued its military occupation of Confederate states.[60]

The pre-1865 military occupation of dozens of Southern towns and cities evolved into the Union army's extensive role occupying five zones created from the ex-Confederate states now under U.S. Army military district commanders. While the victory of the Union armies and the surrender of the Confederate armies accomplished the abolition of slavery, the emancipation of the enslaved, the death of the Confederacy as a functioning nation-state, an asymmetrical war of ex-Confederate terrorism and guerrilla violence aiming to safely protect white supremacy lasted far beyond

60. On the American Civil War death toll, see J. David Hacker, "A Census-Based Count of the Civil War Dead," *Civil War History* 57, no. 4 (2011): 307–48.

Appomattox. The post-1865 armed conflict of extralegal violence and irregular warfare was sanctioned by the majority white, still pro-Confederate population and continued for more than a decade.

General Philip Sheridan reported to President Ulysses S. Grant in 1875 that in Louisiana alone 2,141 black people had been killed and another 2,115 wounded since the "end" of the American Civil War. One high-profile example of the continuing white Southern irregular war of racial control came in the April 1873 Colfax massacre, in which white militia and Confederate veterans killed more than fifty blacks to preserve, as the honorary monument to the three white dead in the event plainly stated, "white supremacy." The final Federal troops would not be withdrawn from the Southern states until 1877, twelve years after the last formal surrender of Confederate troops. In the western region of the South, the irregular wars in Arkansas, Texas, and Missouri continued in a different form as many of the Confederate guerrillas like Frank and Jesse James became outlaws fighting the establishment of legitimate political authority and law in the growing American West.

What is clear is that while regular armies of the Confederacy surrendered in 1865, the violence and armed conflict of the Civil War's unresolved political, social, and cultural issues continued well beyond that date.[61] In many ways, the war aim of the Confederate government—white political, social, and racial control, or *home rule*—was ultimately successful despite regular battlefield defeat in 1865.[62]

---

61. Nicholas Lemann, *Redemption: The Last Battle of the Civil War* (New York: Farrar, Straus, and Giroux, 2006), 11, 26; Eric Foner, *Reconstruction: America's Unfinished Revolution* (New York: Harper and Row, 1988), 437.

62. Foner, *Reconstruction*, 276–77, 437.

5. Civil War Prisons: The Legacy of Responsibility

Benjamin Cloyd

> The National Prisoner of War Museum is dedicated to the men and women of this country who suffered captivity so that others could remain free. Their story is one of sacrifice and courage; their legacy, the gift of liberty.
>
> —*Dedication panel at the National Prisoner of War Museum at Andersonville National Historic Site, Andersonville, Georgia*

The myth of Civil War prisons is actually layers of myths. Both North and South argued, and continued to argue for generations, that they treated the prisoners of war in their custody by the accepted laws of war and, in the case of the South, as well as their economic situation allowed. Both sides also argued that their opponents were cruel and brutal to the poor souls in their custody. While the famous image of the elderly veterans of Gettysburg shaking hands across the infamous stone wall in 1913, fifty years after the battle, is representative of certain postwar sentiments, the treatment of prisoners of war was an open sore long after the original participants had passed away. The truth behind the accumulating and evolving myth of Civil War prisons remains that each side indiscriminately abused the prisoners of the other. But the truth is also that the story is complex; both sides are wrong and both sides are correct in aspects of their arguments.

There is no better example of Civil War mythmaking than the competing interpretations of the combatants' prisoner-of-war policies and their inhumane effects. In their simplest forms these myths explained this morally troubling aspect of the war by positing a dichotomy of good versus evil. The Northern tradition held that the Confederacy's treatment of prisoners of war was singularly and intentionally brutal, even as the North, by contrast, hosted its Southern captives with generosity. Southern lore, meanwhile, argued that the Confederacy cared as well as possible for its prisoners—despite untenable circumstances caused by the Union—and that, in fact, it was Southern soldiers who suffered from starvation and exposure to the elements in the North. To better understand the war, it is imperative to explore why these myths were needed to explain such atrocities.

Civil War prisons, or more precisely the misery experienced by captured soldiers, represented some of the worst aspects of an unrelenting and brutal conflict.

Approximately 56,000 soldiers—out of the nearly 410,000 imprisoned overall—died in captivity between 1861 and 1865. A closer look at the numbers reveals the universal nature of the suffering, as almost 30,000 Union soldiers died in Confederate prisons, while about 26,000 Confederate captives perished in Northern prison camps. Even in the midst of unprecedented destruction, the deaths of so many young men in Union and Confederate prisons created anger, confusion, and controversy. The search for responsibility began, of course, during the war itself. With both Union and Confederate sensibilities shocked and outraged—and even as the bodies accumulated—an elaborate battle of self-justification, one as complex as the campaigns of the armies themselves, commenced before the guns went silent and endured long after Appomattox. Tragedy rarely lasts as long as the stories we tell others, and ourselves, about it. The legacy of Civil War prisons is no exception.

Death in the Camps

There was and is plenty to tell about the tragedy of Civil War prisons. Deaths in the Union and Confederacy's camps represented about 7.5 percent of the military fatalities suffered during the Civil War. The death toll of Civil War prisons certainly explains—and requires—an emotional response. But the scramble to assess responsibility devolved into blame fueled by bitterness. Neither side could come to grips with the atrocities in its prisons. Each, therefore, attempted to evade blame by highlighting the actions and motives of its adversary. Shifting culpability required the construction of narratives that absolved one side while demonizing the other. Such themes reverberate to the present. The task of untangling real and perceived guilt has challenged historians since the war itself. Yet before such liabilities can be assessed, another question must be answered. Why did such suffering happen? In Confederate prisons, 15.5 percent of the Union prisoners of war died. In Union prisons, the death rate among Confederate captives was 12 percent.[1] Given the roughly 5 percent mortality rate expected on the battlefields of the Civil War, the death toll among prisoners of war was stunning. In retrospect, several reasons played a critical role in the devastation.

Part of the surprising trauma of Civil War prisons can be ascribed to prewar expectations and a resulting lack of preparation. When the war began, few Americans predicted the scale of what awaited them. As the Confederacy formed and the Union awaited Lincoln's inauguration, uncertainty gripped the divided nation. It would have been remarkable, indeed, had someone, North or South, begun to plan for the long-term care of prisoners of war. But why would they? While the United States certainly had experience with prisoners of war in earlier conflicts—the American Revolution was notoriously hard on captured soldiers—battlefield precedent from the early 1800s

---

1. The death rates of Civil War prisons are well established. See Lonnie R. Speer, *Portals to Hell: Military Prisons of the Civil War* (Mechanicsburg, PA: Stackpole Books, 1997), xiii–xix.

actually discouraged much preparation in this regard. Both the practice of immediate prisoner exchange following battle, or the custom of parole, in which captives were released after signing an oath not to fight until their formal exchange could be negotiated, in essence had the same effect—prisoners were no longer the responsibility of the captors. Thus, there was little need to develop policies or infrastructure to accommodate large numbers of indefinitely detained captives. Prisoners of war were not—and could not have been—a priority because they should not have existed in large numbers given the rules of war and experience in previous American military engagements.[2]

If initially excusable, the lack of preparation for properly housing, feeding, clothing, nursing, and organizing prisoners of war quickly became less so as the war dragged on and the numbers of prisoners mounted. Yet both sides responded ineffectively to the growing crisis of caring for prisoners of war and acted in a manner that could be described, depending on one's perspective, as at least curious, if not callous. The institutional apparatus in charge of dealing with prison logistics reflected the lack of a sense of urgency surrounding the issue. The Union developed more of a true prison system, at least in theory, led by Brigadier General William Hoffman. The Confederacy, however, waited almost until the end of the war before placing General John Winder in a similar position. The parallels between the two are not exact, but it is accurate to state that both men struggled to exert authority in the face of desperate circumstances. Hoffman's relative lack of status in the massive Union military bureaucracy ensured that, while more organized than its Confederate counterpart, Union care of captive soldiers remained a low priority. Winder, handicapped by the intensifying pressure on Richmond, the main Confederate locale for housing Union prisoners of war, scrambled with fatal consequences to find space for an escalating population of Union captives. This failure was most notably demonstrated at Andersonville, Georgia, in 1864. Neither Hoffman nor Winder enjoyed anything close to ideal circumstances in his assignment. But the generals' ineffective leadership showed how deadly bureaucracy can be when it fails to prioritize the care of human life.[3]

"Deadly" only begins to describe the world inside the walls of Civil War prisons. Well over one hundred locations were either built or transformed into prison camps during the conflict. At twelve of these sites—nine in the Union, three in the Confederacy—over one thousand prisoners were confirmed to have died in captivity.

---

2. Eugene M. Thomas, III, "Prisoner of War Exchange during the American Civil War" (Ph.D. diss., Auburn University, 1976), 3–4. For more background (and a diversity of opinions) on American expectations of prisoner exchange prior to the Civil War, see Speer, *Portals to Hell*, xiii–xix; Charles W. Sanders, Jr., *While in the Hands of the Enemy: Military Prisons of the Civil War* (Baton Rouge: Louisiana State University Press, 2005), 2–24; and James M. Gillispie, *Andersonvilles of the North: The Myths and Realities of Northern Treatment of Civil War Confederate Prisoners* (Denton: University of North Texas Press, 2008), 3–4.

3. For insight on Hoffman, see Leslie G. Hunter, "Warden for the Union: General William Hoffman (1807–1884)" (Ph.D. diss., University of Arizona, 1971). On Winder, see Arch Blakey, *General John H. Winder, C.S.A.* (Gainesville: University of Florida Press, 1990).

In the North, the deadliest prison environments were Alton, Illinois; Camp Chase, Ohio; Camp Douglas, Illinois; Camp Morton, Indiana; Elmira, New York; Fort Delaware, Delaware; Gratiot Street, Missouri; Point Lookout, Maryland; and Rock Island, Illinois. Their Southern counterparts were Andersonville, Georgia; Danville, Virginia; and Salisbury, North Carolina. All these camps (and others not listed here, such as Johnson's Island, Ohio, and Libby Prison, Virginia) developed infamous reputations, but Andersonville, both in terms of its massive size and its nearly 29 percent mortality rate, and Elmira, with an almost 25 percent death rate, became most synonymous with human despair.[4] Private Charlie Mosher's initial impression of Andersonville encapsulated the terrible circumstances faced by prisoners of war: "Many are without hats, coats, shoes, and have nothing on but an old shirt, all in rags, and a worse pair of pants; they scarcely look like human beings at all; whose countenances show that there has been a desperate fight between hope and despair, and that despair has won the day."[5]

The common suffering endured by captives occurred at many different prisons and resulted from a variety of understandable, if no less horrible, day-to-day realities. Given the differences between the many prison camps on both sides, there was no universal prisoner experience. But a number of common factors combined to ensure prisoner misery regardless of setting. The immediate threat to the detainees' health came from disease, which was the overwhelming killer of prisoners of war. If coping with disease presented a major challenge for armies in the field, outbreaks proved even more lethal in the confines of Civil War prisons. Susceptibility to illness was heightened by malnutrition, poor sanitation, and exposure to the elements. Medical care could do little to alleviate the impact of these conditions. Harder to quantify but no less real was the toll from the emotional strain of being held captive and dealing with an uncertain future while likely carrying the burden of having—at least in some sense—failed in their service. Prisoner interaction, especially in larger camps, often became a Darwinian struggle for survival. The relationships between captives and their guards, especially in larger Civil War prisons, were frequently defined by a strange mixture of boredom, hatred, and terror that could turn not only hostile, but fatal. The traumatic nature of captivity that grew from the multifaceted layers of prisoner suffering thus had many contributing causes. And the anxiety of these institutions was heightened by a nagging question: Was it necessary?[6]

---

4. Speer provides a most helpful summary of prison locations and known casualties in *Portals to Hell*, 323–40.

5. Wayne Mahood, ed., *Charlie Mosher's Civil War* (Hightstown, NJ: Longstreet House, 1994), 210.

6. The conditions in Civil War prisons are extensively documented in memoirs and monographs. Four major overviews of Civil War prisons exist and are the best starting point to understand what Civil War prisoners of war endured. See William B. Hesseltine, *Civil War Prisons: A Study in War Psychology* (1930; repr., Columbus: Ohio State University Press, 1998); Speer, *Portals to Hell*; Sanders, *While in the Hands of the Enemy*; and Gillispie, *Andersonvilles of the North*.

As with most frustrating questions, the answer of course was both yes and no. The most truthful answer was that it seemed necessary during the war itself. The very reasons that Civil War prisons—and the suffering that occurred within them—existed proved inseparable from the reasons the conflict began in the first place. At the outset of the war, the question of prisoners of war was about more than just preparation or the possible duration of the fighting. From the perspective of Abraham Lincoln and the Union, captured Confederates were traitors subject to prosecution. Applying the usual punishment of execution, however, had consequences, including the potential of retaliatory killings by the Confederacy. Recognizing that this gap between policy and reality created opportunity, Jefferson Davis and the Confederacy pushed for a formalized process of prisoner exchange as part of a larger strategy of establishing a recognized Confederate sovereignty. Given the conflicting motivations that drove the Lincoln and Davis administrations, it should not surprise that it took until the 1862 acceptance of the Dix-Hill Cartel to agree to official standards of exchange. The Dix-Hill Cartel established a formula to ensure the mutually equal return of prisoners and designated official locations for the transactions. In the end, exchanging prisoners, whether done through the official Dix-Hill agreement or not, was rarely motivated by concern for the captives themselves. Prisoners of war were just one more resource used by both sides in the competition to legitimize their respective causes and gain whatever advantage they could.[7]

The contested status of prisoners of war became even more controversial as Lincoln took careful aim at the institution of slavery. With the announcement of the Emancipation Proclamation and the acceptance of African American soldiers for Union military service, the question loomed as to what would happen once those men fell into Confederate hands. Davis and the Confederate hierarchy refused to consider African American servicemen as deserving of equal treatment, insisting on a policy that captured black prisoners of war would be considered runaway slaves. The practical experience of African American soldiers taken prisoner, or not, seen most notably with the racially motivated massacre of captured black troops at Fort Pillow in 1864, was even worse. Lincoln's response was to stand firm in support of the rights of African American enlistees, demanding that they be subject to exchange like any other soldier. The resulting collapse of the Dix-Hill Cartel thus hinged on slavery. The Lincoln administration's embrace of a tenuous equality for African Americans was noteworthy and admirable. But for prisoners of war on both sides, it doomed thousands to horrible fates. Only the war could resolve the questions of Confederate independence and slavery. Prisoners of war were manipulated in pursuit of those objectives. If at the start of the war no one spent much time thinking about prisoners

---

7. Benjamin Cloyd, *Haunted by Atrocity: Civil War Prisons in American Memory* (Baton Rouge: Louisiana State University Press, 2010), 4–8. For more on exchange, see Thomas, "Prisoner of War Exchange"; Hesseltine, *Civil War Prisons*, chaps. 2, 5, and 10; Sanders, *While in the Hands of the Enemy*, chaps. 5 and 6; and Gillispie, *Andersonvilles of the North*, 37–39, 54–66, 84–95.

of war, the truth was that by the end of the war most Americans deliberately chose to look the other way.[8]

Civil War prisoners of war ultimately suffered for many interrelated reasons. The combination of false expectations, unpreparedness, inefficient organization, and frightful conditions all led to a tragedy further escalated by decisions to sacrifice prisoners of war in behalf of larger wartime goals. But the complexity of that explanation dissatisfied then, and still dissatisfies. In their wartime diaries, the prisoners themselves displayed a perceptive and nuanced awareness of the factors that led to their ordeal. They also expressed bitterness toward their leaders as well as their captors in regard to their situations.[9] This should not surprise—all failure breeds resentment in those most affected by it. Yet the depth of the failure, the scope of what went wrong between 1861 and 1865 in Civil War prisons, rippled beyond those imprisoned. The existence of these prison camps conflicted with both the Union and Confederate narratives of the war and revealed the true nature of the ugly contest. Part of the outrage from both sides stemmed from how prisoners' suffering and their deaths challenged the comfortable cultural ideal of purposeful sacrifice.[10] Perhaps the most galling aspect of the distress was that the prisoners, their families, and by the end of the war, anyone paying close attention knew that this sacrifice had been coerced instead of given. By implication, given that few volunteer to die in prison, their sacrifice became less noble.

Building a Myth

The treatment of prisoners of war punctured the preferred illusion of the Civil War as a battle of good and evil. The complexity of responsibility for the tragedy of Civil War prisons simultaneously demanded and prevented an honest reckoning. The fact that so much blame could and should be attached to the topic allowed for the formation of multiple—yet ultimately self-serving and never quite satisfying—narratives of what had gone wrong. A number of possible explanations, or myths, emerged as Americans rearranged the facts of the war to accommodate the needs of a postwar world. Historian David Blight identified three visible traditions: reconciliation, predominant among Northerners; white supremacy, most associated with white Southerners; and an emancipationist perspective, largely held by African Americans.[11] Caroline Janney and others point out that preserving the integrity of the "Union cause" also remained a driving

---

8. Cloyd, *Haunted by Atrocity*, 8–11.

9. Ibid., 14–20.

10. Drew Gilpin Faust, *This Republic of Suffering: Death and the American Civil War* (New York: Alfred A. Knopf, 2008), 6–17.

11. David W. Blight, *Race and Reunion: The Civil War in American Memory* (Cambridge, MA: Belknap Press of Harvard University Press, 2001), 2.

force for many Northerners for generations.[12] More suggestive than definitive, each limited and refracted through personal experience, these scholarly categories nonetheless remain helpful. What took place (and still takes place) was a fierce and enduring competition among these visions as Americans sought to at least be able to live with what they had done in the prisons and the war. This is why Blight declares that no aspect of the Civil War "caused deeper emotions, recriminations, and lasting invective than that of prisons."[13] Or as Janney describes, "No war memory was as fraught with bitterness and more likely to revive sectional passions than the prisoner-of-war issue."[14] All four of these remembrance legacies are powerful and persuasive in grappling with the meaning of and responsibility for Civil War prisons. None was or is monolithic enough to fully dispel or absorb the others. But of the four, it was the reconciliationist and Unionist perspectives that cast the largest shadow in the case of Civil War prisons.

Reconciliation

The prison controversy had become an open wound by the end of the war, one made even more painful because of the knowledge that the wound was, at least in part, self-inflicted. Robert Penn Warren long ago identified the Northern belief—confirmed by victory—in what he called the "Treasury of Virtue."[15] The fighting and winning of the Civil War by the North, according to Warren, absolved it of any particular failings during the conflict. This "Virtue," like all aspects of honor, required vigorous defense long after the fighting ceased. The search for the responsibility for Civil War prisons was, at its core, about self-justification, and was already well underway by 1865. Both North and South were gripped by a phenomenon first described by William Hesseltine in his groundbreaking 1930 book *Civil War Prisons: A Study in War Psychology* as "war psychosis."[16]

War psychosis not only encouraged self-righteousness but also, in what might be a universal characteristic of war, required self-delusion. It is logical that the side with more manpower and resources would also have the louder voice—amplified by victory—on the topic of Civil War prisons. As prisoners shared accounts of their sufferings and the survivors returned home, their experiences became common knowledge among families and communities. Outrage grew. Northern newspaper coverage and government reports praised the Lincoln administration for providing the best

---

12. Caroline E. Janney, *Remembering the Civil War: Reunion and the Limits of Reconciliation* (Chapel Hill: University of North Carolina Press, 2013), 5–6. See also Gary W. Gallagher, *The Union War* (Cambridge, MA: Harvard University Press, 2011).

13. Blight, *Race and Reunion*, 152.

14. Janney, *Remembering the Civil War*, 256.

15. Robert Penn Warren, *The Legacy of the Civil War* (1961; repr., Lincoln: University of Nebraska Press, 1998), 59–66.

16. Hesseltine, *Civil War Prisons*, 172.

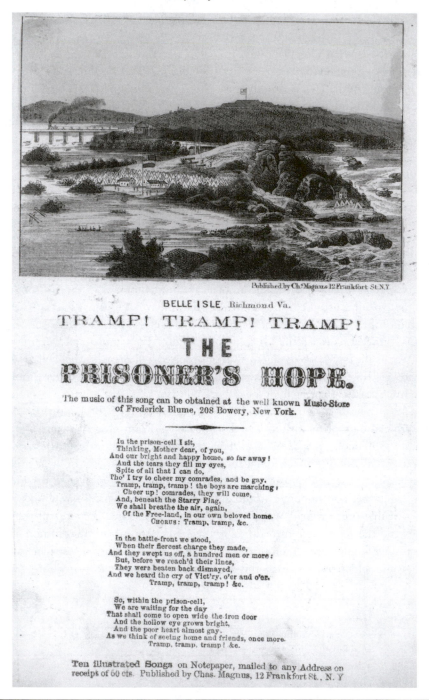

Advertisement for the sheet music to the popular song "The Prisoner's Hope," illustrated with an image of the prisoner of war camp on Belle Island in Virginia. Courtesy of the Library of Congress.

possible care for prisoners of war. It was not enough that the Union be innocent of the atrocities ascribed to the Confederacy; the drumbeat of accusations of deliberate and systematic abuse of captives by the Confederacy was about much more than frustration over the treatment of prisoners of war. Songs like George Root's 1864 "Tramp, Tramp, Tramp!; or, The Prisoner's Hope!" and Henry Tucker's 1865 "We Never Can Forget It, or The Memories of Andersonville Prison Pens" etched into many Northern minds a fixed—and one-sided—image of the legacy of Civil War prisons.

The lyrics to Tucker's account of Andersonville came from the prolific hymn writer Mary Ann Kidder and captured the emotional intensity of the prisoner's perspective:

> How we suffered in our weakness—
> Freezing, starving—none can tell;
> Stagg'ring near the fatal "dead line,"
> Where so many gladly fell;
> Gazing into ghastly faces,
> When all joy and hope had fled;
> Longing, dying for the firelight,
> With no shelter, clothes, or bed.

Kidder's poetry certainly creates a more human portrayal of the subject of prisoners of war. And it must be acknowledged without any begrudging that Northerners were entitled to find meaning and dignity as best they could in the face of tragedy. But so, of course, were others. The Northern obsession with righteousness—and shouting down those who questioned that righteousness—proved remarkably enduring. Kidder's refrain perfectly sums up the animosity on the topic of Civil War prisons that would not fade:

> Freezing! starving! living death!
> Father! can they know at home?
> Oh! we never can forget it
> In all the years to come.[17]

It turns out that "Virtue," especially sizable amounts of it, is best noticed when compared with a lack of it in others. And its vigilant defense also came from the reality that the construction of a singular Northern "Virtue" was not entirely true. The trauma of the Civil War, even for the winners, required this distortion. It allowed Northerners to persist in their causes, mourn their losses, and define their victory for "years to come."

---

17. Henry Tucker, "We Never Can Forget It, or The Memories of Andersonville Prison Pens," lyrics by Mary Ann Kidder (New York: W. Jennings Demorest, 1865), http://lcweb2.loc.gov/diglib/ihas/loc.natlib.ihas.200002110, accessed November 12, 2014. Thanks to Eric Leonard for your assistance.

Henry Wirz, former commander of Andersonville, being read his death sentence. Courtesy of the Library of Congress.

Reconstruction

If by 1865 a potent Northern myth of Civil War prisons already existed, Reconstruction demonstrated just how valuable it could be in the postwar struggle to forge the United States anew. The wartime hostility over the treatment of prisoners perpetuated lingering sectional tensions and fueled the sense of Northern justification in acting from a higher moral ground. This Northern perspective on the prisoner issue—placing singular responsibility for the prison tragedy on the South—was confirmed during the fall of 1865 by the trial and execution of C.S.A. Captain Henry Wirz, the commandant of Andersonville Prison. Created in haste and quickly overcrowded, Andersonville was, is, and will always be the dominant name in the story of Civil War prisons. Andersonville's massive scale and casualties—45,000 Union soldiers experienced its misery, with 13,000 dying there—ensured its infamy. The fact that all this suffering occurred in just over one calendar year, from early 1864 until the end of the war, created a Northern fixation on Wirz as the "demon of Andersonville."[18] Scholars today argue just how exceptional Andersonville really was, but there was no debate

---

18. United States Army Military Commission. *The Demon of Andersonville; or, The Trial of Wirz, for the Cruel Treatment and Brutal Murder of Helpless Union Prisoners in His Hands. The Most Highly Exciting and Interesting Trial of the Present Century, His Life and Execution Containing Also a History*

"Let Us Clasp Hands over the Bloody Chasm."—Horace Greeley.

A cartoon in *Harper's Weekly* during the 1872 presidential election illustrating that the treatment of prisoners was still an issue many did not plan to forget. Image courtesy of Princeton University Library.

that the prison remained a focal point of Northern outrage during Reconstruction and beyond.[19] During 1865, even as Wirz went to the gallows, Andersonville began another of its many transformations. As the final prisoners departed and the Union claimed possession, the work of remembrance began with the creation of Andersonville National Cemetery. It did not stop at mourning the dead.

Fed by the steady release of prisoner memoirs that expanded on the emotions hinted at by Kidder, a sense of Northern moral supremacy, particularly with regard to Civil War prisons, became more entrenched. In recasting prisoners' captivity as an experience of active heroism, battlefield failure gave way to intricate schemes of escaping prison.[20] Senseless suffering became intentional sacrifice, and if during the war the prisoners had been ignored, they no longer needed to be. The retroactive desire to honor Union soldiers who had been imprisoned was incorporated into the traditions of the Grand Army of the Republic.[21] Every election cycle, Republican candidates used

---

of Andersonville, with Illustrations, Truthfully Representing the Horrible Scenes of Cruelty Perpetuated by Him (Philadelphia: Barclay, 1865).

19. For the best assessment of Andersonville, see William Marvel, *Andersonville: The Last Depot* (Chapel Hill: University of North Carolina Press, 1994).

20. Cloyd, *Haunted by Atrocity*, 58–67; For a list of prison narratives, see pages 214–21.

21. Oliver Morris Wilson, *The Grand Army of the Republic under Its First Constitution and Ritual* (Kansas City, MO: Franklin Hudson, 1905), 223–35. Thanks to Eric Leonard for your assistance.

their responsibility to the memory of those who endured—as Indiana congressman and former Union general John P. C. Shanks expressed it during his 1870 reelection campaign, the "wanton and savage cruelty to helpless prisoners of war"—as a political weapon.[22] Thomas Nast used Andersonville to dismiss the presidential qualifications of 1872 Democratic nominee Horace Greeley—who campaigned openly for sectional reconciliation—with an illustration (part of a larger series) titled "Let Us Clasp Hands over the Bloody Chasm." In the image, Greeley eagerly reaches out across the Andersonville stockade to the South, standing on his tiptoes, arms outstretched, even while families mourn at the headstones of fallen prisoners of war below. Nast's usage of Andersonville as a central symbol of Northern righteousness, warning against any premature reconciliation with the Democratic—meaning traitorous—South, evinces the powerful emotions still generated by the search for responsibility in the prison controversy. The willingness to distort once again must also be noted, as Nast blended the stockade grounds and cemetery together to make his point.[23]

Reconstruction thus perpetuated and encouraged the peculiar Northern understanding of Civil War prisons. The myth of Northern purity heightened the appetite for honoring the sacrifice of its prisoners of war and prevented forgiveness of the "wanton and savage" South. The intensity with which it was pursued also revealed that it did not, and perhaps could not, fully satisfy the wrongs of the past.

Remembrance

By the turn of the century, the ongoing rhetorical war to pin the blame for the responsibility of the treatment of prisoners of war on either the North or the South entered a new phase of the struggle. Although the voices of former captives were fewer in number, they remained outspoken and urgent in their desire, as Massachusetts Lieutenant Thomas Sturgis put it in 1911, to "leave our testimony."[24] A fear persisted—there were competing myths of the Civil War, after all—that in time the sacrifices of the 1860s might well be forgotten. Words alone would not suffice to protect history. In 1898, New Jersey dedicated the first state monument to Andersonville. Large quantities of bronze, marble, and granite followed, and within twenty years a majority of Union states created individual tributes to the soldiers who had perished in captivity. The significance of Andersonville was further confirmed in 1910 when the Women's

---

See also Stuart McConnell, *Glorious Contentment: The Grand Army of the Republic, 1865–1900* (Chapel Hill: University of North Carolina Press, 1992).

22. J. P. C. Shanks, *Speech of Gen. J. P. C. Shanks, of Indiana, on Treatment of Prisoners of War* (Washington, D.C.: Judd and Detweiler, 1870), 3.

23. *Harper's Weekly*, September 21, 1872.

24. Thomas Sturgis, "Prisoners of War," in *Personal Recollections of the War of the Rebellion*, ed. A. Noel Blakeman (New York: G. P. Putnam's Sons, 1912), 267.

Relief Corps transferred ownership of the former prison's grounds to the United States government.[25] These efforts represented a permanent claim to the landscape of Andersonville on behalf of those who "suffered captivity," as the National Prisoner of War Museum, located at the Andersonville National Historic Site, reminds us today. Their purpose was to ensure that Americans never forgot the "sacrifice and courage" of Civil War prisoners of war. As in any war—even a rhetorical one—securing territory was critical, and with state monuments spreading not just in the cemetery but next to the old stockade site, this transition ensured that the Northern myth of Civil War prisons would continue its dominance.

Why was this so important? In part, the transformation of Andersonville into a shrine to Northern sacrifice came from the allure of honoring the dead as a form of atonement. It also offered a chance to thank the dwindling group of Andersonville survivors as they disappeared. It evidenced the rising profile of the United States and the self-congratulatory narrative that without the Union's heroism in the 1860s this power would never have been possible. Perhaps most important, it salved old wounds, at least momentarily. But it was also, whether out of confidence or arrogance—or both—a statement of an aggressive determination to preserve the Northern perception of Andersonville as a terrible exception to the noble American character. It continued to deny any responsibility that the Union might have had for the tragedy of Civil War prisons. No matter the motivation, it remained as one-sided as ever and provoked consequences.

The most obvious of these consequences was that the pursuit of the Northern myth of Civil War prisons escalated the postwar contest over remembrance and revealed just how fragile the illusion of reconciliation really was. It had always been fragile, of course. The dominant white Southern memory of the prison controversy, which rejected the Northern premise of reconciliation as false, dated back to the war itself. Throughout the late nineteenth century, a determined effort persisted to exonerate the Confederacy's treatment of prisoners of war. The *Southern Historical Society Papers* mounted a vociferous defense of Confederate prison sites. Numerous former captives who had endured Union prisons penned their own narratives of suffering. Jefferson Davis continued to remind anyone who would listen that the Confederacy did the best it could for its prisoners in the face of overwhelming circumstances. Although the purveyors of this defensive Southern myth were as outnumbered as the wartime generation had been on the battlefield, they remained persistent.[26]

With these old wounds still festering, even after several decades, the renewed attention focused on Andersonville, and in particular the strident tone of the monuments and the language of dedication, offended many white Southerners who resented promises of Northern forgiveness. The lack of similar memorials at the counterpart

---

25. Cloyd, *Haunted by Atrocity*, 88–89.
26. Ibid., 67–74.

prison sites and graves in the North rankled groups like the United Daughters of the Confederacy (UDC). Angrily rejecting the terms of reconciliation proposed by the Northern remaking of Andersonville, the UDC in 1909 unveiled the Wirz monument adjacent to the prison site in the town of Andersonville. Noted by the local newspaper as a "splendid consummation of their work of love and devotion to the cause which they represent," the UDC's effort to depict Wirz as a martyr demonstrated the one-sidedness of the white supremacist myth prevalent in the South.[27] If white Southern-ers could not control the story at the epicenter of Andersonville, they could at least claim the surrounding terrain. The urgency of this struggle to remember, culminating in the Taft administration's acceptance of the prison grounds, showed that both North and South remained sensitive to the failure of Civil War prisons well into the twenti-eth century. The same need that prompted the desire to remember Civil War prisons consistently prevented authentic reconciliation. The truth was that neither side was prepared to admit its past faults, preferring instead to construct alternative realities. It is often easier to try to deflect blame than to accept responsibility.

Race

The monument contest at Andersonville echoed the Civil War in one other important way—both were motivated by questions of race, and both represented failed oppor-tunities to fully answer the questions. Civil War prisoners experienced prolonged cap-tivity rather than exchange because of the controversial status of African American soldiers as prisoners of war, which was one component of the larger national struggle over the future of slavery and what its end might mean for the United States. Civil War prisons were therefore powerful symbols of freedom if viewed from an emancipa-tionist perspective. Even as the dominant myths of the North and South continually sparred over the issue of responsibility, the emancipationist vision of Andersonville and other prison sites focused on celebrating "the gift of liberty." The challenge for African Americans to define and protect "liberty" was (and is) an ongoing one. Claim-ing the prize of freedom turned out to be no easy task and often led to racial turmoil. The postwar usage of the former prison grounds at Andersonville provides one exam-ple of the difficulty of change. In the late 1860s Andersonville briefly hosted a school for African American children that became a target of white violence.[28] Local African American residents at Andersonville faced a vicious white backlash against them dur-ing Reconstruction. "Driven from their homes," missionary H. W. Pierson wrote, the

27. *Americus Times-Recorder*, May 13, 1909, clipping in Andersonville vertical files, Andersonville National Historic Site. On the Wirz monument controversy, see Cloyd, *Haunted by Atrocity*, 101–9; and Janney, *Remembering the Civil War*, 256–61.

28. Peggy Sheppard, *Andersonville Georgia USA* (1973; repr., Andersonville, GA: Sheppard Publica-tions, 2001), 66–68.

"facts show that no matter how horrible and brutal the outrage and personal violence committed upon them there had been no punishment to the perpetrators and no redress to the Freedmen."[29] Part of what sustained people in the face of constant threat was the strength of remembrance. Pierson had come to Andersonville because "these historic grounds, this Gethsemane of the nation," deserved to be properly honored.[30] The desire by those freed by the war to pay homage to such a sacrifice persisted and evolved over the years. It did not take the form of monuments but was instead displayed year after year by the crowds of African Americans who gathered at Civil War prison sites each Memorial Day.[31] Their presence testified to a deep gratitude for what Civil War prisoners had endured. Places that had once destroyed the hopes of thousands of captives now encouraged hopes for generations of African Americans that "the gift of liberty" might yet become more tangible.

The assertive presence of African Americans at commemorations, of course, defied the prevalent Lost Cause tradition among Southern whites. But it also directly challenged the dominant Northern myth of Civil War prisons. Northerners, and especially former prisoners, certainly embraced the concept of meaningful sacrifice, but did so secondarily, as the logical consequence of first assigning the proper responsibility for the suffering experienced by prisoners of war. The emancipationist vision, meanwhile, elevated the sacrifice of prisoners to the point where the issue of responsibility became essentially irrelevant. This made the two narratives incompatible. For Northerners, culpable Southern responsibility remained the driving force behind the need to remember Civil War prisons. It was more comfortable to claim "Virtue" and congratulate the heroism of former prisoners than to face the disconcerting truth that the wartime and Reconstruction efforts at racial equality had been largely abandoned. The preoccupation with the responsibility for Civil War prisons allowed Northerners to build monuments at Andersonville to honor a generalized sacrifice on behalf of a reunited—and supposedly reconciled—nation. It also allowed them to ignore the legacy of ending slavery and enabled ongoing racial discrimination in which all of the reunited nation was complicit. The Northern obsession with responsibility thus not only prevented any admission of guilt for the suffering of Southern prisoners of war but negated one of the essential purposes of that suffering. The concepts of both reconciliation and reunion were thus largely illusions rooted in the desire to avoid further pain, which is certainly understandable given the trauma of the 1860s. Nevertheless, it is strange but true that the pursuit of a mythical responsibility contributed to the denial of a real responsibility to engage with the fundamental racial implications of the Civil War.

---

29. H. W. Pierson, *A Letter to Hon. Charles Sumner, with "Statements" of Outrages upon Freedmen in Georgia, and an Account of My Expulsion from Andersonville, Ga., by the Ku Klux Klan* (Washington, D.C.: Chronicle Print, 1870), 17–18. Thanks to Eric Leonard for your assistance.

30. Pierson, *A Letter to Hon. Charles Sumner*, 17.

31. Cloyd, *Haunted by Atrocity*, 50, 74–76, 104–5, 118.

The Historians

As the early 1900s progressed, the last of the Civil War generation waned. With their passing, even though memorial groups like the UDC persisted, the crowds and commemorations surrounding battlefields and monuments dwindled. So too did the intensity of the emotions stirred by Civil War prisons. Historians finally began to probe the dominant Northern myth of Civil War prisons in a search to understand the tragedy with a more professional precision. The attraction of that myth would prove difficult to overcome. Not until 1911, when Holland Thompson provided the first comparative assessment of Union and Confederate prison camps in volume seven of Francis Trevelyan Miller's series *The Photographic History of the Civil War in Ten Volumes* did anyone dare to suggest in significant detail that perhaps the search for responsibility in the case of Civil War prisons should have a national focus instead of the traditional sectional explanations. It would be another twenty years before a fuller challenge to the entrenched myth, dismissed by former prisoner of war Thomas Sturgis as a product of "unconscious bias," emerged.[32] William B. Hesseltine's 1930 *Civil War Prisons* marked the first determined scholarly stand against the old Northern accusations of intentional Confederate cruelty to their captives. "It is possible now," Hesseltine asserted in his preface, since "two wars have arisen to test the firmness with which the nation was re-welded by 1865," that the time had come "to examine the prisoners and prisons of the Civil War in a scientific spirit." The "organic whole" of the United States was now secure enough to withstand a deconstruction of its mythical past.[33] Part contrarian by nature, Hesseltine, a Virginian who was educated and taught in the North, clearly relished the chance to defend the Confederacy from the charges of the traditional Northern myth.[34]

But why was it so important to properly assess responsibility at this late date? Those who did or did not deserve the blame were, of course, no longer around to care. What motivated Hesseltine—like all scholars who hold themselves to the standards of academic rigor and honesty—in his desire for historical accuracy was the chance to understand the deeper truths that underlie our human controversies. His focus on "war psychology" and "war psychosis," which made it easy for the North to believe its own propaganda regarding supposed Southern degeneracy, could not undo the decades of recriminations over the treatment of Civil War prisoners of war. But it could reframe that suffering in the context of World War I. The scale and cruel conditions of World War I dwarfed even those of the Civil War, rendering the old view of Wirz as "the demon of Andersonville" an anachronism from this more modern,

---

32. Holland Thompson, ed., *Prisons and Hospitals*, vol. 7 of *The Photographic History of the Civil War in Ten Volumes*, ed. Francis Trevelyan Miller (New York: Review of Reviews, 1911); Sturgis, "Prisoners of War," 326–28.

33. Hesseltine, *Civil War Prisons*, xxiii.

34. William Blair, foreword to Hesseltine, *Civil War Prisons*, ix–xxi.

"scientific" perspective. What if responsibility for prisoners of war was detached from leaders such as Wirz, Seddon, and Davis on the one side, or Grant, Stanton, and Lincoln on the other, and was instead viewed, in Hesseltine's words, as an "inevitable" product of "the vicissitudes of warfare"?[35] The need to understand Civil War prisons remained urgent, but it was no longer personal. If Hesseltine expressed frustration with the enduring power of the Northern version of Civil War prisons, it was because myth by its nature often obstructs the perceived potential for progress. From Hesseltine's more objective viewpoint, the Northern myth had become unnecessary. Identifying our myths is one thing. Disentangling from them is quite another. They are seductively adaptive, after all.

The unprecedented horrors of World War I encouraged a deeper examination of the nature of modern war. World War II demanded it. The numbing human cost of World War II made the traditional divisive sectional remembrance of the Civil War, and its prisons in particular, seem obsolete. The most powerful recasting of the old story of Civil War prisons in the aftermath of World War II came not from a historian but from a popular novelist, MacKinlay Kantor. *Andersonville*, published in 1955, was a novel as big as the twenty-five years it took Kantor to finish it.[36] Hailed by historian Henry Steele Commager as "the greatest of our Civil War novels," both the Pulitzer Prize–winning book itself—and the reaction to it—were clearly motivated by the fresh emotions stirred by the indelible suffering of the 1940s.[37] According to scholar Jeff Smithpeters, Kantor's novel reflected the belief "that a real concentration camp and a semblance of a Holocaust had happened in America."[38] Writing in *Civil War History*, Lawrence Thompson described *Andersonville* as a product of "Olympian objectivity," and credited Kantor with helping readers "to find out what made Wirz and millions of his contemporaries behave as they did." Thompson also recognized the novel's overt connection to World War II, pointing out that "no student of Civil War history need be told that Buchenwald and Belsen would have had no special horrors for anyone lucky enough to have survived the pest-ridden valley at Andersonville Station in central Georgia."[39] The novel remains a beautiful exploration of how the brutality of war overwhelms the human capacity for justice and order. And it confirmed how much the old myth of responsibility was changing in the mid-twentieth century. By blurring the Civil War and World War II as roughly equal expressions of modern war, the guilt of the past became no longer a question of the burden of individual responsibility,

---

35. Hesseltine, *Civil War Prisons*, 1.

36. MacKinlay Kantor, *Andersonville* (1955; repr., New York: Plume, 1993). On the impact of *Andersonville*, see Cloyd, *Haunted by Atrocity*, 131–38.

37. Henry Steele Commager, *The New York Times Book Review*, October 30, 1955.

38. Jeff Smithpeters, "'To the Latest Generation': Cold War and Post Cold War U.S. Civil War Novels in their Social Contexts" (Ph.D. diss., Louisiana State University, 2005), 58.

39. Lawrence S. Thompson, "The Civil War in Fiction," *Civil War History* 2 (March 1956): 93–94.

but instead a collective challenge for the present and future—which makes it easier to live with, does it not?

An undeniable commercial success, *Andersonville* was not universally popular. Hesseltine labeled the book a "perversity." Frustrated by the continued spotlight on Andersonville Prison, which ran counter to his efforts to challenge the traditional Northern perspective on Civil War prisons, Hesseltine worried that Kantor was perpetuating "the myth of Andersonville."[40] The singular focus on Andersonville did give Hesseltine's concerns some merit. But what Hesseltine could not recognize at the time was that there never had been just one "myth of Andersonville."

Both men shared more in common than not as they contributed to a new myth of Civil War prisons, a myth born out of allegedly fair-minded historical investigation that supposedly resulted in a true understanding of Civil War prisons and—while it could not totally replace the original sectional divisions—could at least soften some of the old bitterness. Taking a more dispassionate and nonpartisan stance on the responsibility for the suffering of Civil War prisoners was certainly attractive and understandable. This lack of partisanship allowed for the possibility of sectional forgiveness that the old myth of Northern "Virtue" never could. It offered hope that perhaps somehow the universal lessons of war—"their story . . . their legacy"—could yet be understood. The subject of Civil War prisons thus remained vital even after almost a century had passed. If the claims of deliberate brutality once cemented victory, the embrace of supposed impartiality, even "objectivity," removed from both sides the burden of responsibility for that brutality and offered hope that perhaps our capacity for inhumanity was a problem—daunting to be sure—that nevertheless could be solved.

Although each generation reacted to the tragedy of Civil War prisons in the context of its own time, their myths are not as different as first appearance might suggest. Each perception of the past was rooted in the element of pride that so often inflates the importance of personal perspective. Both the Northern myth and the objective myth externalized responsibility and deflected the particulars of blame. Pride must be protected after all. And the objective myth was never capable of fully dispelling the earlier recriminations. Instead it ensured that the old accusations would always be remembered even if kept at a safe distance by the illusion that they no longer offended. But the core of the objective myth retained the old sense of Northern acrimony. It just layered over it. Part of the seduction of myth—what keeps it so usable—is that engagement with it usually leads to something being defined on its terms. Given the limits of human experience and our preference for the familiar, this trade often seems more than fair.

Freed from the more overt controversies of Civil War prisons by the "objective view" pioneered by Hesseltine and popularized by Kantor, recent historians have much more thoroughly, if still not fully, explored the once taboo topic of responsibility for

---

40. William B. Hesseltine, "Andersonville Revisited," *Georgia Review* 10 (Spring 1956): 97–100.

the harsh treatment of Civil War prisoners. No longer having to apologize for the hard feelings of the past has allowed for an explosion of books and articles detailing the individual stories of the major Civil War prisons.[41] As a result a more nuanced argument about Civil War prisons now exists. Lonnie Speer's 1997 *Portals to Hell: Military Prisons of the Civil War* provided a much-needed update to Hesseltine and outlined in more detail the conditions and varying scale of prison camps during the conflict. It is true that the single-volume narratives of the Civil War, such as James McPherson's *Battle Cry of Freedom*, still treat the subject of Civil War prisons as a relative footnote in the war's history.[42] Despite this, there are hopeful signs that prisons are becoming more essential to contemporary interpretations of the Civil War. The rise of Civil War remembrance, sparked by Blight and expanded with Caroline Janney's *Remembering the Civil War: Reunion and the Limits of Reconciliation*, emphasizes that the lingering bitterness that surrounded Civil War prisons obstructed the nation's recovery from the war.[43] But the implications of Civil War prisons will not be more fully understood until prison scholars themselves directly confront the myths of Civil War prisons.

---

41. There are too many works to provide a comprehensive list here, but the following, in chronological order, are representative of the contemporary interpretation of Civil War prisons: William O. Bryant, *Cahaba Prison and the Sultana Disaster* (Tuscaloosa: University of Alabama Press, 1990); Sandra V. Parker, *Richmond's Civil War Prisons* (Lynchburg, VA: H. E. Howard, 1990); Leslie J. Gordon-Burr, "Storms of Indignation: The Art of Andersonville as Postwar Propaganda," *Georgia Historical Quarterly* 75 (1991): 587–600; Joseph P. Cangemi and Casimir J. Kowalski, eds., *Andersonville Prison: Lessons in Organizational Failure* (Lanham, MD: University Press of America, 1992); Louis A. Brown, *The Salisbury Prison: A Case Study of Confederate Military Prisons, 1861–1865* (Wilmington, NC: Broadfoot, 1992); Marvel, *Andersonville*; George Levy, *To Die in Chicago: Confederate Prisoners at Camp Douglas, 1862–1865* (Gretna, LA: Pelican, 1999); Dale Fetzer and Bruce Mowday, *Unlikely Allies: Fort Delaware's Prison Community in the Civil War* (Mechanicsburg, PA: Stackpole Books, 2000); David R. Bush, "Interpreting the Latrines of the Johnson's Island Civil War Military Prison," *Historical Archeology* 34 (2000): 62–78; Benton McAdams, *Rebels at Rock Island* (DeKalb: Northern Illinois University Press, 2000); Michael P. Gray, *The Business of Captivity: Elmira and Its Civil War Prison* (Kent, OH: Kent State University Press, 2001); Michael Horigan, *Elmira: Death Camp of the North* (Mechanicsburg, PA: Stackpole Books, 2002); Robert S. Davis, *Ghosts and Shadows of Andersonville: Essays on the Secret Social Histories of America's Deadliest Prison* (Macon, GA: Mercer University Press, 2006); Glenn M. Robins, "Race, Repatriation, and Galvanized Rebels: Union Prisoners and the Exchange Question in Deep South Prison Camps," *Civil War History* 53 (2007): 117–40; John K. Derden, *The World's Largest Prison: The Story of Camp Lawton* (Macon, GA: Mercer University Press, 2012); and Evan A. Kutzler, "Captive Audiences: Sound, Silence, and Listening in Civil War Prisons," *Journal of Social History* 48 (2014): 239–63.

42. James M. McPherson, *Battle Cry of Freedom* (New York: Ballantine Books, 1988), 791–802; David Goldfield, *America Aflame: How the Civil War Created a Nation* (New York: Bloomsbury Press, 2011), 321–25.

43. Blight, *Race and Reunion*; Janney, *Remembering the Civil War*. See also Benjamin Cloyd, "Civil War Prisons, Remembrance, and the Promise of Reconciliation," in *Civil War Prisons II*, ed. Michael Gray (Kent, OH: Kent State University Press, forthcoming). There are many excellent works on Civil War remembrance—two recent articles are excellent starting points to the field. See Robert Cook, "The Quarrel Forgotten? Toward a Clearer Understanding of Sectional Reconciliation,"

This is starting to happen. A work by Charles Sanders, Jr., *While in the Hands of the Enemy: Military Prisons of the Civil War,* probes the prison tragedy in an attempt at a more precise accounting of responsibility for the miserable treatment of prisoners of war by both sides. He finds that "although organizational incompetence and the absence of resources certainly contributed to the horrors in the camps, the roots of Civil War prisoners' suffering and death lay in decisions and directives that were deliberately chosen and implemented by Union and Confederate leaders."[44] Sanders' work represents a return to the original roots of the prison controversy, which began largely out of the outraged search for responsibility. But this time, instead of privileging either the North or South, Sanders refuses to excuse or find guiltless either the Lincoln or Davis administrations for their "deliberately chosen" treatment of prisoners of war. Not everyone accepts his position, however. James Gillispie's *Andersonvilles of the North: The Myths and Realities of Northern Treatment of Civil War Confederate Prisoners* gives a much needed modern look at the Union prison system and asserts that the prevalence of disease—the major killer of Civil War prisoners of war—cannot be blamed on the Union authorities. Certainly "Northern officials were far from perfect," but Gillispie argues convincingly that "Federal prisoner of war policies and conditions in their prisons were quite humane and enlightened for the time."[45] We seem to have come full circle, with the Union once more at least relatively exonerated. Both scholars are thorough, fair, and determined in their pursuit of the topic. So who is right? The answer depends on which part of the myth of Civil War prisons one prefers. Despite the valuable insights provided by both Sanders and Gillispie, there remains more than a faint echo of the enduring influence of the old myth of human culpability in both works. The peculiar combination of the older myth of deliberate responsibility and the newer myth of objective universality still fails to satisfy. The essential problem with the myth of Civil War prisons is that it challenges us to explain what seems unresolved but, in fact, is already known. We know the reasons why the prisoners died. No matter which of the root causes is emphasized, their deaths were, are, and always will be tragic. The real question seems to be, why do we have so much trouble admitting that we know? The debate over Civil War prisons seems repetitive. But in the most important ways it is only beginning.

Kantor's novel sparked renewed interest in visiting Andersonville during the late 1950s and beyond. The four-year-long Civil War Centennial and the ongoing relevance of the issue of the treatment of prisoners of war during the Vietnam War (1955–75) combined the historical significance and commercial potential of Civil War prisons with the national desire to, once again, find (or make) meaning out of

---

Journal of the Civil War Era 6 (September 2016): 413–36; and Nina Silber, "Reunion and Reconciliation, Reviewed and Reconsidered," *Journal of American History* 103 (June 2016): 59–83.

44. Sanders, *While in the Hands of the Enemy*, 298.

45. Gillispie, *Andersonvilles of the North*, 245–46.

suffering.[46] In 1970, Andersonville became Andersonville National Historic Site. The National Park Service was tasked with, according to the U.S. Senate's statement justifying the creation of the new vision of Andersonville, the presentation of "a memorial" to "all Americans who have served their country, at home and abroad, and suffered the loneliness and anguish of captivity. It is the undaunted spirit of men such as these that keeps America the Nation that it is."[47] The attraction of a more patriotic remembrance of the Civil War prison tragedy is undeniable. It reached an apex with the 1998 opening of the National Prisoner of War Museum at Andersonville. The language of the dedication panel in the museum's lobby is inspiring. Words such as "sacrifice," "courage," "free," and "liberty" assert a confident purpose to the contributions made by every generation of American prisoners of war. The transformation of Andersonville from the epicenter of Civil War bitterness to a common symbol of American appreciation for sacrifice and service is nothing short of remarkable. There is beauty and hope in the power of unity to overcome the divisions of the past. And as is evident in the contemporary commemorations at Andersonville, there is an urgent human need to pay tribute to the disappearing generations of warrior-POWs from World War II, Korea, and Vietnam. The new patriotic remembrance of Civil War prisons seems more satisfying than the older versions of the myth.[48] But it could not exist without them. Each evolving version of the myth fits the needs of the present. In the end, the patriotic remembrance is not a solution to the perplexing legacy of Civil War prisons—it is only the current and outermost layer of the myth.

The tragedy of Civil War prisons has had a positive effect. The standard of treatment of prisoners of war, at least on paper, has been clarified and codified over the years. Lincoln's adoption of the Lieber Code in 1863, a policy designed to promote the ethical conduct of war, might be the strongest statement of the president's "humane intentions" toward Confederate prisoners of war. And echoes of the Lieber Code can be seen in the Hague and Geneva Conventions.[49] It is true that exploring the history of prisoners who endured inspires the hope that such suffering can be avoided in the future. But to claim that a unified legacy of American prisoners of war exists is too much. We have already seen that "the gift of liberty" was and is contested. And as the Civil War long ago revealed, and the ongoing demands of fighting terrorism continue to remind, when under pressure, pragmatism usually trumps humanitarianism. The suspicion persists that despite our increasingly elegant constructions of humane standards of behavior, we are always on the edge of abandoning them. Deep down the myth of Civil War prisons is about regret. There has been, and will continue to be, a sorrow that the Civil War—and certainly the suffering experienced by

---

46. Cloyd, *Haunted by Atrocity*, 138, 144–50, 164–67.

47. 91 Cong. Rec. S35,403 (Oct. 7, 1970).

48. Cloyd, *Haunted by Atrocity*, 164–79.

49. Gillispie, *Andersonvilles of the North*, 104, 196. See also John Fabian Witt, *Lincoln's Code: The Laws of War in American History* (New York: Free Press, 2012).

prisoners of war confirms this—was in part a failure whether it ended in victory or defeat. The use of the word "legacy" as a critical component of the myth of Civil War prisons is in part about healing from this failure, both then and now. No amount of impatience or criticism should distract from the reality that even more than 150 years has not yet been long enough to recover from resentment. It might take much longer yet. For generations the myth of Civil War prisons has been—and it still is—a crutch (and do not forget that crutches can be weapons too). It allows us to bear the burden of responsibility for what happened inside the prisons of the Civil War, and many other places, at many other times, until we are more ready to recognize and forgive the past, and perhaps even ourselves.

As we have seen, neither the traditional Northern nor Southern interpretation of the prisoner-of-war controversy fully correlates with historical evidence. The largely anecdotal evidence on which these myths were based was selectively created and embellished to serve the personal and sectional needs of remembrance. Once constructed, these myths hardened into layers over time and not only formed the lenses through which each side viewed the prisons but also became part of the arsenal in the continuing conflict over the meaning of the entire war. Consequently, removing such distortions to get a fresh and more accurate glimpse of the causes, events, and legacy of the prisoner-of-war camps has been, and remains, a daunting task.

6. The Lost Causers' Favorite Target: Grant the Butcher

Edward H. Bonekemper, III

[Grant] is a butcher and is not fit to be at the head of an army. . . . He loses two men to the enemy's one. He has no management, no regard for life.[1]
—*Mary Todd Lincoln*

It was not enough to idolize Robert E. Lee; Ulysses S. Grant's reputation had to be destroyed.[2]
—*Joan Waugh*

It is an article of faith among most students of the Civil War that Lee was the greatest general of the war, if not American history. Any bookstore's Civil War shelf will carry titles such as *The Genius of Robert E. Lee*, and, of course, Ken Burns' popular series was worshipful of the general to the point that Lee himself would have dismissed the man as a sycophant. Lee's reputation is not completely unearned. He had a chain of successes that no other Confederate general was able to come close to matching. The problem, however, that the Lee cult has to overcome is that in the end he was defeated. It is difficult to argue that someone was the greatest when he was forced to surrender his army and return home to an occupied capital in defeat. To counter this reality, the myth has arisen that his conqueror, Ulysses S. Grant, was simply a butcher who indiscriminately drove men to their deaths with no skill or strategic sense, just an understanding that Lee would run out of men first. Thus, Lee's reputation as the great fencer remains intact. The problem with this interpretation is that it is simply not true. Modern Civil War historians point to the strategy and tactics of both men and, perhaps most importantly, the numbers of men under their command and their respective casualty rates. Grant was a better strategist and tactician than he is given credit for, and Lee's great successes disappeared the first time he met an opponent who was not inherently flawed.

---

1. Daniel Mark Epstein, *The Lincolns: Portrait of a Marriage* (New York: Ballantine Books, 2009), 431; David Herbert Donald, *Lincoln* (New York: Simon and Schuster, 1995), 515.

2. Joan Waugh, *U. S. Grant: American Hero, American Myth* (Chapel Hill: University of North Carolina Press, 2009), 186.

The protagonists. Confederate General Robert E. Lee and Union General Ulysses S. Grant. When Grant was promoted to commander of all Union military forces in 1864, the Northern public wanted to see its great general defeat the South's strategic master. Images courtesy of the Library of Congress.

Grant's Civil War Career

Throughout the Civil War, the armies under Ulysses S. Grant played crucial roles in the Union victory. Grant has justly been credited as one of the great leaders of American military history. Early in the war, in February 1862, Grant led a combined army-navy operation that captured Forts Henry and Donelson on the Tennessee and Cumberland rivers, respectively. That victory resulted in Union control of both rivers; the fall of Nashville; Confederate abandonment of vital Columbus, Kentucky, on the Mississippi River; and the surrender of a fourteen-thousand-man army. As a result of such achievements, Grant became a national hero.

Two months later, Grant was caught by surprise at Shiloh, Tennessee, but saved his army and turned possible defeat into a stunning victory that foiled a grand Rebel offensive. Despite that victory, "Bloody Shiloh," which produced more than seventeen hundred Union soldiers killed and more than eight thousand seriously wounded, resulted in the first widespread criticism of Grant's generalship. The *New York Times* blamed "the massacre at Shiloh" on "drunkenness, or incompetency, or both" and claimed that his earlier promotions were based solely on Grant's ability of "sounding his own trumpet."[3]

In mid-1863, Grant conducted one of the greatest campaigns in U.S. military history—his famous and decisive Vicksburg Campaign. His goal was to capture Vicksburg, the last significant Confederate bastion on the Mississippi. After several unsuccessful efforts, Grant launched a brilliant, risky initiative. He marched his troops down the west bank of the river, conducted a major amphibious crossing into Mississippi, won five battles in eighteen days while outnumbered in enemy country, besieged Vicksburg, and accepted the surrender of the city and a thirty-thousand-man Rebel army. The Mississippi was now totally in Federal hands. For the second time, Grant was a national hero. Admiration for these masterstrokes was equally wholehearted more than a century after the fall of Vicksburg. The U.S. Army Field Manual 100–5 (May 1986) describes the Vicksburg Campaign as "the most brilliant campaign ever fought on American soil" and states, "It exemplifies the qualities of a well-conceived, violently executed offensive plan."[4]

That autumn, President Abraham Lincoln named Grant commander of most Western Union forces and sent him to save a hungry and semi-besieged Union army. Following the Battle of Chickamauga, the Union Army of the Cumberland was trapped in Chattanooga, Tennessee. Grant established a "cracker" (supply) line within five days of his arrival, organized reinforcements, captured Lookout Mountain and Missionary Ridge, and broke out of Chattanooga within a month. He sent Confederate General Braxton Bragg's Army of Tennessee scurrying back to Georgia at a cost of almost six thousand Union casualties—to the Rebels' almost seven thousand. Although compelled to attack a fortified enemy who held the high ground, he had achieved another major offensive victory with reasonable casualties. That action set the stage for William T. Sherman's successful Atlanta Campaign of 1864. Although less well known than Gettysburg, Chattanooga is considered by many historians to be one of the key turning points of the war.[5] Grant's Chattanooga victory also made him a national hero for the third time.

Grant triumphed in the Western and Middle theaters, suffering around 37,000 casualties (the largest number while on the defensive at Shiloh, where he negligently ignored the possibility of a surprise enemy attack), and imposed 84,000 casualties on the enemy.

Having ended Confederate control in the Mississippi Valley and eastern Tennessee, as well as winning Lincoln's confidence in his willingness to fight and his ability

3. "Our Washington Correspondence," *New York Times*, April 22, 1862.

4. Al W. Goodwin, Jr., "Grant's Mississippi Gamble," *America's Civil War* 7 (1994): 50–56 at 54; Terrence J. Winschel, "Vicksburg: 'Thank God. The Father of Waters Again Goes Unvexed to the Sea,'" *America's Civil War* 16 (2003): 18–19 at 19.

5. Gordon Rhea, Richard Rollins, Stephen Sears, and John Y. Simon, "What Was Wrong with the Army of the Potomac?," *North & South* 4 (2001): 12–18 at 18.

to achieve victory, Grant was summoned to Washington in March 1864. The Union Army of the Potomac had squandered opportunities to pursue Lee's Army of Northern Virginia after the battles of Antietam (1862) and Gettysburg (1863), and it had recoiled after the first major battle of each offensive campaign against Lee (the Seven Days' Battles, Fredericksburg, and Chancellorsville). That army had demonstrated, in the judgment of one Civil War historian, "superior numbers and equipment alone did not win the war. Success was contingent upon the outcome of battles and campaigns, and the Army of the Potomac only became successful when it found someone who could use its resources to the utmost."[6]

In recognition of Grant's many successes, Congress approved a special gold medal for him, and he was promoted to lieutenant general and commander of all Union armies. The imminence of the presidential election made quick victory even more imperative.[7] The pressure was on Grant to produce early, positive results. He organized a coordinated national strategy, kept pressure on the Confederates on all fronts, and drove Lee's army back to Richmond in a bloody campaign through the Wilderness, Spotsylvania Court House, the North Anna River, Cold Harbor, and Petersburg. Grant had succinctly instructed Major General George Meade, who commanded the Army of the Potomac, "Lee's army will be your objective point. Wherever Lee goes, there you will go also."[8]

Although Meade led the main Union army in Virginia, Grant was the overall commander of the movement, known as the Overland Campaign. It was a long, grinding campaign and became the source of most future criticism of Grant. It did, however, lead to overall victory, and Grant understood something his predecessors did not: the sooner the war ended, the fewer casualties there would be in the long run.[9] This same strategy would be strongly embraced by American leadership in the Second World War. In the spring of 1865, Grant's troops cut off the last open railroad into Petersburg, broke through Lee's lines, outraced what was left of the fleeing Army of Northern Virginia, and compelled its surrender at Appomattox Courthouse on April 9, 1865.

Ultimately, dual Union campaigns resulted in the capture of Atlanta by Sherman in September 1864 and the surrender of Robert E. Lee's army to Grant. By the end of 1864, Grant's multi-front national campaign had succeeded in capturing Atlanta, Savannah, Mobile, and the Shenandoah Valley; reelecting President Lincoln; virtually destroying the Army of Tennessee at Franklin and Nashville; and laying the groundwork for the final defeat of Lee and the Confederacy.

---

6. Ibid.

7. Russell F. Weigley, *The American Way of War: A History of United States Military Strategy and Policy* (New York: Macmillan, 1973), 128–29.

8. John Y. Simon et al., eds., *The Papers of Ulysses Grant*, 32 vols. (Carbondale: Southern Illinois University Press, 1967–2012), 1:xv, 10:274.

9. Waugh, *U. S. Grant*, 88.

Moreover, Grant's generous terms of surrender at Appomattox won him much esteem among the men he defeated. General James Longstreet, who fought against Grant in both Tennessee and Virginia, referred to Grant as a man of "generous heart, a lovable character, a valued friend."[10] Another foe, General John B. Gordon, the infamous post-Reconstruction governor of Georgia, U.S. senator, and Ku Klux Klan leader, wrote that Grant had "truly great qualities—his innate modesty, his freedom from every trace of vain-glory, his magnanimity in victory, his genuine sympathy for his brave and sensitive foemen, will give him a place in history no less renowned and more to be envied than that secured by his triumphs."[11]

Under Grant's leadership the Union army had won the Civil War. Brilliant and dogged in war and magnanimous in victory, he was recognized as a national hero once again and achieved international acclaim for his generalship.

So what happened to Grant's military reputation?

The Myth

Given the economic ruin of the South and its massive manpower losses resulting from the Civil War (one quarter of its white, fighting-aged men were dead), ex-Confederate leaders such as Gordon attempted to justify the war they had started. The resulting Myth of the Lost Cause included assertions that the South never had a chance to win, that the North won by brute force and "total war," and that Robert E. Lee fought bravely, was defeated by sheer numbers, and was one of the greatest generals in history. During the hundred years following the war, the myth took on the aspect of religion, and Lee, Jefferson Davis, and Stonewall Jackson were the holy trinity. It became critical to preserve the image of Lee's near perfection because his reputation was so closely tied to the validity of the Myth of the Lost Cause.

To deify Lee, Lost Cause advocates found it convenient, possibly necessary, to denigrate Grant. Because Confederate soldiers were considered far superior to the Union enemy and their General Lee above reproach, vanquished Rebels had to find reasons elsewhere for the Confederacy's defeat. The primary issue was explaining how Lee ended up losing the war to, of all people, Ulysses S. Grant, the disheveled-looking former shopkeeper and "drunk" who was anything but the image of an elite warrior and cavalier. Advocates of the Myth of the Lost Cause criticized Grant as having barely any military talent and were successful in labeling Grant a "butcher," thereby staining his reputation for over a century.

---

10. James Longstreet, *From Manassas to Appomattox* (Philadelphia: J. B. Lippincourt, 1896; repr., New York: Da Capo Press, 1992), 17.

11. John B. Gordon, *Reminiscences of the Civil War* (Baton Rouge: Louisiana State University Press, 1993), 463–65.

How could Grant have defeated Lee in less than a year in the East and thereby won the Civil War? Lost Cause creators focused primarily on the Overland Campaign and found the reason for his success in the superior resources and manpower of the North. They claimed that Grant won only by brute force and butchered his own troops to achieve that victory.

A classic example of anti-Grant rhetoric is the 1866 attack by Richmond newspaperman Edward Pollard in his book *The Lost Cause*:

> [Grant] was one of the most remarkable accidents of the war. That a man without any marked ability, certainly without genius, without fortune, without influence, should attain the position of leader of all the Federal armies, and stand the most conspicuous person on that side of the war, is a phenomenon which would be inexplicable among any other people than the sensational and coarse mobs of admiration in the North.[12]

This passage seethes with Pollard's contempt for both the victorious Grant and the triumphant North. Its inaccuracies, bias, overstatements, and strange criteria for judging success speak for themselves. But it did set the tone for a century-long criticism of Grant as well as lay the basis for the myth of "the Lost Cause," a term coined by Pollard.

One historian, taking issue with this view of Grant, has noted that the general has been falsely regarded as a "hammerer and a butcher who was often drunk, an unimaginative and ungifted clod who eventually triumphed because he had such overwhelming superiority in numbers that he could hardly avoid winning."[13] Another concurs and laments that Grant "remains a clumsy butcher to many Americans, who look to a warped historical record that draws heavily on the efforts of Lost Cause writers."[14] According to historian Gary Gallagher, Grant acquired the unfortunate and unfair label of "butcher" because of the high number of Union casualties associated with some of his victories. He stands accused of unnecessarily slaughtering his own men in order to achieve victory, thereby promoting the goals of personal ambition.[15]

Actually, the claim that Grant was butchering his own soldiers predated the rise of the Lost Cause myth; it began with his 1864 campaign in Virginia. Southern newspapers referred to him as the "Butcher of the Wilderness."[16] One Southerner

---

12. Edward A. Pollard, *The Lost Cause: A New Southern History of the War of the Confederates* (New York: E. B. Treat, 1866; repr., New York: Gramercy Books, 1994), 509.

13. T. Harry Williams, *McClellan, Sherman and Grant* (New Brunswick, NJ: Rutgers University Press, 1962), 81.

14. Gary W. Gallagher, introduction to *The Myth of the Lost Cause and Civil War History*, by Gary W. Gallagher and Alan T. Nolan (Bloomington: Indiana University Press, 2010), 7.

15. Ibid.

16. "Letter from Richmond," *Memphis Daily Appeal*, June 16, 1864.

said at the time, "We have met a man this time, who either does not know when he is whipped, or who cares not if he loses his *whole* army."[17] The criticism even arose among some on the Union's side. During this campaign, Mary Todd Lincoln, the president's wife, expressed the opinion quoted at the opening of this chapter, namely that Grant, who had no concern whatsoever for the lives of his soldiers, was not fit to command an army. It has been surmised that Mrs. Lincoln might have been miffed because Grant had declined an invitation to a presidential dinner and banquet in order to leave Washington and travel to discuss a coordinated campaign strategy with Sherman.[18] During what came to be called Grant's Overland Campaign, Union Secretary of the Navy Gideon Welles wrote in his diary, "Still there is heavy loss, but we are becoming accustomed to the sacrifice. Grant has not great regard for human life."[19] Soon after the war, a *New York Times* article stated that Grant relied "exclusively on the application of brute masses, in rapid and remorseless blows."[20] A paper presented to the Military Historical Society of Massachusetts by its founder, Harvard-trained historian John C. Ropes, noted that Grant felt a "burning, persistent desire to fight, to attack, in season and out of season, against entrenchments, natural obstacles, what not."[21]

The "butcher" accusations proliferated in the early postwar period. The Confederate guns at Appomattox had barely been stilled and stacked when General Robert E. Lee issued General Order Number 9, his farewell to his troops, on April 10, 1865. He began his brief salute to his soldiers' gallantry by stating, "After four years of arduous service marked by unsurpassed courage and fortitude, the Army of Northern Virginia has been compelled to yield to overwhelming numbers and resources."[22] He did not accuse his victorious opponent of butchery or crass disregard for the lives of the soldiers under his command, but his statement that the Army of Northern Virginia had yielded only to "overwhelming numbers" was the foundation for the myth of Grant, the heavy-handed exploiter of vastly superior forces. In his book of 1866 cited above, Pollard continued in this vein, writing that Grant "contained no spark of military genius; his idea of war was to the last degree rude—no strategy, the mere application of the vis inertia [force of inertia]; he had none of that quick perception on the field

---

17. Herman Hattaway, "The Changing Face of Battle," *North & South* 4 (2001): 34–43 at 42.

18. Epstein, *The Lincolns*, 431; Donald, *Lincoln*, 515.

19. Gideon Welles, *Diary of Gideon Welles* (Boston: Houghton Mifflin, 1911), 2:45. The similarity of Welles' and Mary Todd Lincoln's language might have resulted from the closeness of the first lady and Welles' wife, Mary Jane. Epstein, *The Lincolns*, 431.

20. William Swinton, *Campaigns of the Army of the Potomac* (New York: Richardson, 1866), 440.

21. John C. Ropes, "Grant's Campaign in Virginia in 1864," *Papers of the Military Historical Society of Massachusetts*, 4:495, quoted in Gordon C. Rhea, *Cold Harbor: Grant and Lee, May 23–June 6, 1864* (Baton Rouge: Louisiana State University Press, 2002), xii.

22. Robert E. Lee, General Order 9, Army of Northern Virginia, Confederate States of America, Gilder Lehrman Institute of American History Collection.

of action which decides it by sudden strokes; he had no conception of battle beyond the momentum of numbers."[23]

Beginning in the 1870s, former Confederate officers, who further promoted and popularized the Myth of the Lost Cause, played a prominent role in criticizing Grant—especially in comparison to Lee. Trusted Lee lieutenant, the colorful General Jubal Early wrote in 1872, "Shall I compare General Lee to his successful antagonist? As well compare the great pyramid which rears its majestic proportions in the Valley of the Nile, to a pygmy perched on Mount Atlas."[24] One of Lee's staff officers and his lone aide at Appomattox Courthouse, Colonel Walter Herron Taylor, wrote in his memoirs,

> It is well to bear in mind the great inequality between the two contending armies, in order that one may have a proper appreciation of the difficulties which beset General Lee . . . and realize the extent to which his brilliant genius . . . proved more than a match for brute force, as illustrated in the hammering policy of General Grant.[25]

Grant's stance on racial issues also earned the ire of Southerners. While commander of the army, Grant suspended prisoner exchanges due to the threat of the Confederate government to execute white officers leading black soldiers and to enslave their soldiers. As president of the United States, Grant was a strong advocate for blacks' civil rights in both the North and South. He favored greater use of Federal troops to protect blacks from the Ku Klux Klan and widespread violence in the South. He wrote, "As time passes, people, even of the South, will begin to wonder how it was possible that their ancestors ever fought for or justified institutions which acknowledged the right of property in man."[26]

Grant's entrance into presidential politics also brought about criticism of his military leadership. In the 1868 presidential election, Grant's status as "the man who won the Civil War" was his chief attraction. If the Democratic Party had any hope of defeating him, his military record had to be impugned. What better way to do this than claim that he had a complete disregard for the lives of those who were his strongest supporters, the Union veterans?

The 1880s publication of *Century Magazine*'s series *Battles and Leaders of the Civil War*, containing the recollections of the war's participants, provided former

---

23. Pollard, *Lost Cause*, 510.

24. Gary W. Gallagher, "'Upon Their Success Hang Momentous Interests': Generals," in *Why the Confederacy Lost*, by Gabor Boritt (New York: Oxford University Press, 1992), 79–108 at 90–91, quoting Jubal A. Early, *The Campaigns of Gen. Robert E. Lee: An Address by Lieut. General Jubal A. Early, before Washington and Lee University, January 19, 1872* (Baltimore: Murphy, 1872), 44.

25. Walter H. Taylor, *General Lee: His Campaigns in Virginia, 1861–1865, with Personal Reminiscences* (Norfolk, VA: Nusbaum Books, 1906; repr., Lincoln: University of Nebraska Press, 1994), 231.

26. Ulysses S. Grant, *Personal Memoirs of U.S. Grant* (New York: Jenkins and McCowan, 1885), 1:169–70.

Confederates with another opportunity to assail Grant. One ex-Rebel general wrote, "What a part at least of his own men thought about General Grant's methods was shown by the fact that many of the prisoners taken during the [Overland] campaign complained bitterly of the 'useless butchery' to which they were subjected."[27] Indeed, it is true that many Northerners joined Southerners in glorifying Lee and his army and in attacking Grant as a butcher in the pages of *Century*.[28]

In the mid-twentieth century, another Richmond newspaper reporter turned historian, Douglas Southall Freeman, also criticized Grant. Freeman and the graduate students he trained dominated Civil War historiography for more than fifty years. In his four-volume *R. E. Lee*, he faulted Grant for hammering Lee's forces instead of maneuvering more. But even Freeman conceded that Grant's efforts had not been in vain: "Lee did not lose the battles but he did not win the campaign. . . . And in some subtle fashion General Grant infused into his well-seasoned troops a confidence they had never previously possessed."[29] A disciple of Freeman, Clifford Dowdey was harder on Grant than Freeman. He described Grant as a "boring-in type of attacker, who usually scorned finesse."[30] Later he wrote, "Absorbing appalling casualties, [Grant] threw his men in wastefully as if their weight was certain to overrun any Confederates in their path. In terms of generalship, the new man gave Lee nothing to fear," and described Grant as "an opponent who took no count of his losses."[31]

In his 1943 book, Virginian Robert Douthat Meade wrote, "In the spring of 1864 Grant took personal command of the Union Army in Virginia and, with a heavily superior force, began his bludgeoning assaults on Lee's weakened but grimly determined troops."[32] A 1953 dust jacket on noted historian Bruce Catton's book said (contrary to Catton's own views), "[The Army of the Potomac's] leader was General Ulysses S. Grant, a seedy little man who instilled no enthusiasm in his followers and little respect in his enemies."[33]

Although he relied on Catton's work that extolled Grant's military talents and personal attributes, William McFeely treated Grant with much less sympathy in

27. E. M. Law, "From the Wilderness to Cold Harbor," in *Battles and Leaders of the Civil War*, by Robert Underwood Johnson and Clarence Clough Buel (Secaucus, NJ: Castle, 1884–88; repr., New York: Thomas Yoseloff, 1956), 4:118–44 at 143.

28. Richard M. McMurry, *Two Great Rebel Armies: An Essay in Confederate Military History* (Chapel Hill: University of North Carolina Press, 1989), 50.

29. Douglas Southall Freeman, *R. E. Lee* (New York: Charles Scribner's Sons, 1935), 3:433–34, 447.

30. Clifford Dowdey, *Lee's Last Campaign: The Story of Lee and His Men against Grant, 1864* (New York: Little, Brown, 1960; repr., Wilmington, NC: Broadfoot, 1988), 93.

31. Clifford Dowdey, *Lee* (New York: Little, Brown, 1965; repr., Gettysburg, PA: Stan Clark Military Books, 1991), 433.

32. Robert Douthat Meade, *Judah P. Benjamin: Confederate Statesman* (1943; repr., Baton Rouge: Louisiana State University Press, 2001), 284–85.

33. Bruce Catton, *The Army of the Potomac: A Stillness at Appomattox* (New York: Doubleday, 1953).

a 1981 biography. McFeely's portrayal of Grant was of a man who was unmoved by the death around him. He claimed that "Grant's strategy was to make sure more Southerners than Northerners were killed. It was a matter of simple arithmetic." Of the Overland Campaign, McFeely wrote, "In May 1864 Ulysses Grant began a vast campaign that was a hideous disaster in every respect save one—it worked. He led his troops into the Wilderness and there produced a nightmare of inhumanity and inept military strategy that ranks with the worst such episodes in the history of warfare."[34] A later historian cited McFeely's work as a biography written by an academic historian who was influenced by the Vietnam War and denigrated Grant's critical role in the Union victory.[35]

Even innocuous sources reinforced the myth with irrelevant or inaccurate statements. Among these was *Generals in Gray* (1959). In a short Lee biography, it inaccurately stated, "Casualties of almost three to one in [Lee's] favor, and the advantage of fighting behind entrenched lines, however, could not compensate for the undiminished resources and determination of the Federals."[36] Even though he wrote that "Grant was the greatest general of the war," distinguished British military historian John Keegan nevertheless inaccurately commented, "In the West, Grant won success by risk-taking and unceasing aggressiveness, but his soldiers paid the price. Most of Grant's battles were costly in casualties."[37]

Another historian explained Grant's reputation problem:

> Grant enjoyed little of the "glory" for his contributions to the [Army of the Potomac's] ultimate success, and was the recipient of much of the blame for the "disasters." Despite moving continually forward from the Wilderness to Petersburg and Richmond, ultimately to Appomattox, and executing the campaign that ended the war in the East, Grant has received little credit, and is most remembered for the heavy losses of Cold Harbor, which tagged him with the reputation of a "butcher."[38]

A good current example of piling on Grant is the *Oxford Encyclopedia of the Civil War* (2011), which claimed that the Union army took 75,000 casualties in the six-week

---

34. William S. McFeely, *Grant: A Biography* (New York: W. W. Norton, 1981), xii, 114–15, 122, 157, 165.

35. Jean Edward Smith, *Grant* (New York: Simon and Schuster, 2001), 14–15.

36. Ezra J. Warner, *Generals in Gray: Lives of the Confederate Commanders* (Baton Rouge: Louisiana State University Press, 1959), 182.

37. John Keegan, *American Civil War: A Military History* (New York: Alfred A. Knopf, 2009), 329; John Keegan, "A Brit Rates Our Generals," *Civil War Times* 48 (2009): 54–59 at 58. In fact, Grant's "Western" casualties were almost fifty thousand fewer than his enemies' casualties. See the discussion below of Grant's casualties.

38. Gregory A. Mertz, "No Turning Back: The Battle of the Wilderness," *Blue & Gray Magazine* 12 (1995): 8–20, 48–50 at 50.

Overland Campaign and at Cold Harbor lost 8,000 men in ten minutes ("about 1,000 per minute").[39] Both numbers are inaccurate and excessive. Grant's casualties in the Overland Campaign were about 55,000. During the brief, disastrous charge at Cold Harbor, Grant probably incurred about 3,500 casualties. His total casualties for the entire day were about 6,000.[40]

The "butcher" label, like most myths, does not go away easily. According to one commentator, "Grant has often been depicted as a butcher whose only strategy was to overcome the smaller enemy force by attrition, knowing that he could replace his losses more easily than Lee."[41] Another notes, "The ghost of 'Grant the Butcher' still haunts Civil War lore."[42] And another historian reluctantly concluded, "Grant the butcher is a hard myth to extinguish."[43]

Undermining the Myth

Although remnants of the "Grant the Butcher" myth continue to appear from time to time, historians have exposed many of its flaws. The following is a summary of the pendulum swing favorable to Grant that has largely dispelled the anti-Grant myth among those who study Civil War history—if not the general public.

A leading Civil War historian, James McPherson, provided this insight into Grant and his memoirs:

> Grant's strength of will, his determination to do the best he could with what he had, his refusal to give up or to complain about the cruelty of fate help explain the success both of his generalship and his memoirs. These qualities were by no means typical among Civil War generals. Many of them spent more energy clamoring for reinforcements or explaining why they could not do what they were ordered to do than they did in trying to carry out their orders.[44]

As he was dying from throat cancer and in order to provide a secure financial future for his family, Grant wrote his remarkably lucid and revealing *Memoirs* in 1884–85.

---

39. William L. Barney, *The Oxford Encyclopedia of the Civil War* (New York: Oxford University Press, 2011), 152–53.

40. See the exhaustive study of these casualties in Gordon Rhea, "Cold Harbor: Anatomy of a Battle," *North & South* 5 (2002): 40–62 at 59–61; and Rhea, *Cold Harbor*.

41. Don Lowry, *No Turning Back: The Beginning of the End of the Civil War, March–June 1864* (New York: Hippocrene Books, 1962), 519.

42. Rhea, *Cold Harbor*, xi.

43. E. B. Long, "Ulysses S. Grant for Today," in *Ulysses S. Grant: Essays and Documents*, ed. David L. Wilson and John Y. Simon (Carbondale: University of Illinois Press, 1981), 22.

44. James M. McPherson, "The Unheroic Hero," *New York Review of Books* 46 (February 4, 1999): 16–19 at 16.

Keegan wrote, "If there is a single contemporaneous document which explains 'why the North won the Civil War,' that abiding conundrum of American historical enquiry, it is the *Personal Memoirs of U.S. Grant.*"[45] Grant began writing about the war with four articles for the *Century Magazine* series *Battles and Leaders of the Civil War*. In mid-1884, he wrote articles on Shiloh, Vicksburg, Chattanooga, and the Wilderness. These articles formed the basis for his memoirs.[46]

In his memoirs, Grant noted that Southern historians were creating the Myth of the Lost Cause: "With us, now twenty years after the close of the most stupendous war ever known, we have writers—who profess devotion to the nation—engaged in trying to prove that the Union forces were not victorious; practically, they say, we were slashed around from Donelson to Vicksburg and to Chattanooga; and in the East from Gettysburg to Appomattox, when the physical rebellion gave out from sheer exhaustion."[47] Some pro-Grant studies by former members of Grant's staff also emerged after the war. One of those was by Adam Badeau, a detailed insider's account of Grant's campaigns that stressed the quickness and deception that kept the Confederates off-balance and outnumbered in each separate encounter during his Vicksburg Campaign.[48] Another aide, Horace Porter, offered a sympathetic appraisal of Grant's traits and successes that reflects his closeness to Grant:

> [Grant] was unquestionably the most aggressive fighter in the entire list of the world's famous soldiers. . . . For four years of bloody and relentless war he went steadily forward, replacing the banner of his country upon the territory where it had been hauled down. He possessed in a striking degree every characteristic of the successful soldier. His methods were all stamped with tenacity of purpose, originality, and ingenuity.[49]

Significant praise for Grant, other than from his subordinates and fellow officers, first came from overseas. British military historian and theorist Major General J. F. C. Fuller strongly endorsed the greatness of Grant in books that appeared in 1929 and 1932. He concluded that Grant was a superior strategist, possessed common sense, recognized what needed to be done to win the war, and deserved the major credit for doing so. He found that Lee consistently throughout the war lost a higher percentage of his troops than Grant or other adversaries he faced, and that Lee, much more than

---

45. John Keegan, *The Mask of Command* (New York: Viking, 1987), 202.

46. McPherson, "The Unheroic Hero," 16; John G. Leyden, "Grant Wins Last Battle by Finishing Memoirs," *Washington Times*, March 23, 2002.

47. Ulysses S. Grant, *Personal Memoirs of Ulysses S. Grant* (New York: Charles L. Webster, 1885–86; repr., New York: Cosimo Books, 2007), 61

48. Adam Badeau, *Military History of Ulysses S. Grant, from April, 1861, to April, 1865* (New York: D. Appleton, 1880), 1:203–95.

49. Horace Porter, *Campaigning with Grant* (New York: Century, 1897; repr., New York: Smithmark, 1994), 513.

Grant and for no good reason, sacrificed his troops in frontal assaults and continued to do so until he had no more to sacrifice.[50]

Despite his inaccurately faulting Grant for a supposedly high casualty rate (as we saw above), another Englishman, John Keegan, also praised Grant. Discussing Grant in a 1987 book chapter entitled "Grant and Unheroic Leadership," he praised Grant's fighting skills and concluded, "But in retrospect, great though Grant's generalship is seen to be, it is his comprehension of the nature of the war, and of what could and could not be done by a general within its defining conditions, that seems the more remarkable."[51]

Comprehensive sympathetic treatment of Grant also came in numerous Civil War histories written by Bruce Catton.[52] A contemporary of Catton, T. Harry Williams was a renowned Civil War scholar and also a strong proponent of Grant. Williams found Grant superior to Lee and others in *Lincoln and His Generals* (1952) and to his fellow Union generals in *McClellan, Sherman and Grant* (1962). In the former book, Williams concluded, "Grant was, by modern standards, the greatest general of the Civil War."[53] Similarly, Southerner Shelby Foote described Grant's assets and his liabilities. In a sentence summarizing public reaction to Grant's victories at Forts Henry and Donelson, he caught the essence of Grant: "People saw Grant as the author of this deliverance, the embodiment of the offensive spirit, the man who would strike and keep on striking until this war was won."[54]

Other historians concluded that Grant was responsible for recognizing the North's need to effectively use its superior resources and did so. Hattaway and Jones in their *How the North Won* concluded that Grant's seizure of Forts Henry and Donelson and his approval of Sherman's March to the Sea were decisive events.[55] Even Grant's costly Overland Campaign, the focus of most Lost Cause critics, has been viewed in a more sympathetic manner. A 1986 encyclopedia article on Grant concluded:

> Provided with mammoth resources for the 1864 Virginia campaigning, Grant would go into textbooks as a butcher who slashed and pounded his

---

50. J. F. C. Fuller, *The Generalship of Ulysses S. Grant* (London: J. Murray, 1929); J. F. C. Fuller, *Grant and Lee: A Study in Personality and Generalship* (London: Eyre and Spottiswoodee, 1932).

51. Keegan, *Mask of Command*, 229.

52. Catton first wrote of Grant in the second and third volumes of the famous Civil War trilogy *Mr. Lincoln's Army* (1951), *Glory Road* (1952), and *A Stillness at Appomattox* (1953). Having come to admire Grant above other Civil War generals, Catton then wrote *U.S. Grant and the American Military Tradition* (1954; the bulk of which is entitled "The Great Commander"), *This Hallowed Ground: The Story of the Union Side in the Civil War* (1956), *Grant Moves South* (1960; describing Grant's Civil War career through Vicksburg in glowing terms), and *Grant Takes Command* (1968; taking him through the end of the war).

53. T. Harry Williams, *Lincoln and His Generals* (New York: Alfred A. Knopf, 1952), 312.

54. Shelby Foote, *The Civil War: A Narrative* (New York: Random House, 1956), 1:215.

55. Herman Hattaway and Archer Jones, *How the North Won: A Military History of the Civil War* (1983; repr., Urbana: University of Illinois Press, 1991), ix, xv, 638–39.

way to triumph, heedless of cost. This image is false. . . . Grant sought to outmaneuver rather than outfight [Lee]. . . . He bypassed Lee in mid-June by an artful turning movement toward Petersburg. Frustrated there, Grant employed various indirect offensives that eventually lengthened Lee's lines beyond the breaking point, making inevitable Lee's surrender 9 Apr. 1865. In his most decisive campaign, Grant succeeded not by brute force but by agility, speed, and craft.[56]

In 1992, Gary Gallagher criticized the selectiveness and merits of Early's and others' criticisms of Grant:

Jubal Early, Confederate general and post-Reconstruction governor of South Carolina. Early was a powerful champion of Lost Cause mythology. Image courtesy of the Library of Congress.

> Absent from Early's work, as well as that of other writers who portrayed Grant as a butcher, was any detailed treatment of Grant's brilliant campaign against Vicksburg, his decisive success at Chattanooga, or his other western operations. Moreover, critics failed to grasp that Grant's tactics in 1864 went against his preferred style of campaigning. He fought Lee at every turn primarily because he wished to deny Jefferson Davis the option of shifting Confederate troops from Virginia to Georgia where they might slow Sherman's progress.[57]

The works of Geoffrey Perret and Brooks D. Simpson characterized a return to Catton's sympathetic approach (after McFeely's deviation). Perret praised Grant's

---

56. "Ulysses S. Grant" Patricia L. Faust, ed., *Historical Times Illustrated Encyclopedia of the Civil War* (New York: Harper and Row, 1986), 320.

57. Gallagher, "'Upon Their Success'," 91.

"military genius" and credited him with creating two concepts that the U.S. Army has utilized since: converging columns (Grant's 1864–65 national strategy of simultaneous attacks on a point or area) and wide envelopment (Grant's sweeping around Lee's right flank throughout 1864 and 1865).[58] Simpson described a non-idealized Grant and praised his common sense, imagination, and perseverance. On the issue of Grant's tactics, Simpson concluded:

> He was less successful at shaking the perception that he was a ham-handed tactician who freely wasted the lives of his own men. This reputation was largely based on the pervasive impression of his generalship left by the 1864 campaign in Virginia. That during the Vicksburg and Chattanooga campaigns combined, Grant's forces suffered fewer losses than did Lee's troops at Gettysburg escaped most people's notice; that he was far more frugal with human life than his leading Confederate counterpart . . . is recognized by only a few. He preferred to take prisoners than to slay foes; he emphasized movement and logistics over slugging it out.[59]

Moreover, Grant, who had been a quartermaster in the Mexican War, as opposed to Lee, who served as one of Winfield Scott's top aides and was above the day-to-day drudgery of supplying men, was a master of logistics. He ensured that his armies were as well supplied and well fed as humanly possible. Jean Edward Smith's 2001 book *Grant* is an excellent, sympathetic biography of Grant. Smith points to Grant's decisiveness at Fort Donelson, his Vicksburg Campaign's amphibious crossing, his moving forward after the Wilderness, and his surreptitious crossing of the James River as examples of Grant's greatness. He contends that Grant was the strategic master of his Confederate counterparts, had a lower casualty rate than Lee, and demonstrated his strategic skills by focusing on enemy armies rather than geographic goals.[60]

Indeed, in recent years, detailed studies of specific aspects of the Civil War have also complimented Grant's overall operations and practices. A study of staff use concluded that Grant was unique in finding creative ways to assemble and fully utilize a professional personal staff in a manner that made them "his right hand of command."[61] A study of military intelligence determined that Grant viewed the uncertainty of war as a fertile ground for opportunity, used his own initiative to shift the burden of uncertainty onto the enemy, and was able to prevent his concern about what the enemy

---

58. Geoffrey Perret, *Ulysses S. Grant: Soldier and President* (New York: Random House, 1997), 321–22.

59. Brooks D. Simpson, *Ulysses Grant: Triumph over Adversity, 1822–1865* (New York: Houghton Mifflin, 2000), 463.

60. Smith, *Grant*.

61. R. Steven Jones, *The Right Hand of Command: Use and Disuse of Personal Staffs in the Civil War* (Mechanicsburg, PA: Stackpole Books, 2000), 176–219.

was doing from precluding his taking the offensive.[62] Grant's ideas about army organization, from staff to military intelligence, paved the way for many of the modern military profession's doctrines and practices.

In the six-year period spanning 1994 to 2000, Grant's conduct of the Overland Campaign received exhaustive and generally positive treatment in four comprehensive books by Gordon C. Rhea. He contends that Grant has been unfairly tagged as a "butcher," that his casualties were proportionately less than Lee's, and that Grant was an innovative and effective general who focused on and achieved his strategic objectives.[63] Of Grant's "butcher" reputation, Rhea wrote, "Judging from Lee's record, the rebel commander should have shared in Grant's 'butcher' reputation. After all, Lee lost more soldiers than any other Civil War general, including Grant, and his casualties in three days at Gettysburg exceeded Union casualties for any three consecutive days under Grant's orders."[64]

Alfred Young has produced a definitive, detailed statistical study of Lee's losses in the Overland Campaign. He concludes that Lee's army had a strength of 96,000 men (far exceeding the 78,000 claimed by Major Taylor of Lee's staff), including reinforcements received during the campaign, and its total casualties were 33,646. Young's conclusions are based on book-length, unit-by-unit calculations of strength and casualties.[65] Grant's casualties in that same campaign were 52,788 out of an original complement of 118,000.[66] Comparatively, Grant's predecessors as Army of the Potomac commanders incurred more casualties (about 144,000) than Grant and, except for inflicting heavy casualties on Lee's army, had no concrete results to show for them.[67] They lacked Grant's dogged perseverance. Following their three years of strategic failure, Grant won the war in less than a year. If superiority in resources was the only reason for Grant's Eastern Theater victories, his predecessors should have converted those resources to victories. They did not. One of Grant's strengths was

62. William B. Feis, *Grant's Secret Service: The Intelligence War from Belmont to Appomattox* (Lincoln: University of Nebraska Press, 2002), 267–68.

63. Gordon C. Rhea, *The Battle of the Wilderness, May 5–6, 1864* (Baton Rouge: Louisiana State University Press, 1994); Gordon C. Rhea, *The Battles for Spotsylvania Court House and the Road to Yellow Tavern* (Baton Rouge: Louisiana State University Press, 1997); Gordon C. Rhea, *To the North Anna River: Lee and Grant, May 26–June 3, 1864* (Baton Rouge: Louisiana State University, 2000); Rhea, *Cold Harbor.*

64. Rhea, *Cold Harbor,* xii.

65. Alfred C. Young, III, "Numbers and Losses in the Army of Northern Virginia," *North & South* 3, no. 3 (March 2000): 14–29; Alfred C. Young, III, *Lee's Army during the Overland Campaign: A Numerical Study* (Baton Rouge: Louisiana State University Press, 2013), 15–16, 218–25, 242–43.

66. Edward H. Bonekemper, III, *Grant and Lee: Victorious American and Vanquished Virginian,* rev. ed. (Washington, D.C.: Regnery History, 2012), 301.

67. Charles A. Dana, *Recollections of the Civil War* (1893; repr., New York: Collier Books, 1963), 187–89.

his willingness and ability to marshal all available Union resources and use them to achieve victory.

In the face of all this praise for Grant's generalship, many historians (especially those of the Lost Cause persuasion) have continued to denigrate Grant in order to deify Lee. Therefore, it is necessary to undertake a comprehensive analysis of Grant with a focus on his Civil War record and especially on his alleged butchery of his own troops.[68] Astoundingly, despite the century-long drumbeat of "Grant the Butcher," no one until recently had ever bothered to exhaustively explore the war-long casualties incurred and inflicted by Grant's armies.

Grant's Civil War military exploits included winning crucial campaigns in the Western, Middle, and Eastern theaters; capturing three enemy armies (while no one else on either side captured any); and winning the war.[69] Since Grant had been on the strategic and tactical offensive throughout the war to meet the North's burden of affirmatively winning the war (in contrast, the Confederacy only had to avoid defeat), Grant's armies' casualty records are somewhat surprising. Grant's victorious armies in three theaters suffered 153,642 casualties while imposing 190,760 on the enemy—a positive balance of 37,118.[70] A Grant-Lee comparative analysis reveals that Lee's army's casualty record was unaffordable by the Confederacy. Lee's losing army in a single theater suffered 208,922 casualties while imposing 240,322 on its foes. The outmanned Confederacy simply could not afford 209,000 casualties in a single (losing) theater—55,000 more than Grant's armies suffered in three theaters.[71]

In 2009, another historian briefly and pointedly examined the war-long comparative casualties of Grant and Lee:

> Both [Grant and Lee] presided over campaigns that resulted in huge casualties—significantly more as a percentage of his army's strength in Lee's case. Indeed, the "Grant the Butcher" characterization simply does not stand up to scrutiny. In the five major operations he oversaw before facing Lee in 1864's Overland Campaign (Belmont, Forts Henry and Donelson, Shiloh, Vicksburg and Chattanooga), Grant's losses totaled roughly 35,000 killed, wounded and missing. Lee's pre-Overland Campaign losses, in comparison, approached 90,000. In the Overland and Petersburg campaigns, when Federal armies outnumbered Confederates by about 2-to-1, Grant suffered another 126,500 casualties to Lee's 71,000. With these numbers as a yardstick, Lee must be reckoned the bloodier

---

68. Edward H. Bonekemper, III, *A Victor, Not a Butcher: Ulysses S. Grant's Overlooked Military Genius* (Washington, D.C.: Regnery, 2004); republished as *Ulysses S. Grant: A Victor, Not a Butcher; The Military Genius of the Man Who Won the Civil War* (Washington, D.C.: Regnery, 2010).

69. Ibid., especially 252–63.

70. Ibid., 279–319.

71. Bonekemper, *Grant and Lee*, 434–502.

general—in an absolute sense in the first years of the war and a relative sense during the 1864–65 campaigns.[72]

In major battles studied by two casualty experts, Lee's army suffered about 121,000 killed and wounded, while Grant's armies suffered about 94,000 killed and wounded. In those major battles, they concluded, Lee's army suffered an average of about 20 percent killed and wounded in each battle, while Grant's armies suffered about 18 percent killed and wounded.[73]

Ulysses Grant got off to a bad start among Civil War and postwar participants and historians, but his military accomplishments have received increasing, if somewhat erratic, recognition since about 1930. One of the significant ramifications of Grant's being labeled a butcher by many historians is that his successes have been seriously slighted. Civil War historians have reexamined this issue, and many have concluded that Grant's aggressive but creative approach to the war was consistent with the North's need for an affirmative victory. Indeed, far from being the butcher of the battlefield, Grant determined what the North needed to do to win the war and did it. Grant's record of unparalleled tactical and strategic success—including Forts Henry and Donelson, Shiloh, Port Gibson, Raymond, Jackson, Champion's Hill, Big Black River, Vicksburg, Chattanooga, the Wilderness, Spotsylvania Court House, Petersburg, and Appomattox—establishes him as the greatest general of the Civil War. Serious historical reestablishment of his multi-theater, war-winning record continues.

---

72. Gary W. Gallagher, "Why Doesn't Grant Get the Love?," *Civil War Times* 48 (2009): 20–21 at 21.

73. Grady McWhiney and Perry D. Jamieson, *Attack and Die: Civil War Military Tactics and the Southern Heritage* (Tuscaloosa: University of Alabama Press, 1982), 19, 24, 25, 158.

7. Marching through Georgia: The Myth of Sherman's Total War

Wesley Moody

> The sum of these [Sherman's] villainies has passed into Northern history as a weight of martial glory. But the day will yet come when the hero of such a story, instead of enjoying as now the plaudits of ferocious and cowardly mobs, will obtain the execrations of civilized mankind.[1]
> —*Edward A. Pollard, Richmond newspaper editor, 1866*

> [Sherman] was unnecessarily cruel, bringing hunger and misery to innocent people. He used terror as a weapon of war.[2]
> —*John M. Gibson, Civil War author, 1961*

One of the most cherished myths in Civil War history is that of General William Tecumseh Sherman and the destruction he inflicted across Georgia and South Carolina. Not only did it take Georgia and South Carolina nearly one hundred years to recover from the devastation, but it changed the nature of warfare by inventing what twentieth-century historians termed "total war."[3] According to this narrative, Sherman and his army laid waste to a large portion of the Southeast in an attempt to bring the war to Southern civilians. He wanted to make them feel the pain of the war they supported in order to break their will to resist and sought to destroy the infrastructure that supported their rebellion. Sherman's army left a fifty-mile-wide streak of blackened earth behind as the army marched across the South. They looted civilian property and burned everything in their path, including the entire city of Columbia, South Carolina. Only the brick fireplaces remained as lone symbols of what had existed before the Yankee hordes had marched through. This was a new type of warfare. Prior to the appearance of the brutal Sherman onto the stage, war was a chivalrous affair fought

---

1. Edward A. Pollard, *The Lost Cause* (New York: E. B. Treat, 1866; repr., New York: Random House, 1994), 612.

2. John M. Gibson, *Those 163 Days: A Southern Account of Sherman's March from Atlanta to Raleigh* (New York: Bramhall House, 1961), 11.

3. John B. Walters, "General Sherman and Total War," *Journal of Southern History* 14 (1948): 447–80.

General William T. Sherman. The Ohio-born West Point graduate was an obscure figure in 1860 but was an international celebrity by the war's end. Image courtesy of the Library of Congress.

between armies and with the exception of taxes and conscription, civilians were rarely bothered.[4]

This popular narrative has found its way into most textbooks, popular histories, and scholarly works on other aspects of the war. The myth was enshrined in popular culture with the 1939 movie *Gone with the Wind* and in the controversial, but very popular, 1915 film *The Birth of a Nation.* Although Sherman had other accomplishments that helped bring victory to the Union cause, he is mostly remembered for the "March to the Sea" and his statement "War is Hell."[5] Although this view of General Sherman as the brutal total warrior seems nearly universally accepted, historians who specialize in the Western Theater of the Civil War and biographers of the general have moved away from it.[6] Mark Grimsley, the accepted specialist of Union policy toward Southern civilians, shows that Sherman's actions do not come close to the brutality claimed in the myths.[7]

There are two major aspects of this myth. The first is the destructiveness of Sherman's March to the Sea. To be sure, there was destruction. This was a war, and in

4. The best examples of these myths by twentieth-century authors can be found in Earl S. Miers, *The General Who Marched to Hell: Sherman and the Southern Campaign* (New York: Alfred Knopf, 1951); Gibson, *Those 163 Days*; and Walters, "General Sherman and Total War."

5. Wesley Moody, *Demon of the Lost Cause: Sherman and Civil War History* (Columbia: University of Missouri Press, 2011), 1–2.

6. For example, Lee Kennett, *Sherman: A Soldier's Life* (New York: HarperCollins, 2002); Robert L. O'Connell, *Fierce Patriot: The Tangled Lives of William Tecumseh Sherman* (New York: Random House, 2014); and John F. Marszalek, *Sherman: A Soldier's Passion for Order* (New York: Macmillan, 1993).

7. Mark Grimsley, *The Hard Hand of War: Union Military Policy toward Southern Civilians, 1861–1865* (Cambridge: Cambridge University Press, 1997), 190–203.

no time in history has it been pleasant to be in the path or the wake of an army on the march. This is one of the reasons this is a persistent myth. There was destruction in Georgia and South Carolina. No one wanted to be along the route of Sherman's army in 1864–65. The question remains, however: What was the nature, purpose, and extent of the destruction? The second aspect of this myth is that the type of warfare Sherman is accused of waging was somehow unique and new, that Sherman had instituted a new type of warfare often called "total war." The idea that civilians and a country's infrastructure were somehow off limits before Sherman showed the world a new way is almost ludicrous. History is unfortunately filled with many examples that long predate the American Civil War.

General Sherman Takes Atlanta

William T. Sherman had risen from obscurity at the start of the war and overcome many obstacles during the conflict to become one of the leading generals of the United States by 1864. His friendship with, loyalty to, and support of Ulysses Grant not only greatly benefited the Union cause but also made the careers of both men. When Grant was given command of all Union forces, Sherman replaced him as commander of forces in the Western Theater, and would play the key role in Grant's Spring Campaign of 1864. The Confederate army had become skilled at moving forces between theaters of operations in time to meet Union advances. This kept the Union from taking advantage of its numerical superiority. Grant's strategy was for all major Union armies to go on the offensive simultaneously, thus preventing the Confederates from shifting men between fronts. When Grant presented the plan to Lincoln, the president summed it up as only he could have: "If a man can't skin, he must hold a leg while somebody else does."[8]

Grant's strategy was successful. While his forces held the Confederate army under Robert E. Lee in Virginia in place, Sherman was able to drive the second-largest army of the Confederacy out of northern Georgia and capture Atlanta, one of the South's most important railroad junctions and manufacturing centers, on September 2, 1864. This victory helped guarantee Lincoln's reelection in 1864. The day Sherman's army fought the last major battle of the Atlanta campaign was the same day that the Democratic Convention nominated George McClellan as its presidential candidate on the platform that the war was unwinnable.[9]

---

8. John G. Nicolay and John Hay, *Abraham Lincoln: A History* (New York: Century, 1909), 8, 348. President Lincoln's secretaries, Nicolay and Hay launched a minor but complex controversy over whom to credit for the "skinning" quotation. They refuted Grant's version, as stated in his memoirs, that this was Lincoln's statement.

9. The Democratic Party platform was that the Civil War was unwinnable. The party's candidate moderated that by campaigning on the platform that the war was unwinnable with Lincoln as commander in chief. This confusion caused problems for the Democrats in the 1864 campaign.

Sherman would spend the next two months occupying Atlanta and working to prevent the remnants of the Confederate Army of Tennessee, under the command of John Bell Hood, from cutting his supply line, a single railroad line running through the mountains to Chattanooga, Tennessee.

The March

In November 1864, Sherman made his bold move. After much consultation with Grant and the president, Sherman abandoned his supply line and moved toward the interior of Georgia. Sherman's goal was not Georgia but Robert E. Lee and his Army of Northern Virginia. Sherman believed, correctly as events proved, that the war would end when Lee was finished. If Sherman could move a large force to the Atlantic coast, his force could be transported by sea to join Grant and bring the war to a conclusion.[10]

Sherman left the unfinished task of destroying the Confederates' western army to General George H. Thomas. This was a task that the Virginia-born Thomas proved more than suited for. When Sherman reached Savannah the news was waiting that Thomas had won decisive victories over Hood and the Confederate army. The war in the West was all but over. Sherman had taken a huge gamble in moving away from Hood, and that gamble had been successful. Sherman is not given enough credit for setting up the situation that led to the destruction of Hood, nor is Thomas given the praise he deserves for the effect he had on the outcome of the war.[11]

Abandoning Atlanta was a controversial move. It had been a hard-fought victory, and leaving it would give the impression of wasted effort and lives spent in vain. Confederates reoccupied the city as soon as Sherman's force left. To keep Atlanta from returning to its old role as a vital railroad hub and manufacturing center, public buildings, manufacturing establishments, and railroad tracks were destroyed. It is the common belief in most parts of Georgia that Sherman leveled Atlanta. The city's seal is a Phoenix rising from the ashes, and the most memorable (and graphic) scene in *Gone with the Wind* is when Scarlett and Rhett flee the conflagration that was once Atlanta. Recently, Atlanta resident Stephen Davis, in *What the Yankees Did to Us*, cataloged Sherman's "crimes" against Atlanta. Although Davis' tone resembles that of the earliest Southern writers of the war, Davis demonstrates that the damage was not nearly the complete destruction that is often portrayed and admits that a great deal of the damage

---

Sherman's capture of Atlanta proved that the war was winnable and was a large nail in the coffin of an already troubled Democratic campaign. James McPherson, *The Battle Cry of Freedom: The Civil War Era* (London: Oxford University Press, 1988), 774–76.

10. William T. Sherman to Ulysses S. Grant, November 6, 1864, in *The War of the Rebellion: A Compilation of the Official Records of the Union and Confederate Armies*, United States War Department (Washington, D.C.: United States War Department, 1892), ser. 1, vol. 39, pt. 3, 659–60.

11. O'Connell, *Fierce Patriot*, 166–67.

was done by Confederates in defense of the city and during the normal unpleasantness of Union and later Confederate occupation. The damage was considerably less than Richmond suffered at the hands of withdrawing Confederate forces in 1865.[12]

The question of the destruction in Atlanta, as in any occupied city during any war, is a complicated one. As the Union army approached Atlanta in the spring of 1864, the city of Atlanta was a fortified town. It was occupied by the Confederate army and Georgia militia. Buildings were occupied, supplies were requisitioned, and no fence was safe from soldiers looking for firewood. Houses and other buildings were destroyed to build defensive lines. Adding to the destruction, Sherman bombarded the city. General Hood complained to Sherman that this was a violation of the rules of civilized warfare. Sherman, who kept a copy of Emmerich de Vattel's *The Law of Nations*, knew better. Atlanta was a fortified city, and like Winfield Scott in front of the walled city of Veracruz, he was justified in treating it like a medieval castle. Once Hood determined Atlanta was untenable, he ordered the city abandoned and its military stores destroyed. Thus, there was a great deal of destruction before the first Union soldier stepped foot in Atlanta. Even the film that best represents the Lost Cause myth, *Gone with the Wind*, portrays the destruction of Atlanta as the work of retreating Confederates and panicking civilians. What followed was two months of occupation and the same type of destruction that one might expect from more than a hundred thousand men occupying the city.

Dealing with the civilian population was a headache. Sherman had commanded the occupied city of Memphis earlier in the war and did not want to repeat the troubles that caring for a captive and hostile populace entailed. Consequently, within a week of taking the city, Sherman informed General Hood that he was ordering the evacuation of Atlanta's civilian population. He would provide food and transport for those who wished to go north, and those who wished to go south he would escort as far as Rough and Ready, a small village between the Union and Confederate lines. To General Hood, the act "transcends, in studied and ingenious cruelty, all acts ever before brought to my attention in the dark history of war."[13] Sherman responded that it was by no means unprecedented, inasmuch as Hood's predecessor had done the exact same thing in north Georgia just a few months earlier. After providing a laundry list of Southern deprivations, Sherman wrote, "God will judge us in due time, and he will pronounce whether it be more humane to fight with a town full of women and the families of a brave people at our back or to remove them in time to places of safety among their own friends and people."[14]

---

12. Stephen Davis, *What the Yankees Did to Us: Sherman's Bombardment and Wrecking of Atlanta* (Macon, GA: Mercer University Press, 2012), 356–60.

13. John Bell Hood to William T. Sherman, September 9, 1864, in *Memoirs of General William T. Sherman*, by William T. Sherman (New York: D. Appleton, 1876; repr., New York: Da Capo Press, 1984), 2:119.

14. William T. Sherman to John B. Hood, September 10, 1864, in Sherman, *Memoirs*, 2:119–21.

The Atlanta City Council also sent a letter of protest to the general. Sherman's response has become the most quoted of his many writings. Sherman had a tendency to say or write much more than was necessary. In a letter that did not need to be written, Sherman told the council that "war is cruelty, and you cannot refine it." Taken out of the context, the statement can be used to argue that Sherman wanted war to be cruel and did what he could to make it so. Instead, Sherman was arguing that war was an unpleasant business by its nature. Armies exist to break things and kill people, and it was the South that started the Civil War. He pointed out that Atlanta was a center of munitions manufacturing and could not elicit sympathy when the war came to it. But when peace came and the people of Atlanta were loyal once more to the United States, he would share "his last cracker, and watch with you to shield your homes and families against danger from every quarter."[15]

Sherman's chief engineer, Orlando Poe, was in charge of the official destruction of Atlanta's war-making capabilities. His orders were to use fire only as the last step. Fires were set but not on Poe's orders. Atlantans are justified, however, in criticizing Sherman for not doing enough to keep his soldiers from taking private vengeance. In a statement that is surprisingly not his most famous, Sherman in exasperation told his senior staff as he gestured toward some of his men, "There are the men who do this. Set as many guards as you please, they will slip in and set fire."[16]

Upon leaving Atlanta on November 15, 1864, Sherman sent nonessential personnel back to Tennessee along with units to aid General Thomas and divided his remaining 62,000-man force into two separate wings, the first commanded by General Oliver Otis Howard and the second under General Henry Slocum. Each wing was then divided into two columns. This was a common practice to increase the speed of a marching army so the men would not be packed onto a handful of roads. As was also common practice, small signal rockets were carried to signal between the columns. Barns and unoccupied houses were also set on fire as signals, another common practice of armies on the move.[17]

Had Sherman's troops, without a supply line, been stopped in central or south Georgia, it would have been disastrous not only for his army but for the Union cause as a whole. Sherman's army needed to move quickly to prevent a Confederate force from blocking its path. The need for speed necessitated that, for the most part, his soldiers travel lightly. The large amount of headquarters baggage an army usually carried was left behind, and the army brought very little artillery. As noted, around forty thousand soldiers were dispatched to Tennessee. To a degree, Sherman's force was able to self-select. With the large amount of men and equipment moving to the rear, the men who wanted to avoid the dangers of marching deeper into enemy territory had

---

15. William T. Sherman to James M. Calhoun, September 12, 1864, in Sherman, *Memoirs*, 2:125–26.

16. Sherman quoted in Kennett, *Sherman*, 260.

17. Ibid., 263.

plenty of opportunity to advance to the rear. The irony is that the men who "escaped" to Tennessee fought in two major, exceedingly bloody battles, Nashville and Franklin, while the men with Sherman faced far less danger.[18]

Sherman's force carried enough food and supplies to make the roughly three-hundred-mile March to the Sea. Individual rations were carried, and cattle were driven behind the army. Once they reached Savannah, Sherman's men could be supplied by the U.S. Navy. In fact, Sherman's force made little dent in its supplies because, for the most part, the army requisitioned supplies from the people of Georgia, just as the Confederate government had done for the previous three years. This was not only standard military practice since the first organized armies marched into enemy territory, but it had important strategic value as well. If Sherman's troops had been stopped or delayed by a Confederate force, a shortage of supplies could have had catastrophic results. By not eating the supplies they brought with them, Sherman had a guarantee against most eventualities.[19]

Sherman issued specific orders for living off the land. Field Order 120 was issued November 9, 1864, during the planning stage of the March. One sentence from the whole order is the most quoted: "The army will forage liberally on the country during the march." There is, however, much more to the order. Each brigade would organize its own foraging party commanded by a "discreet officer." They were not to enter private dwellings, and only Sherman and the two corps commanders had the authority to destroy anything. Destruction would be limited to those areas where the army faced hostility from guerrillas, a policy accepted by the rules of war.[20]

Before leaving Atlanta, Sherman wrote the governor of Georgia, Joseph E. Brown, and proposed that if Georgia returned to the Union, all foodstuffs and supplies requisitioned by the Union army would be paid for by the War Department. This offer was rebuffed, and Brown and the state legislature promised to fight with rifle in hand to defend the state capital, which was then located in Milledgeville.[21]

Sherman's force moved quickly southeast in the general direction of Georgia's Atlantic coast. His west wing threatened but bypassed Macon, and his east wing threatened but bypassed Augusta. Although Augustans after the war would be offended that they were not deemed important enough to lay siege to, Sherman had sound military reasons for bypassing the two cities. By his threatening these major cities, what troops were available to defend Georgia were tied up in a useless defense of those urban centers, and Sherman's men reached Savannah only having to fight a minor engagement at Griswoldville on November 22. Between Atlanta and Savannah, the only city Sherman entered was the state capital, Milledgeville. Macon, the

18. Moody, *Demon of the Lost Cause*, 28.

19. Kennett, *Sherman*, 263.

20. William T. Sherman, Special Field Orders No. 120, November 9, 1864, in *The War of the Rebellion*, ser. 1, vol. 39, pt. 3, 713–14.

21. Gibson, *Those 163 Days*, 44–45.

state's fifth-largest city, had five times the population of Milledgeville. But Milledgeville was the capital, and it had symbolic value. Governor Brown did not keep his word to personally defend the city. He fled but not before arming and releasing the convicts at the state penitentiary.[22]

The reason Sherman avoided major cities like Macon or Augusta is that their capture would have taken time. If successful, his army would be slowed even further with the task of dealing with the conquered populations. Sherman's men captured Fort McAllister on December 13, 1864, giving him access to the Atlantic Ocean. Before reaching the coast, Sherman had considered bypassing Savannah, but the relatively easy fall of Fort McAllister and the ease of resupply by water for a possible siege convinced him to change his plans and take the city before continuing north toward Virginia.[23]

On December 21, 1864, Sherman marched his army into Savannah. In his famous telegraph to President Lincoln, Sherman presented the city to him as a Christmas gift. Savannah fared better than probably any Confederate city occupied by Union troops. There are a number of reasons for this. The city was taken without a fight, as Confederate General William Hardee had evacuated his troops from the city the night before, having decided Savannah was untenable. Hardee was a well-respected professional who understood the pointlessness of destroying the city before it fell into Union hands. Also, if Savannah remained in Union hands until the end of the war, there was simply no need for Sherman to destroy its war-making capabilities. Yet if Sherman's intention had been to punish the South, as is so often claimed, then Savannah had asked for it. Savannah had aided Charleston during the Fort Sumter crisis long before Georgia voted to leave the Union.[24]

Although his entrance into Savannah ended the March to the Sea, Sherman was not done. By the end of the month he was moving north through South Carolina. This proved much more difficult than the movement through Georgia. Sherman had to cross rivers and swamps in South Carolina, as opposed to the dry pineland in south Georgia. Sherman would occupy Columbia, the South Carolina capital, and it would fare worse than Atlanta. Who was responsible for the damage to Columbia is debated to this day. As the advanced units of Sherman's force moved into Columbia, the rear guard of General Wade Hampton's Confederate cavalry was moving out of the other side of the South Carolina capital. Hampton's men set fires and looted stores as they abandoned the city. On Hampton's orders, cotton bales were set aflame in order to deprive the Union army of a war prize. The incoming Union troops worked to put out the fires, but smoldering cotton floated in the air. Throughout the night fires sprang up throughout the city. Some of the fires were, indeed, set by Union soldiers.

22. Ibid.

23. William T. Sherman to Ulysses S. Grant, December 16, 1864, in *The War of the Rebellion*, ser. 1, 44:726–27.

24. Wesley Moody, *The Battle of Fort Sumter: First Shots of the American Civil War* (New York: Routledge, 2016), 84; Bruce Catton, *This Hallowed Ground* (New York: Doubleday, 1956), 361.

Included among Sherman's men were a growing number of men liberated from Confederate prisoner-of-war camps, with an obvious score to settle. Moreover, a city the size of Columbia obviously had a lawless element, and there were Unionists and Confederate deserters and draft dodgers with a grievance against the South Carolina government. Consequently, arson and the resultant destruction would be hard to control. As Barton A. Myers shows in Chapter 4 of this book, there were many players in the war in addition to the official forces of the Union and Confederate governments. Whoever bore the greatest guilt, it is indisputable that when the Union army moved out of Columbia, the majority of the city lay in ruins.

Although Sherman had ordered the destruction of Confederate buildings, he consistently denied the charge that he had deliberately burned Columbia to punish the South for secession. There are a number of problems with that charge. If Sherman had deliberately ordered the city destroyed, placing his headquarters in the center of the city would have been an odd choice, to say the least. Why would Sherman deny burning Columbia? The burning of Columbia would have enhanced his reputation among Northerners. The question of who destroyed Columbia was investigated by an Anglo-American commission created by the Treaty of Washington. The commission was tasked with adjudicating claims against the U.S. and British governments. Because property owned by British citizens was destroyed in Columbia, the commission held hearings on the destruction of the city. It was by no means a rubber stamp for either country, as its decisions were unpopular with both sides. The commission, after weighing the available evidence, found that Sherman was not responsible for the destruction of Columbia.[25]

At the beginning of March 1865, Sherman's forces began crossing into North Carolina. This state fared much better than Georgia and South Carolina. Faced with no partisan resistance, Sherman's army moved quickly through the state. With Union naval forces in command of North Carolina's major ports, logistics was not a concern. Perhaps most important, there was a major Confederate army in the neighborhood forcing Sherman to keep his army from spreading out too much. Joseph E. Johnston was given command of the remnants of Hood's army, and pulling together as many men as he could, he had positioned them between Sherman and Lee's Army of Northern Virginia. The armies met in one of the last battles of the war. After a Union victory, Johnston surrendered his army to Sherman. The surrender terms were so lenient that Sherman was accused of treason in the North by the secretary of war and some members of the press.[26] If the accusation of treason could be taken seriously

---

25. Moody, *Demon of the Lost Cause*, 114.

26. Sherman met with Grant, Lincoln, and Admiral David Dixon Porter and discussed the strategy for the last month of the war. It was agreed to offer lenient surrender terms in order to get Confederate soldiers back on their farms as soon as possible. When Confederate General Joseph Johnston met with Sherman to discuss the surrender of the Confederate army, he was accompanied by former U.S. vice president and Confederate secretary of war, John Breckinridge. The Confederate secretary

in 1865, it brings into question just how brutal Sherman had been on his last campaign. Sherman arrived in Virginia too late to take part in the defeat of the Army of Northern Virginia. Regardless, the war ended with Sherman's reputation secured as one of the Union's greatest generals, second only to Grant himself.[27]

Sherman's Immediate Postwar Reputation

The myth of Sherman the brutal destroyer took time to emerge. Sherman before, during, and after the war made many public statements against the use of military violence. His memoirs are far more hostile to those who brought on the war than they are to the enemies he faced in battle. Sherman's most famously quoted statement, "War is Hell," was an assertion of his anti-war sentiments, not a suggestion of how war should be fought, as it is often interpreted.[28]

Indeed, Sherman the monster was by no means the common view in the South during the lifetime of most veterans of the war. It was not until the following generation that the story of Sherman as heartless destroyer of the South began to take shape. There are events in the decades that immediately followed the war that could not have occurred or even have been contemplated had Sherman been viewed as he is today. Sherman and his main antagonist during the war, Joseph Johnston, became good friends in the postwar years. Johnston would visit Sherman, and the two old men would get on the ground and go over old maps and battles more like two former opposing football coaches than two men who had been locked in deadly combat with the fate of nations at stake. It is highly unlikely that Johnston would have had such

---

offered Sherman the surrender of all Confederate forces, not just those under the direct command of Johnston. In exchange for this war-ending offer, Breckinridge wanted terms beyond the strictly military. The wily politician outmaneuvered the professional soldier. Sherman agreed to terms that allowed Confederate soldiers to remain armed and state governments to remain in place. Sherman forwarded the treaty to Washington, where it was rejected. General Grant traveled to North Carolina and while remaining behind the scenes allowed Sherman to fix his own error. The situation could have ended there had not Secretary of War Stanton decided to use the situation to his own political advantage, making the treaty public knowledge along with accusations of disloyalty and allowing the Confederate president to escape. Northern newspapers parroted the secretary's accusations. Sherman followed the advice of his more politically astute brother, U.S. Senator John Sherman, and made no response, although Sherman could not resist snubbing the secretary at the Grand Review in Washington. Eventually, the story was replaced in newspapers by the political events that followed the war, and the Sherman-Johnston agreement has become a footnote.

27. Kennett, *Sherman*, 265–82; Catton, *This Hallowed Ground*, 393.

28. Although there is disagreement about the origins of the quotation, it was most likely given many times in slightly different forms. The most well-documented was in a speech Sherman gave to a Grand Army of the Republic meeting in Columbus, Ohio. Speaking in 1880 to the sons and grandsons of the veterans, he said, "There is many a boy here today who looks on war as all glory, but, boys, it is all hell. I look upon war with horror; but if it has to come I am here." Quoted in O'Connell, *Fierce Patriot*, 326.

a close relationship with Sherman had his opponent been the brutal monster that later generations accused him of being. Another antagonist, General John Bell Hood, reached out to Sherman for help in the postwar years, and Sherman tried to help the disabled veteran sell his military papers to the U.S. government. Although Sherman was unsuccessful in selling Hood's papers before the Confederate general passed away, it was not for lack of trying. Had Sherman been the ruthless warrior he is depicted as in popular lore, it is unlikely Hood would have approached him for aid.[29]

Sherman was also approached after the war by both the Republican and Democratic parties with suggestions that he run for president. Any Democratic candidate, if he had a chance of winning, would have to take all the Southern states and make serious inroads into the North.[30] The fact that the Democratic Party thought Sherman could win is telling, as it was counting on him winning the states of South Carolina and Georgia, an impossible task if even half the stories now told about Sherman had been true. Beyond politics, Sherman was the guest of honor at the Atlanta Cotton Expo in 1881, was named Duke of Louisiana at a Mardi Gras ball in New Orleans in 1879, and was generally well received when he toured the South on several occasions during the immediate postwar period.[31]

There was obviously some bitterness, but the Southern view of Sherman by those who lived through the war was simply the view of the victor by the vanquished. He was not the most popular man in the South but no less popular than any other Union general. In fact, Southerners had a softer view of Sherman than of most other Northern generals because of his postwar politics. Unlike Grant, who supported civil rights and other Republican Reconstruction policies, Sherman remained, at least philosophically, a Whig and thus did not want to see many changes in the postwar South—a position that endeared him to many Southerners.[32] He was, according to a former Confederate officer who had served with Sherman while the general was the superintendent of the Louisiana State Seminary of Learning and Military Academy (later Louisiana State University) in the year preceding the outbreak of war, "a bitter enemy in war but a good friend in peace."[33]

Emergence of a Myth

The transition of Sherman into the brutal monster who violated the laws of civilized nineteenth-century warfare has a number of origins. C. Vann Woodward wrote in his

---

29. O'Connell, *Fierce Patriot*, 181; Kennett, *Sherman*, 329–30.

30. O'Connell, *Fierce Patriot*, 323; Kennett, *Sherman*, 301.

31. Moody, *Demon of the Lost Cause*, 65–66, 91.

32. Kennett, *Sherman*, 329.

33. David F. Boyd, quoted in Germaine Reed, *David French Boyd: Founder of Louisiana State University* (Baton Rouge: Louisiana State University Press, 1977), 189.

iconic *The Burden of Southern History* that Southerners lived through an experience like no other Americans. They had been defeated in war, and most lived under their conquerors. Woodward argued that this naturally affects how Southerners view their history. Defeat is much easier to accept if it does not mean that the victors were superior.[34] It has been much easier to believe that the South lost because the North did not play by the rules of civilized warfare. Historically, there was also a much more practical reason behind this than how Southerners felt. If Northerners could be shown to have fought the war in a less than noble fashion, then they lost the ability to take the moral high ground in the postwar political debate over the future of the country and the defeated South.

According to this view, President Lincoln started the war by cheap, underhanded tricks at Fort Sumter, and Grant had no concern for the lives of his own men as he defeated Southern armies, and all Union armies were brutal and uncivilized to Southern civilians.[35] For a number of reasons, however, Sherman and his army were a much more convenient tool than Lincoln and even Grant "the butcher" for Southern mythmakers to demonstrate this brutality. Sherman's March to the Sea put him and his army into more direct contact with Southern civilians than the actions of other Union antagonists. For the most part, Union armies moved through battlefields from which civilians had already fled or, fearful of the loss of their property, had moved their slaves. According to this view, Sherman's troops were the exception—a large force moving through cotton-belt areas previously unscarred by war.

Additionally, a common theme in Southern postwar writing was the bravery and strength of Southern women and the loyalty of their slaves. The loyal slave is a myth that is reemerging with a different twist, as we see in Brooks D. Simpson's chapter on black Confederates. Stories of the brave Southern woman defeating the evil Yankee were a staple of Southern tales relating to the March to the Sea. Scarlett O'Hara's mortal clash with a deserter in *Gone with the Wind* might be the most famous example. The stories of slaves who not only remained loyal to their owners but outsmarted the Union invader were equally plentiful. In one example, from an 1899 article in *The Confederate Veteran* magazine, Vice President Alexander Stephens is saved from capture by Sherman's men by his quick thinking and loyal slaves. This was pure fiction, as Stephens turned himself in to Union forces at his first opportunity.[36] Sherman's March to the Sea gave Southerners more opportunity to tell these mythical, usually absurdly false stories than any other Union campaign.

---

34. C. Vann Woodward, *The Burden of Southern History* (Baton Rouge: Louisiana State University Press, 1960), 19.

35. Moody, *The Battle of Fort Sumter*, 105. For a discussion of Grant, see Chapter 6.

36. Anne Sarah Rubin, *Through the Heart of Dixie: Sherman's March and American Memory* (Chapel Hill: University of North Carolina Press, 2014), 46–49; "Blue Coats at Victory Hall," *Confederate Veteran* 7 (1899): 303–5; William C. Davis, *An Honorable Defeat: The Last Days of the Confederacy* (New York: Harcourt, 2001), 313–14.

Although postwar Southerners played a huge role in creating the myths that surround Sherman and his March to the Sea, no one individual played a larger role than the general himself. Any book written to support the myth will quote Sherman liberally. In the series of letters between Sherman, Grant, and General Henry Halleck, Sherman lays out his argument for making "Georgia howl" and how he would "cripple their military resources."[37] The problem with Sherman as a witness is, as one recent biographer put it, there is a vast difference between what Sherman said and what Sherman did.[38] Although Sherman claimed he would destroy the ability of Georgia to wage war, what he actually did does not live up to this pledge.

Tour guides and local historical societies love to tell visitors how Sherman's army destroyed everything in their charming little towns. They are also proud to show off their antebellum homes. Aware of the obvious inconsistency, they are quick to tell a story of why this one building was spared by Sherman, usually through his personal intervention. One common theme is a connection with the Masons. The usual story is the owner of the home was a Mason, and with a show of regalia or a secret sign, Sherman would spare the building. Sherman probably would have had a hard time understanding the secret signs and symbols, since he was not a Mason.[39]

Another common story is that Sherman had dated a woman from the home and so spared it. As has often been pointed out, if Sherman had dated as many women as these myths claim, he would have had little time for a military career. A third legend that appears in a great deal of the literature is that the smells coming out of a specific kitchen were so fantastic that the home was spared. Had Sherman eaten all the pies it is claimed that were given to him, he would have been unable to mount his horse by the time he reached the Atlantic.[40]

If one begins to add up the number of places that were spared due to special circumstances, the destruction starts to seem not nearly so great. In 1955, University of Georgia professor of geography D. J. de Laubenfels used the reports of Sherman's officers to trace the army's route to Savannah. What de Laubenfels found was that the majority of the plantation homes that Sherman supposedly targeted were still standing. They were under threat from age, neglect, and dry rot, which explains why so many of them are not standing today. It is often estimated that Sherman did a hundred million dollars' worth of damage to Georgia. De Laubenfels wrote that the majority of the damage done to Georgia was from loss of livestock. Confederate requisition officers had already taken a large bite out of the livestock numbers long before

---

37. Sherman to Grant, October 9, 1864, in *The War of the Rebellion*, ser. 1, vol. 39, pt. 3, 162.

38. O'Connell, *Fierce Patriot*, xv.

39. Rubin, *Through the Heart of Dixie*, 52–57.

40. Ibid., 63–64.

CONTRABANDS ACCOMPANYING THE LINE OF SHERMAN'S MARCH THROUGH GEORGIA.—FROM A SKETCH BY OUR SPECIAL ARTIST.

An image from *Harper's Weekly* of a few of the thousands of freed slaves that followed Sherman's army to Savannah. Image courtesy of the Library of Congress.

Sherman arrived. Horses were especially vulnerable because Confederate cavalrymen were expected to supply their own mounts.[41]

Lost labor made up a large portion of the damage. Nearly ten thousand slaves followed Sherman's army to the "sea." Of course, all slaves were freed by the end of the war, whether they followed Sherman or not. Counting the value of freed slaves in the oft-given $100 million figure is misleading. Sherman and his army ended slavery in only selected areas of the South for less than a year, and economists are quick to point out that the value of slaves was not lost; their value was transferred to the new owners, the former slaves themselves.[42]

In examining the damage done to Georgia and South Carolina, there is the uncomfortable question for Southerners of how much of the destruction was carried out by the Confederates themselves. Confederate cavalry commander General Joseph Wheeler was ordered by Generals John Bell Hood and Braxton Bragg to destroy everything that could be used by Sherman's army. There are letters in Southern newspapers, predating the "March," complaining about the destruction caused by Wheeler's men. In response, General Wheeler felt that his command was getting an unfair reputation.

---

41. D. J. de Laubenfels, "Where Sherman Passed By," *Geographical Review* 47 (1957): 381–95.

42. Peter Temin, "The Post-Bellum Recovery of the South and the Cost of the Civil War," *Journal of Economic History* 36 (1976): 898–901.

Wheeler believed his men were being blamed for the damage done by Confederate deserters and armed convicts from the Georgia state prison in Milledgeville, who had been released by the state government in the misguided hope they would help resist Sherman. These men were operating in the lawless void left behind by the Union army. According to Wheeler, he sent a force to trail Sherman in order to "apprehend the marauders," not to defend Southern civilians against the Yankee horde.[43]

One of the weaknesses of oral history, on which so much of the Southern version of the events of Sherman's March is based, is that storytellers want the approval of their audience. In the postwar period, recounting how Sherman's army destroyed your crops, stole your livestock, and dug up grandma's silver made a much better tale than the truth that you were victimized by fellow Southerners. Obviously, it would be impossible to reexamine all the destruction and assign blame for individual acts. However, that there were other parties involved is a severe blow to the myth.

According to the myth, Sherman's goal was to destroy the South's ability to wage war by attacking its infrastructure and the morale of the civilian population. Like the United States Army Air Corps destroying German factories and railyards in the Second World War, Sherman would march through Georgia and South Carolina in order to destroy the South's ability to make war. Like so many aspects of the myth, it does not stand up to closer scrutiny. During the March to the Sea, Sherman avoided Georgia's remaining industrial and population centers. Macon, Columbus, and Augusta were all bypassed. Macon, the first natural target for Sherman after leaving Atlanta, was a railroad hub and manufacturing center. Its arsenal produced cannon, and the Macon Armory was on the verge of becoming the largest producer of Enfield rifles outside of Britain. Macon was also the location of the Confederate States Central Laboratory, a key center for the production and testing of artillery.[44]

Columbus, to the south of Macon, was in the top five Confederate cities ranked by industrial output. Local factories made tents, uniforms, rain gear, and wagons. The South's largest shoe factory was in Columbus. With river access to the Gulf of Mexico, Columbus was an important naval construction center. The Navy Yard built ironclad warships, while the ironworks produced the engines.[45]

Augusta, on the South Carolina border, was the largest producer of gunpowder in the Confederacy. It was also the home of a large pistol factory and many other manufacturing establishments producing goods for the war effort.[46] Although Sherman's army came close to these three important cities, he bypassed them all. If his goal had been to destroy the South's ability to wage war, why did he bypass factories producing war goods to trample on cotton fields and break some cotton gins? If his goal had been to destroy

---

43. "General Wheeler's Command," *Fayetteville Observer*, January 19, 1865.

44. Kenneth Coleman, ed., *A History of Georgia* (Athens: University of Georgia Press, 1991), 191.

45. Ibid.

46. Ibid.

Sherman's men carrying out the difficult task of destroying railroad. Sherman's chief engineer complained that the men rarely did a thorough job. Image courtesy of the Library of Congress.

the morale of the South by showing that he could travel anywhere he wanted, why would he bypass such low-hanging fruit?

Defenders of the myth will point out that with the destruction of the railroad, it would not matter how much these cities produced because their goods could not be moved to where they were needed. Sherman's men ripping up railroad tracks is a common image in stories of the March to the Sea. "Sherman's neckties," a phrase commonly cited as an example of this supposedly systematic destruction of the railroad system, refers to the practice of Union soldiers heating and bending the iron track so that the railroad could not be repaired without the aid of a rolling mill, the nearest of which was inconveniently located in Richmond, Virginia. Such "neckties" were a reality, but their numbers are exaggerated. In point of fact, destruction of the railroad system was not accomplished to such a degree as to destroy Georgia's ability to wage and support the war. Sherman's chief engineer, Orlando Poe, and his judge advocate, Major Henry Hitchcock, complained to the general that the infantry was not doing a very good job of destroying the rail system. Sherman agreed but made no changes. Sherman was much more effective at destroying the railway network around Atlanta during his campaign to take that city when it was of strategic importance.[47] It seems unlikely that after Atlanta the South's rail lines were of major concern to him.

Another issue that calls into question the myth is the speed that Sherman traveled through Georgia and South Carolina. Sherman left Atlanta on November 15, 1864; his army arrived on the outskirts of Savannah on December 20, 1864. In just over a month his 62,000-man army covered roughly three hundred miles. After staying in Savannah for over a month, Sherman continued north through South Carolina and

---

47. Kennett, *Sherman*, 271.

into North Carolina, where he fought one of the last battles of the war against General Joseph Johnston on March 19, 1865. After Savannah his force covered almost four hundred miles. His army marched on average eight miles a day. That was a respectable speed for an army before the invention of the truck.[48] If Sherman's intention had been the deliberate destruction of Georgia and South Carolina, why did he rush through those states?

Had Sherman's goal been, as he claimed, to take the war to Southern civilians and to destroy the South's ability to make war, he missed the best opportunities to do just that when he bypassed major industrial centers and, as well, simply did not give his men enough time to do the damage he told his superiors he expected them to do. So why was Sherman selling the myth? He was extremely career oriented and wanted one of the top spots in the army when the war was over. Everyone knew that there would be a massive reduction in the size of the military after the Confederacy was defeated. There would be a large number of captains and majors in the postwar army who had been generals at the end of the Civil War. It was obvious that Sherman's objective was to reach Virginia and help defeat Lee's army.[49] So what would happen if Sherman and his army came up short? What would happen if Grant defeated Lee before Sherman was able to take part? What would happen if Thomas, an extremely capable general, instead of waging a simple mopping-up operation, defeated Hood and the remnants of his army in grand style? After the victory in Atlanta, Sherman risked marching off to obscurity. In fact, Sherman did not reach Virginia in time, and Thomas won two of the great decisive battles of the war, but Sherman still managed to grab the attention he craved. Sherman's goal was to take a decisive part in the end of the war. Since he was unable to do this, he invented the idea of destroying the South's ability to wage war. This worked. Although Thomas won the twin victories that ended the war in the Western Theater, Sherman emerged as the second great Union general of the war. It was Sherman who went on to become the commanding general of the postwar U.S. Army.

A recent popular biographer of the general has called him "Sherman the showman." "Uncle Billy" Sherman abandoned his West Point spit-and-polish manner to appeal to his volunteer soldiers by affecting a disheveled look in his perfectly tailored Brooks Brothers uniform. In other words, he changed who he was from the beginning of the war in order to reach his military and professional goals.[50] This was also what he did with the hype surrounding his March to the Sea. By championing the myth of a destructive march through Georgia, Sherman made it impossible to argue that he was unimportant in bringing about Union victory.

The second part of the myth is that Sherman's March to the Sea represented a new and revolutionary approach to warfare. There are several major problems with this myth.

---

48. Gibson, *Those 163 Days*, 33, 72, 163, 221.

49. O'Connell, *Fierce Patriot*, 177.

50. Ibid., xiii–xiv.

First, the idea that anything that Sherman and his army is accused of doing was somehow unique in the annals of warfare is problematic. Noncombatants have always suffered in war. The Greek historian Herodotus, considered the first Western historian, described the depredations of the army of Xerxes that were aimed at the civilian populations of ancient Greece. Likewise, the Spartans and the Athenians leveled each other's fields and homes during the Peloponnesian War (431–404 BCE). Those are two examples that antebellum Americans, steeped in classical history, would have known well. That medieval wars were limited to combatants on the battlefield is a myth for another book in this series. During the Hundred Years War (1337–1453), the English army, too small to lay siege to French cities, targeted civilians in order to draw out the French army. The Thirty Years War (1618–48) was horrific beyond description, with millions of noncombatants killed.

Much closer to the lifetime of Americans of the Civil War era were the Napoleonic Wars (1803–15). Indeed, General Lee was eight years old when Napoleon was defeated at Waterloo. Civil War generals had studied the battles of the French emperor Napoleon extensively, and some even tried to emulate his battle plans on American soil.[51] One of the many reasons that Napoleon had been successful was that his armies were highly mobile because they lived off the land. They were not hindered by long supply lines as their adversaries were. Sometimes the farmers and merchants were reimbursed, and sometimes they were not, but they had no choice whether to sell. It was not until his enemies adopted a defensive scorched-earth policy that Napoleon was defeated.

Beyond living off the land, Napoleon's army was famous for its destruction and brutality in occupied areas. This was mostly due to the revolutionary nature of his army. The men targeted churches and the homes and property of the wealthy. The wars in Spain and Portugal were horrific in destruction and the brutal treatment of civilians.[52]

An even more recent example was the Texas Revolution (1835–36). This would have been a recent memory for the Civil War generation. General Antonio López de Santa Anna waged total war against Texas as many of its settlers tried to secede from the United States of Mexico. He and his army leveled homes, destroyed fields, and slaughtered cattle and a fair number of Texans. Santa Anna planned to show both Texans and the rest of Mexico that it was not wise to cross General Antonio López de Santa Anna. Sherman had by no means invented a new type of warfare, nor did he emulate the deeds of Santa Anna or Napoleon's armies.[53]

Santa Anna's brutality proved, almost predictably, to be counterproductive. "Remember the Alamo and Goliad" became the rallying cry of Texas rebels as they went on to win their independence. Throughout the Civil War, and recorded history, it was defeat in battle and the loss of cities and other strategic sites that destroyed morale.

---

51. Carol Reardon, *With a Sword in One Hand and Jomini in the Other: The Problem of Military Thought in the Civil War North* (Chapel Hill: University of North Carolina Press, 2012).

52. Richard A. Preston and Sydney F. Wise, *A History of Warfare and Its Interrelationships with Western Society* (New York: Praeger, 1970), 162.

53. Will Fowler, *Santa Anna of Mexico* (Lincoln: University of Nebraska Press, 2007).

The fall of Vicksburg and the defeat at Gettysburg had been crushing blows to Confederate morale. The loss of Atlanta a year later had a similar effect. The loss of Georgia's remaining manufacturing centers would have likewise severely damaged the Confederate will to continue the war. But Sherman bypassed Georgia's three still-functioning industrial cities. At the end of his March to the Sea, Sherman captured Savanah, a port city, and two coastal fortresses. That traditional strategic move was what was celebrated in Northern newspapers, not his supposed destruction of private property.[54]

If, as the myth claims, Sherman's March to the Sea was destructive to Southern morale, why did Southern newspapers and politicians, whose goal it was to boost morale, ensure that the story of the March to the Sea was well known to the public and even exaggerated? Newspaper editors and the Confederate government understood that the type of "barbarity" that Sherman was accused of would have the opposite effect of destroying morale. Early in the war, in a reference to the embargo placed on trade with the secessionist South, Confederate President Jefferson Davis, in an effort to fire up Southern resolve, predicted that "mankind will shudder at the outrages committed" "on the sick, women, and children."[55] It was obvious to Davis that the more brutal an enemy was, the more determined people were to resist. President Lincoln and General Grant understood this. It was why the Union, including Sherman, offered generous terms to Confederate armies in 1865. When Germany invaded Belgium in World War I, Southern writers compared it to the March to the Sea.[56] It is reasonably argued that German crimes in Belgium were greatly exaggerated as effective propaganda by the British.[57] Portraying the enemy as evil is always an effective way of rallying the population, which seriously calls into question the idea of using brutality to subdue an enemy.

Regardless of the obvious problems, there are a number of reasons why this myth became and remains a favorite among students of the conflict. As noted, like so many myths about the war, it came about as a way to explain the Confederate loss. The Old South was considered by Southerners the greater society. In the words of the opening of the movie *Gone with the Wind*, "There was a land of Cavaliers and Cotton Fields called the Old South . . . Here in this pretty world Gallantry took its last bow. Here was the last ever to be seen of Knights and their Ladies Fair, of Master and of Slave. Look for it only in books, for it is no more than a dream remembered. A Civilization gone with the wind." How could such a grand civilization be defeated by unprincipled, money-grubbing Yankees and their immigrant minions, drawn from the slums of the North? The explanation was simple: the Northerners unable to win on the battlefield against great leaders like Robert E. Lee turned to unprincipled tactics, such as

---

54. "The Latest and Last Aspect of the War," *New York Times*, December 20, 1864.

55. "Meeting of the Rebel Congress—Special Message of Jefferson Davis," *New York Herald*, July 22, 1861.

56. Henry E. Shepard, "Historic Ironies," *Confederate Veteran* 26 (January 1918): 17.

57. Adam Hochschild, *King Leopold's Ghost: A Story of Greed, Terror, and Heroism in Colonial Africa* (New York: Houghton Mifflin, 1998), 296.

making war against women and children. How could chivalric Southerners possibly be expected to defeat an enemy who did not play by the rules of civilized warfare?

Beyond the Civil War, the story of The March served other useful purposes. Historians cannot help but look at history through the lenses of their own times and the problems of their present. This is very much the case with Sherman's March to the Sea. Twentieth-century historians have used him to make arguments about warfare in their own time. One of the earliest examples of this is the British military writer B. H. Liddell Hart. The controversial Liddell Hart wrote biographies of Scipio Africanus, the great Roman general; Attila the Hun; and Sherman. All of Liddell Hart's works written in the 1920s and 1930s had one very specific goal; he used his subjects to criticize the military strategists and generals of the First World War, who relied on deadly frontal assaults against entrenched positions and machine guns. The military leaders he wrote about all used what Liddell Hart termed the "indirect approach." Liddell Hart considered Sherman one of the great generals. He based his evaluation of Sherman, for the most part, on his Atlanta campaign against Joseph Johnston. With the exception of his failed frontal assault at Kennesaw Mountain, Sherman mainly did not strike at the center of Johnston's line but continually outflanked him. This, Liddell Hart argued, is what the generals of World War I should have done. Although this is what Liddell Hart meant by the indirect approach, the definition took on a life of its own. The indirect approach began to be identified with Sherman's supposed war on civilians.[58]

Sherman and his indirect approach to warfare took on another life after World War I with the strange marriage of Lost Cause historians and air power enthusiasts. The term "total war" is itself an invention of Italian General Giulio Douhet. In his 1921 book, *Il dominio dell'aria* (Command of the Air), Douhet argued for the use of strategic airpower to destroy the opponent's infrastructure. This became the accepted policy of most nations during World War II, especially Germany, Great Britain, and the United States. With the introduction of nuclear weapons into arsenals around the world, the idea of what the battlefield actually is had to be reevaluated. According to Southern historians, Sherman set the precedent for total war. If infantry and cavalry destroying railways, factories, and other civilian property was acceptable, then destroying the same things by dropping high explosives, conventional or nuclear, from the air would also be acceptable. John Bennett Walters, who was much better at writing titles than he was at writing books and journal articles, forever linked Sherman with the idea of total war. Walters' "General Sherman and Total War" appeared in the highly influential *Journal of Southern History* in 1948 at the peak of the fight between the U.S. military services over who should dominate.[59] An argument that Sherman helped win the war by using total war tactics fit with the Air Force's philosophy.

---

58. B. H. Liddell Hart, *Sherman: Soldier, Realist, American* (1929; repr., New York: Frederick A. Praeger, 1958), 106–10, 127–32, 264–65.

59. John Bennett Walters, "General Sherman and Total War," *Journal of Southern History* 14 (1948): 447–80.

Walters returned in 1973 with a book-length version of his journal article. The timing was perfect for both Walters and the myth. *Merchant of Terror* was published toward the end of the Vietnam War (1955–75). The American military had been accused of unnecessary brutality and even war crimes during the last decade of the war. The lesson from Walters' book was obvious. If American forces were capable of atrocities in 1864, it was reasonable to believe they occurred in 1964 and following. Eleven years later, James Reston, Jr., offered a much less nuanced argument in his book *Sherman's March and Vietnam*. Reston argued that Sherman set the precedent for atrocities that he believed occurred in Vietnam, such as the 1968 massacre at My Lai.[60]

Although modern biographers of the general and historians of the Western Theater of the Civil War have moved away from the picture of Sherman the total warrior bent on bringing utter destruction to the American South, the Sherman myth is one that is not likely to leave us anytime soon. It is a persistent myth for many reasons. There was damage and destruction, some done by Sherman and his men, some done by others. Sherman's army did live off the land. However, Sherman's motive was to pass quickly through Georgia, not to destroy that state's capability to make war. Nor was anything Sherman did or was accused of doing somehow new in the annals of warfare. The story circulating in today's academic circles is more nuanced than "he did or he did not." But because the myth cannot simply be disproved, it is unlikely to go away.

Perhaps the major reason that the myth that Sherman instituted a new and brutal form of warfare that shocked the civilized world is so persistent is simply that it makes for a good story. From *Gone with the Wind* to E. L. Doctorow's recent novel *The March*, Sherman's adventures contain more potential drama and even comedy than so many other aspects of American history. The image of the Union soldiers carrying everything from live chickens to furniture is as great an image as that of former slaves wearing their owners' best clothes as they escaped with Sherman's men. Even I am guilty of using aspects of the myth for this reason. In my class on Florida history, when discussing the introduction of bloodhounds into the United States during the Second Seminole War, I tell the story of the Union soldiers targeting bloodhounds because they were used to hunt runaway slaves. There was one soldier who was about to kill the lapdog of a Southern plantation owner. When she protested that it was not a bloodhound, his supposed response was "Yes, but we don't know what it will grow into." The story is problematic on many levels, and it is very difficult to place within Sherman's campaign, but it is a great story.

Ironically, it is those who visit Gettysburg and lament what might have been who are the strongest champions of the Sherman myth, a myth the man they hate would have greatly approved. No one who accepts the myth will ever say that Sherman was unimportant.

---

60. John Bennett Walters, *Merchant of Terror: General Sherman and Total War* (New York: Bobbs-Merrill, 1973), xiii, 163–64; James Reston, Jr., *Sherman's March and Vietnam* (New York: Macmillan Publishing Company, 1984), 56–64.

Epilogue: Notes from a Southerner

Sometimes being a Southerner and a Civil War historian can be awkward. There is the belief, held by many Southerners as well as Northerners, that if I do not accept the view of the Civil War spelled out in the catechism of the United Daughters of the Confederacy, then I am a traitor to the land of my birth. As someone who wrote a book arguing that Sherman was not that bad, I have felt this acutely. I reject this. It defies all sense and logic that I have to accept things that are counterfactual to be a good Southerner. If the president of the Sons of Confederate Veterans, Confederate General Joseph E. Johnston, and I were in the same room, the general would agree with me. He was, after all, a pallbearer in Sherman's funeral. Johnston might have been accused of being a poor general, but never was he accused of not being a good Southerner. If Robert E. Lee joined our little discussion group, he would reject the assertion that Grant was simply a butcher who won only because he threw overwhelming numbers into the fight with little regard for their lives. Lee was a great general; had he faced in Grant a general whose only skill was sending men to their death, it would have been a one-sided slaughter. As a Southerner, how can I be faulted for agreeing with Lee?

The other issue with being a Southerner and a historian is the issue of slavery. Most of our ancestors, but not all, were on the wrong side of that issue. It can be argued that it was complicated and that people on the other side were not entirely pure in their motives. While this might be true, the fact is that slavery would have survived in North America with a Confederate victory. As a Southerner, I take heart in General Grant's observation in his memoirs, "I felt like anything rather than rejoicing at the downfall of a foe who had fought so long and valiantly and had suffered so much for a cause, though that cause was, I believe, one of the worst for which a people ever fought, and one for which there was the least excuse."[1] Or in the words of the legendary country singer Johnny Horton, "You fought for your folks, but you didn't die in vain. Even though you lost, they speak highly of your name. 'Cause you fought all the way, Johnny Reb." Our ancestors were led down a bad path by scheming politicians, but once they got there they fought hard.

There are also parts of the modern Confederate canon that are disparaging to Southern military achievement. Once again, consider General Grant. I consider him one of the greatest generals produced by the United States. Emperor Napoleon III of France pulled his troops from Mexico out of fear they might have to face Grant as the Civil War drew to a close. With a well-supplied, battle-hardened, numerically

---

1. Ulysses S. Grant, *Personal Memoirs of U.S. Grant* (New York: Jenkins and McCowan, 1885), 2:629–30.

superior army, Grant took more than a year to defeat the Southern forces under Lee. That the Confederate army lasted as long as it did is an impressive feat that is minimalized when one diminishes the skill of the opposing general.

For my fellow Southerners who are African Americans, pride in the Confederate military achievement is not a viable option. To them the Confederacy should stand as a symbol of what they have overcome. Jacksonville, Florida, used to have a high school named

Although Nathan B. Forrest High School has been renamed, other schools named for Confederate leaders remain in Jacksonville, Florida, such as Robert E. Lee High School. As Jefferson Davis' military adviser, Lee believed that Florida's major cities were not worth defending. It's odd that he is thus honored by a city he believed should be abandoned.

for Nathan Bedford Forrest. I find it odd that an academic institution was named after a man who is infamous for his negative views of education and was barely literate. However, the real controversy stems from the fact that he is credited with founding the Ku Klux Klan. Before the name of the high school was changed, I had a young African American student who had recently graduated and played four years of football as a Forrest High School General. In my introductory U.S. history class, I ask my students to read a biography, and this student chose to read about Forrest. I was a bit surprised until he admitted to me that, although he had spent so much time at the school named after Forrest, he knew nothing about the man. I did not give the ending away. I asked him to come to my office when he completed his voyage of discovery.

After he finished, I asked him whether he thought the name should be changed. He was adamant that the name should remain. He wished only that he had known more about the general when he was a student there. He felt he would have been more motivated to achieve as a way to spite the Klan's founder. I assured my student that Forrest would be extremely annoyed that he received an education at a school named in Forrest's honor and was now earning a college education.

There is an old saying that living well is the best revenge. That is probably a healthier attitude than attempting to scrub any mention of the Confederacy or the antebellum world from the public sphere. St. Augustine, Florida, a city with history to spare, has done a wonderful job memorializing its Civil Rights history. That its monuments are in the presence of the Confederate memorials that witnessed the Civil Rights movement makes them more powerful than had the Confederate statues been hauled away in a Joseph Stalin–like purge.

The last word has not been written on the Civil War, nor will it be anytime soon. What direction the literature will take is impossible to predict. Historians as a group are poor seers of the future. Over the last two decades, social history has dominated Civil War writing. Gender, class, and race have recently been the subjects pursued by the top scholars. What happened on the battlefield and even in the political world has taken a back seat to everything else. The term "Civil War Era" has replaced "Civil War" in the titles of journals and organizations so as not to lead people to the false belief that Civil War historians study only military history. The trend toward social history is one that nobody, at least in academic circles, sees ending. Yet this year the Society of Civil War Historians gave its top award to a book about small-unit tactics, a development that I doubt even the author of that book saw coming. Whether that is the beginning of a major change or an exception, we cannot know. The fact that in the society's official announcement of the award, military history is disparaged as a field leaves me, a military historian, less than hopeful.

With all the myths, misinformation, and errors admitted and some of them disputed in this little book, I only hope that, as we move forward, honest research and accuracy remain our dual overall goals but that we do not forget our myths. They are an important part of the story.

Wesley Moody

On Presidents' Day 2012, Ford's Theatre National Historic Site unveiled a thirty-four-foot-tall, eight-foot-thick stack of books about Abraham Lincoln to represent the more than fifteen thousand that have been written about the sixteenth president in the more than 150 years since his death. That, of course, only makes up a percentage of the massive number of books written about every aspect of the Civil War. If, as the editors and authors of this book hope, we have whetted your appetite and you want to read more on the Civil War, you might be overwhelmed with so many books available. Also, as the author of each of the seven chapters has pointed out, there are many books that perhaps are best avoided. We have prepared a short list of books on the subjects covered in this work.

The list is obviously influenced by the myths covered in this book. Almost all major figures have at least one biography. Most major battles have numerous books written about them. Gettysburg has probably been written about more than any other individual event. We have not included any suggestions along those lines (although Stephen Sears' *Gettysburg* is a wonderful book). Both the Society of Civil War Historians (http://scwhistorians.org) and the Louisiana State University Library's *Civil War Book Review* (http://www.cwbr.com) offer book reviews on most new Civil War books.

General Books

Beringer, Richard E., Herman Hattaway, Archer Jones, and William N. Still, Jr. *Why the South Lost the Civil War.* Athens: University of Georgia Press, 1991.

Gallagher, Gary W. *The Confederate War: How Popular Will, Nationalism, and Military Strategy Could Not Stave Off Defeat.* Cambridge, MA: Harvard University Press, 1997.

Hattaway, Herman, and Archer Jones. *How the North Won: A Military History of the Civil War.* Urbana: University of Illinois Press, 1991.

McPherson, James. *Battle Cry of Freedom: The Civil War Era.* New York: Oxford University Press, 1988.

Woodward, C. Vann. *The Burden of Southern History.* Baton Rouge: Louisiana State University Press, 1960.

The Original Myth: The Lost Cause

Blight, David W. *Race and Reunion: The Civil War in American Memory.* Cambridge, MA: Belknap Press of Harvard University Press, 2001.

Brundage, W. Fitzhugh. *The Southern Past: A Clash of Race and Memory.* Cambridge, MA: Harvard University Press, 2005.

Connelly, Thomas L. *The Marble Man: Robert E. Lee and His Image in American Society.* Baton Rouge: Louisiana State University Press, 1977.

Coski, John M. *The Confederate Battle Flag: America's Most Embattled Emblem.* Cambridge, MA: Harvard University Press, 2005.

Cox, Karen L. *Dixie's Daughters: The United Daughters of the Confederacy and the Preservation of Confederate Culture.* Gainesville: University Press of Florida, 2003.

Davis, William C. *The Cause Lost: Myths and Realities of the Confederacy.* Lawrence: University Press of Kansas, 1996.

Foster, Gaines M. *Ghosts of the Confederacy: Defeat, the Lost Cause, and the Emergence of the New South, 1865 to 1913.* New York: Oxford University Press, 1987.

Gallagher, Gary W. *Jubal A. Early, the Lost Cause, and Civil War History: A Persistent Legacy.* Milwaukee: Marquette University Press, 1995.

Gallagher, Gary W., and Alan T. Nolan, eds. *The Myth of the Lost Cause and Civil War History.* Bloomington: Indiana University Press, 2000.

Wilson, Charles Reagan. *Baptized in Blood: The Religion of the Lost Cause.* Athens: University of Georgia Press, 1980.

Confederate States' Rights: A Contradiction in Terms

Bensel, Richard F. *Yankee Leviathan: The Origins of Central State Authority in America, 1859–1877.* Cambridge: Cambridge University Press, 1991.

Bernath, Michael T. *Confederate Minds: The Struggle for Intellectual Independence in the Civil War South.* Chapel Hill: University of North Carolina Press, 2010.

Binnington, Ian. *Confederate Visions: Nationalism, Symbolism, and the Imagined South in the Civil War.* Charlottesville: University of Virginia Press, 2013.

Davis, William C. *Look Away! A History of the Confederate States of America.* New York: Free Press, 2003.

Degler, Carl N. *The Other South: Southern Dissenters in the Nineteenth Century.* New York: Harper and Row, 1974.

Dew, Charles B. *Apostles of Disunion: Southern Secession Commissioners and the Causes of the Civil War.* Charlottesville: University Press of Virginia, 2001.

Faust, Drew Gilpin. *The Creation of Confederate Nationalism: Ideology and Identity in the Civil War South.* Baton Rouge: Louisiana State University Press, 1988.

Freehling, William W. *The South vs. the South: How Anti-Confederate Southerners Shaped the Course of the Civil War.* Oxford: Oxford University Press, 2001.

McCurry, Stephanie. *Confederate Reckoning: Power and Politics in the Civil War South.* Cambridge, MA: Harvard University Press, 2010.

Neely, Mark E., Jr. *Southern Rights: Political Prisoners and the Myth of Confederate Constitutionalism.* Charlottesville: University Press of Virginia, 1999.

Quigley, Paul. *Shifting Grounds: Nationalism and the American South, 1848–1865.* Oxford: Oxford University Press, 2011.

Rable, George C. *The Confederate Republic: A Revolution against Politics.* Chapel Hill: University of North Carolina Press, 1994.

Sheehan-Dean, Aaron. *Why Confederates Fought: Family and Nation in Civil War Virginia.* Chapel Hill: University of North Carolina Press, 2007.

Thomas, Emory. *The Confederacy as a Revolutionary Experience*. Englewood Cliffs, NJ: Prentice-Hall, 1971.

Was Abraham Lincoln a Racist?

Burlingame, Michael. *Abraham Lincoln: A Life*. 2 vols. Baltimore: Johns Hopkins University Press, 2008.

Donald, David Herbert. *Lincoln*. New York: Simon and Schuster, 1996.

Foner, Eric. *The Fiery Trial: Abraham Lincoln and American Slavery*. New York: W. W. Norton, 2010.

White, Ronald C. *A. Lincoln*. New York: Random House, 2010.

African Americans in Confederate Military Service: Myth and Reality

Brasher, Glenn. *The Peninsula Campaign and the Necessity of Emancipation: African Americans and the Fight for Freedom*. Chapel Hill: University of North Carolina Press, 2014.

Levine, Bruce. *Confederate Emancipation: Southern Plans to Free and Arm Slaves during the Civil War*. New York: Oxford University Press, 2006.

McPherson, James. *The Negro's Civil War: How American Blacks Felt and Acted during the War for the Union*. New York: Doubleday, 1965.

The Myth of the "Great" Conventional Battlefield War

Castel, Albert, and Thomas Goodrich. *Bloody Bill Anderson: The Short, Savage Life of a Civil War Guerrilla*. Mechanicsburg, PA: Stackpole Books, 1998.

Degler, Carl N. *The Other South: Southern Dissenters in the Nineteenth Century*. New York: Harper and Row, 1974.

Fisher, Noel C. *War at Every Door: Partisan Politics and Guerrilla Violence in East Tennessee, 1860–1869*. Chapel Hill: University of North Carolina Press, 1997.

Freehling, William W. *The South vs. the South: How Anti-Confederate Southerners Shaped the Course of the Civil War*. New York: Oxford University Press, 2001.

Goodrich, Thomas. *Bloody Dawn: The Story of the Lawrence Massacre*. Kent, OH: Kent State University Press, 1991.

Jones, Virgil Carrington. *Gray Ghosts and Rebel Raiders*. New York: Holt, Rinehart, and Winston, 1956.

Leslie, Edward E. *The Devil Knows How to Ride: The True Story of William Clarke Quantrill and His Confederate Raiders*. New York: Random House, 1996.

McKnight, Brian D., and Barton A. Myers, eds. *The Guerrilla Hunters: Irregular Conflicts during the Civil War*. Baton Rouge: Louisiana State University Press, 2017.

Myers, Barton A. *Rebels against the Confederacy: North Carolina's Unionists*. New York: Cambridge University Press, 2014.

Ramage, James A. *Rebel Raider: The Life of General John Hunt Morgan*. Lexington: University Press of Kentucky, 1986.

Sutherland, Daniel E. *A Savage Conflict: The Decisive Role of Guerrillas in the American Civil War.* Chapel Hill: University of North Carolina Press, 2009.

———, ed. *Guerrillas, Unionists, and Violence on the Confederate Home Front.* Fayetteville: University of Arkansas Press, 1999.

Urwin, Gregory J. W., ed. *Black Flag over Dixie: Racial Atrocities and Reprisals in the Civil War.* Carbondale: Southern Illinois University Press, 2004.

Civil War Prisons: The Legacy of Responsibility

Brown, Louis A. *The Salisbury Prison: A Case Study of Confederate Military Prisons, 1861–1865.* Wilmington, NC: Broadfoot, 1992.

Cloyd, Benjamin. *Haunted by Atrocity: Civil War Prisons in American Memory.* Baton Rouge: Louisiana State University Press, 2010.

Davis, Robert S. *Ghosts and Shadows of Andersonville: Essays on the Secret Social Histories of America's Deadliest Prison.* Macon, GA: Mercer University Press, 2006.

Derden, John K. *The World's Largest Prison: The Story of Camp Lawton.* Macon, GA: Mercer University Press, 2012.

Gillispie, James M. *Andersonvilles of the North: The Myths and Realities of Northern Treatment of Civil War Confederate Prisoners.* Denton: University of North Texas Press, 2008.

Gray, Michael P. *The Business of Captivity: Elmira and Its Civil War Prison.* Kent, OH: Kent State University Press, 2001.

Hesseltine, William B. *Civil War Prisons: A Study in War Psychology.* 1930. Reprint, Columbus: Ohio State University Press, 1998.

McAdams, Benton. *Rebels at Rock Island.* DeKalb: Northern Illinois University Press, 2000.

Sanders, Charles W., Jr. *While in the Hands of the Enemy: Military Prisons of the Civil War.* Baton Rouge: Louisiana State University Press, 2005.

Speer, Lonnie R. *Portals to Hell: Military Prisons of the Civil War.* Mechanicsburg, PA: Stackpole Books, 1997.

The Lost Causers' Favorite Target: Grant the Butcher

Grant, Ulysses S. *Personal Memoirs of U.S. Grant.* 2 vols. New York: Jenkins and McCowan, 1885.

McFeely, William S. *Grant: A Biography.* New York: W. W. Norton, 1981.

Porter, Horace. *Campaigning with Grant.* New York: Century, 1897. Reprint, New York: Smithmark, 1994.

Rhea, Gordon C. *The Battle of the Wilderness, May 5–6, 1864.* Baton Rouge: Louisiana State University Press, 1994.

Simpson, Brooks D. *Ulysses Grant: Triumph over Adversity, 1822–1865.* New York: Houghton Mifflin, 2000.

Smith, Jean Edward. *Grant.* New York: Simon and Schuster, 2001.

Waugh, Joan. *U. S. Grant: American Hero, American Myth.* Chapel Hill: University of North Carolina Press, 2009.

Marching through Georgia: The Myth of Sherman's Total War

Grimsley, Mark. *The Hard Hand of War: Union Military Policy toward Southern Civilians, 1861–1865*. Cambridge: Cambridge University Press, 1997.

Kennett, Lee. *Sherman: A Soldier's Life*. New York: HarperCollins, 2002.

Marszalek, John F. *Sherman: A Soldier's Passion for Order*. New York: Macmillan, 1993.

Moody, Wesley. *Demon of the Lost Cause: Sherman and Civil War History*. Columbia: University of Missouri Press, 2011.

O'Connell, Robert L. *Fierce Patriot: The Tangled Lives of William Tecumseh Sherman*. New York: Random House, 2014.

Rubin, Anne Sarah. *Through the Heart of Dixie: Sherman's March and American Memory*. Chapel Hill: University of North Carolina Press, 2014.

Sherman, William T. *Memoirs of General William T. Sherman*. New York: D. Appleton, 1876.

CONTRIBUTOR BIOGRAPHIES

Michael T. Bernath is the Charlton W. Tebeau Associate Professor of History at the University of Miami. He earned his Ph.D. from Harvard University in 2005. He is the author of *Confederate Minds: The Struggle for Intellectual Independence in the Civil War South.*

Edward H. Bonekemper, III, is the author of five books on the Civil War. He earned his master's degree from Old Dominion after completing his law degree at Yale. After a career in the United States Coast Guard and as Assistant Chief Counsel for the U.S. Department of Transportation, Bonekemper retired to his passion of Civil War history. He is a well-regarded speaker, having appeared at the Smithsonian and national battlefields across the country.

Benjamin Cloyd is the author of *Haunted by Atrocity: Civil War Prisons in American Memory.* He earned his Ph.D. from Louisiana State University in 2005. He is currently Academic Dean for the Raymond Campus at Hinds Community College.

Ian Patrick Hunt is the Chief of Acquisitions and Research at the Abraham Lincoln Presidential Library and Museum in Springfield, Illinois. He is currently a Ph.D. candidate at Southern Illinois University and intends to complete his dissertation on the secession crisis in the summer of 2017. He has advised on numerous publications, television programs, and movies regarding the Civil War and Abraham Lincoln and is a consultant to the U.S. State Department Public Diplomacy Program.

Wesley Moody is Professor of History at Florida State College at Jacksonville. He is the author or editor of three books on the American Civil War: *Demon of the Lost Cause: Sherman and Civil War History; The Diary of a Civil War Marine;* and *The Battle of Fort Sumter.*

Barton A. Myers is Assistant Professor of History at Washington and Lee University. He was previously a postdoctoral fellow at Cornell University. He is the author of two books on the American Civil War: *Rebels against the Confederacy: North Carolina's Unionists* and *Executing Daniel Bright: Race, Loyalty, and Guerrilla Violence in a Coastal Carolina Community, 1861–1865.* The latter won the 2009 Jules and Frances Landry Award for the best book on a Southern studies topic.

Brooks D. Simpson is the ASU Foundation Professor of History at Arizona State University. He earned his Ph.D. from the University of Wisconsin–Madison. He is the author or editor of seven books on the American Civil War, most recently *The Civil War: The Third Year Told by Those Who Lived It.*

INDEX

West Virginia, xv, 39, 76, 84
Wheeler, Joseph, 94, 156–57
Whig Party, 16, 18, 32, 34
Wilderness, Battle of the, 128, 133
Winder, John, 105
Wirz, Henry, 112–13, 115, 118–19

Women's Relief Corps, 114–15
World War I, 63, 118–19, 161, 162
World War II, 119, 123, 128, 157, 162

Yancey, William, 17
Yellow Fever, 82